Other Books and Se

1901-1907 Native American Census Sene
Ottawa, Peoria, Quapaw, and Wyandotte ¡
Territory)

GW01402614

1932 Census of The Standing Rock Sioux
1924-1932

Census of The Blackfeet, Montana, 1897- 1901 Expanded Edition

Eastern Cherokee by Blood, 1906-1910, Volumes I thru XIII

Choctaw of Mississippi Indian Census 1929-1932 with Births and Deaths 1924-
1931   Volume I
Choctaw of Mississippi Indian Census 1933, 1934 & 1937, Supplemental Rolls to
1934 & 1935 with Births and Deaths 1932-1938, and Marriages 1936-1938
Volume II

Eastern Cherokee Census Cherokee, North Carolina 1930-1939
Census 1930-1931 with Births And Deaths 1924-1931 Taken By Agent L. W. Page
Volume I
Eastern Cherokee Census Cherokee, North Carolina 1930-1939
Census 1932-1933 with Births And Deaths 1930-1932 Taken By Agent R. L.
Spalsbury   Volume II
Eastern Cherokee Census Cherokee, North Carolina 1930-1939
Census 1934-1937 with Births and Deaths 1925-1938 and Marriages 1936 & 1938
Taken by Agents R. L. Spalsbury And Harold W. Foght Volume III

Seminole of Florida Indian Census, 1930-1940 with Birth and Death
Records, 1930-1938

Texas Cherokees 1820-1839 A Document For Litigation 1921

Choctaw By Blood Enrollment Cards 1898-1914 Volumes I thru XVII

Starr Roll 1894 (Cherokee Payment Rolls) Districts: Canadian, Cooweescoowee,
and Delaware Volume One
Starr Roll 1894 (Cherokee Payment Rolls) Districts: Flint, Going Snake, and
Illinois   Volume Two
Starr Roll 1894 (Cherokee Payment Rolls) Districts: Saline, Sequoyah, and
Tahlequah; Including Orphan Roll   Volume Three

Cherokee Intruder Cases Dockets of Hearings 1901-1909 Volumes I & II

Indian Wills, 1911-1921 Records of the Bureau of Indian Affairs
Books One thru Seven;
Native American Wills & Probate Records 1911-1921

Other Books and Series by Jeff Bowen

Turtle Mountain Reservation Chippewa Indians 1932 Census with Births & Deaths, 1924-1932

Chickasaw By Blood Enrollment Cards 1898-1914 Volume I thru V

Cherokee Descendants East An Index to the Guion Miller Applications Volume I
Cherokee Descendants West An Index to the Guion Miller Applications Volume II (A-M)
Cherokee Descendants West An Index to the Guion Miller Applications Volume III (N-Z)

Applications for Enrollment of Seminole Newborn Freedmen, Act of 1905

Eastern Cherokee Census, Cherokee, North Carolina, 1915-1922, Taken by Agent James E. Henderson   Volume I (1915-1916)
Volume II (1917-1918)
Volume III (1919-1920)
Volume IV (1921-1922)

Complete Delaware Roll of 1898

Eastern Cherokee Census, Cherokee, North Carolina, 1923-1929, Taken by Agent James E. Henderson   Volume I (1923-1924)
Volume II (1925-1926)
Volume III (1927-1929)

Applications for Enrollment of Seminole Newborn Act of 1905 Volumes I & II

North Carolina Eastern Cherokee Indian Census 1898-1899, 1904, 1906, 1909-1912, 1914 Revised and Expanded Edition

1932 Hopi and Navajo Native American Census with Birth & Death Rolls (1925-1931) Volume 1 - Hopi
1932 Hopi and Navajo Native American Census with Birth & Death Rolls (1930-1932) Volume 2 - Navajo

Western Navajo Reservation Navajo, Hopi and Paiute 1933 Census with Birth & Death Rolls 1925-1933

Visit our website at **www.nativestudy.com** to learn more about these and other books and series by Jeff Bowen

CHEROKEE CITIZENSHIP COMMISSION DOCKETS 1880-1884 AND 1887-1889
VOLUME I

Jan. 29, 1881
Case #85   Subina Beason
                      (Vs)   Petition for
                 Cherokee Nation   Citizenship

Tahlequah, C.N. July. 14th, 1887

The above case submitted by both parties after
hearing the testimony, Jan. 31, 1881.
The testimony of William Harnage shows that the
claimant is his niece and a Cherokee by blood.
The Commission therefore hereby issued this then
decree admitting the said Subina Beason to all the
rights, privileges, and franchises of Cherokee
citizenship by blood. Jan 31, 1881.
                         Roach Young, President
                         William Harnage
                         G.W. Mayes
J.B. Mayes   Asst. Comm
       Clerk Commission

TRANSCRIBED BY
JEFF BOWEN

NATIVE STUDY
Gallipolis, Ohio
USA

Originally published:
Baltimore, Maryland
2009

Reprinted by:

Native Study LLC
Gallipolis, OH
www.nativestudy.com
2020

Library of Congress Control Number: 2020916859

ISBN: 978-1-64968-058-7

Made in the United States of America.

This series is dedicated to Joyce Tranter,
for giving me the inspiration of a lifetime.
And also to Dominick Lane Dugan.
Remember Isaiah 40:31
God bless!

INTRODUCTION

This publication was previously published by another publisher in 2009 and has now been reproduced by Native Study LLC. There are five volumes in this series concerning the Cherokee Citizenship Commission Dockets 1880 to 1889. This is material that was never before transcribed containing 2,288 Cherokee docket decisions.

This is somewhat of an explanation concerning the reasoning behind the proceedings that led the Cherokee tribal courts to take charge of these docket hearings.

The Cherokee relied upon their leaders to guide them but they ended up hanging in the balance after the Civil War, with their loyalties split worse than ever and their country ravished. Fathers and brothers were off fighting a war that didn't even concern them. By the time the war was over the Cherokee people had lost any form of stability. The men fighting the war came back to the same old political hatreds and in-fighting. The Nation was being over run with many that claimed they were Cherokee, hoping to benefit from false claims of citizenship. These people, known as intruders, did nothing but make it more difficult for the Cherokees because of the pressures from the Government to control their boundaries. The blood Cherokees that were seeking their homeland were again in question as to who they were. They found nothing but scrutiny and distrust, the war had made them choose a side, and the U.S. Government didn't care for the choice of the majority.

Intruder after intruder was encroaching on Cherokee land and what was to seem like a never ending battle. Many Cherokee citizens had lost their rights while intruders that didn't belong stayed using up what little resources there were. The government was telling the Cherokee leaders to settle their own intruder problems or else they would have to intercede. In an effort to clarify who were true Cherokee citizens and who were not, or who had been wrongfully taken off of the rolls, was a problem.

There were part-bloods, full-bloods, and no bloods along with mass confusion, prejudice, vendettas, and deceptions. The intruders wanted a free ride and were willing to use the confusion as a camouflage to achieve their purpose and greed.

This was a situation where the government was threatening to come in and turn the Cherokee Nation into a Federal Territory because it appeared to them that the Tribal Council would not be able to organize an effort to control the problem. But this wasn't the issue at hand as far as the Cherokee were concerned. They felt as if, according to their treaty stipulations, the United States was responsible for intruder removal. They felt as if the United States had let things get out of hand and that the government had not lived up to its contractual agreement. According to treaty stipulations this was true, but, they were told to either come up with a solution or lose their rights as a sovereign nation.

From William G. McLoughlin's book , *After the Trail of Tears, The Cherokees Struggle for Sovereignty 1839-1880,* it references on page 354, "Still, the Nation remained very uneasy about the fundamental question of its right to define who were its own citizens and its right to expect the United States to remove those who the Nation judged were not. Ever since 1872, federal agents had refused to expel from the Nation those former slaves whom the Nation considered 'aliens' and since 1874, federal agents had been under instructions from the Bureau of Indian Affairs to compile their own list of black or white persons who, in their opinion, had some claim to citizenship despite previous rulings of the Cherokee Courts on their claims."

On page 355-356, "On the basis of the affidavits and reports submitted, the Secretary of Interior, Zachariah Chandler, sent E.C. Watkins to the Nation in 1875, to investigate the citizenship problem and gather information that Chandler could use to ask Congress to take action on behalf of these 'men without a country'. Watkins reported in February, 1876, that many of those on Ingall's list were 'clearly entitled' to Cherokee citizenship. Oochalata denied it. He counter charged that Ingalls was meddling in Cherokee affairs and wrote to the Bureau of Indian Affairs to complain. Receiving no satisfactory response, he wrote directly to President Grant on November 13, 1876, enclosing a petition from the Cherokees Cooweescoowee District, complaining that the agent had not removed thousands of intruders in their area though ordered to do so by the Council. Some of these intruders were former slaves from the Deep South, but most were white U.S. citizens from Kansas, Missouri, and Arkansas.

Grant referred this letter to Commissioner J.Q. Smith. Annoyed that Oochalata had gone over the head of the Interior Department to the President, on December 8, Smith wrote Oochalata a long, assertive, and highly provocative letter outlining for the first time the department's position on this question. Smith said that from the evidence he had received, both from various federal agents and from the investigations of E.C. Watkins, the Cherokee Nation had failed to deal consistently and impartially with the problems of former slaves and others who claimed Cherokee citizenship. Therefore, the Bureau of Indian Affairs would continue to compile its own list of those who had 'prima facie' evidence for citizenship [whether the Cherokee courts had acted negatively on their claims or not], and it would take no action to remove them until the Cherokees carried four stipulations to resolve the issue. First, the Council must establish a clear, legal procedure providing due process for adjudicating all prima facie claims. Second, the rules by which such cases were decided must be approved by the Secretary of the Interior to ensure their impartiality. Third, he suggested that the Cherokee Circuit Courts be designated as the appropriate bodies for such hearings. Finally, claimants' appeals of the decisions of the Cherokee Circuit Courts must be forwarded to the Secretary of the Interior, and no claimant for citizenship should be removed from the Nation until the Secretary had made his own ruling. In effect, Smith asserted the right of the Bureau of Indian Affairs to decide who was and was not a Cherokee citizen. A crucial decision concerning the issue of the sovereignty of Indian nations was about to be reached.

Oochalata was stunned and wrote a 139-page letter to Smith explaining why this procedure was totally unacceptable and contrary to law, treaties, precedent, and the U.S. Constitution."

On page 357, "Acting on instructions from Oochalata, the Cherokee Delegation sent another letter to President Grant on Jan. 9, 1877, insisting that treaty rights, the Trade and Intercourse Act, and precedent gave the Nation the right 'to determine the question as to who are and who are not intruders.' The president referred their letter to Secretary of the Interior, Carl Schurz, who, on April 21, 1877, told the delegation that he supported Smith's four stipulations for settling the matter. Oochalata ignored this response and in August, 1877, sent to the new Commissioner of Indian Affairs, Ezra A. Hayt, a list of all the intruders whom the Cherokees wished to be immediately removed. On Nov. 7, Hayt replied flatly that the Bureau of Indian Affairs would not do so: 'while the department reserves to itself the right to finally determine who are and are not intruders under the law, **it expects the Cherokee Nation Council to enact some general and uniform law by which the Cherokee courts shall hear and determine the rights of claimants to citizenship,** subject only to the review of the Secretary of Interior after a final adjudication has been reached.'"

On page 358-9, "The department's claim that it had the right to judge intruders was, in Oochalata's opinion, 'a new doctrine for construing treaty or contracts in writing, to add to it verbally, a new clause, after the expiration of 92 years from date of that compact or treaty and without the consent of [one] party. . . . It is a dangerous doctrine to which I can never agree.'

While he urged the Council to send a protest through its delegation, Oochalata also asked it to enact a law that would establish a court to decide citizenship claims in a legal and uniform manner. The Council complied on Dec. 5, 1877, but the compromise was fatally weakened by the Council's failure to address two aspects of the law governing the Citizenship Court's actions.

First, the law provided no guidelines for deciding cases that would meet the demands of the Bureau of Indian Affairs, and consequently, in cases involving former slaves, the Citizenship Court relied, as the Cherokee Supreme Court had in 1870-71, simply on the wording in the Treaty of 1866. Second, the Council explicitly refused to allow the right of the Secretary of the Interior to review the decisions of the Court, stating that the Cherokee Citizenship Court was 'a tribunal of last resort'. The three persons appointed to the court, were John Chambers, O.P. Brewer, and George Downing. Also referred to as the Chamber's Commission, the Court began to hold hearings early in 1878. All persons claiming to have grounds for citizenship were required to present them or be declared intruders."

On pages 359-360, McLoughlin continues, "By the end of 1878, Oochalata struggling to find some new approach to the problem. On Dec. 3, he went over the head of the Bureau of Indian Affairs again, and wrote to Pres. Rutherford B. Hayes, forwarding a complete account of all of the cases adjudicated by the Citizenship Court and asking him to order the expulsion of those rejected and all other intruders. He told Hayes that the Cherokee Nation had an 'inherent national right' to define its own citizens, while the United States had a well-established obligation to expel non-citizens. Suspecting that Hayes would reject this request, Oochalata approached Commissioner Ezra A. Hayt and tried to work out a compromise. He said that the Cherokees would stop confiscating the property of those former slaves judged to be intruders pending the appointment of a joint commission of Cherokees and members of the Bureau to review the rejected claims. Hayt agreed only on the condition that decisions of this commission must be unanimous or the Bureau would retain the right to make its own decision in each case. Oochalata and the delegation could not accept such a condition, and the negotiations broke down. Finally, as a last resort, the council decided to submit a series of questions to the Secretary of Interior, Carl Schurz, about their right to determine citizenship and the obligation of the United States to accept their determinations. They asked Schurz to present their questions to Attorney General Charles Devens for his opinion. They sent the letter on March 3, 1879, and after Hayt informed Devens of his views on the matter, Devens held hearings at which both sides presented their views. Realizing the importance of the decision, the Cherokees spent the money necessary to hire the best lawyers they could find to assist them. Hayt said that the status of at least one-thousand persons was at issue, the Council argued that there were over twice that many intruders whom the Department was refusing to move.

Throughout the dispute, the Bureau of Indian Affairs declined to act against intruding squatters from Kansas who made no pretense to citizenship.

"The three questions that the Council asked Devens to answer were: Did the Cherokee Nation have the right to determine its own citizenship? Did the former slaves who were citizens have any share in the use of Cherokee land or in the money derived from the sale of the Cherokee land? Was it, or was it not, the duty of the Federal government to remove intruders under treaty stipulations and Trade and Intercourse Act? By the time Devens sent his reply, the Citizenship Court had heard 416 claims for citizenship and rejected 338."

Devens' opinion was clearly in the negative as far as the Cherokee Nation's sovereignty and decision processes were concerned. On page 364, McLoughlin observes, "Clearly, as since the days of Andrew Jackson, Federal refusal to honor the requirement of removing intruders was to be the means of forcing the Indian nations to do what they did not want to do." Ochalata would not run again as the election of August 1879 neared and Dennis W. Bushyhead became the new chief on August 4, 1879 but in the end it didn't matter who was chief the fight to keep Cherokee sovereignty along with self government was all but lost by 1880. On pages 365-366, McLoughlin wrote, "The turning point was reached in 1887 when Congress passed the Dawes Severalty Act. The act expressed what was now the national consensus among white voters (including Indian reformers, railroad magnates, and entrepreneurs) -that the solution to "'the Indian question'" was to denationalize the tribes in the Indian Territory, survey and allot their land in severalty, and establish a white-dominated territorial government over "'Oklahoma'" the Choctaw word for "'red man.'"

The sovereignty of the Western Cherokee tribe was taken, and to this day they still don't have a true land base as a nation. Even though others were able to take away the land that was promised to remain theirs forever; nobody was able to take away their right and ability to choose who was a true citizen and who was not. The dockets transcribed within this series are exactly as they appeared on the microfilm copies from the original court records involving citizenship during the time periods of 1880-1889.

These dockets were referenced and transcribed from microfilm series; 7RA25-0001 (American Genealogical Lending Library), Cherokee Citizenship Commission Docket Books, 1880-1884 and 1887-1889.

Jeff Bowen
Gallipolis, Ohio
NativeStudy.com

Cherokee Citizenship Commission Docket Books
Tahlequah, Cherokee Nation (1880-84, 1887-89)
Volume I

January 5, 1880

The Commission on Citizenship convened on the above date agreeable to an Act of the National Council voted November 26, 1879.

Roach Young (President)
G.W. Mayes
Wm Harnage
Associate Commissioners

John Springston (Interpreter)
Saldin Hall - Attorney

J.B. Mayes
Clerk

Jan. 5, 1880
Case #1

D.W. RAGSDALE   Petition for Citizenship
vs   in the Cherokee Nation
Cherokee Nation

Tahlequah, Jan. 27, 1880

The Commission after hearing all the testimony in the above case, are thoroughly convinced that the above named claimant, D.W. Ragsdale, is a Cherokee by blood and is therefore entitled to all the right and privileges of other Cherokees - and do hereby decide to admit the said D.W. Ragsdale to citizenship - with all the right, privileges and franchise that belong to any other Cherokee.

Roach Young President
Wm Harnage
G.W. Mayes

J.B. Mayes   Associate Commissioners
Clerk Commission

Jan 8, 1880
Case #2

LEWIS ROLSTON
vs   Petition for Citizenship
Cherokee Nation

The above case continued until the September term, 1880, by the Cherokee Nation. Ord for 15 Sept.

1

Cherokee Citizenship Commission Docket Books
Tahlequah, Cherokee Nation (1880-84, 1887-89)
Volume I

The above named claimant, Lewis Rolston, claims his right to citizenship in the Cherokee Nation on grounds of Cherokee blood being a relative of the late Judge John Landrum and James Kell of Delaware Dist, C.N. well known Cherokees.

The testimony in the case favors conclusively to the Commission that the Petitioner's claim is well founded - that he is an immediate descendant of the Kell family, long known to be Cherokees by blood.

The commission therefore hereby decides to admit the said Lewis Rolston to all the rights, privileges and franchise of Cherokee citizenship by blood.

Roach Young, President Comm.
William Harnage
G.W. Mayes

J.B. Mayes,   Asst. Commissioners
　　　　Clerk Comm.

Jan. 14, 1880
Case #3

JAMES S. HARRIS
vs   Petition for Citizenship
Cherokee Nation

The above named claimant, James S. Harris, set forth, has plea to citizenship in the Cherokee Nation on account of his Cherokee blood. The fact of his being a Cherokee by blood is proven in the testimony to the satisfaction of the Commission.

The Commission, therefore, hereby issues this then decree admitting the above named James S. Harris (claimant), to all the rights, privileges, and franchise of Cherokee citizenship by blood.

Roach Young, President
Rendered Feb. 5, 1881   William Harnage
G.W. Mayes
J.B. Mayes   Associate Commissioners
　　　　Clerk Commission

Jan. 14, 1880
Case #4

LAFAYETTE HARLIN

2

Cherokee Citizenship Commission Docket Books
Tahlequah, Cherokee Nation (1880-84, 1887-89)
Volume I

vs   Petition for Citizenship

Cherokee Nation

The above case continued until the September term, 1880, by the Cherokee Nation, ord. for 10th Sept, continued until 13th.

The above claimant has been reported as having taken a reservation on the neutral lands under the Treaty of 1866, between the United States and the Cherokee Nation. The testimony shows that the father of claimant did take a reservation on said land under said Treaty.

But the Commission is of the opinion from the testimony that the claimant did not take a reservation on said land.

Therefore, the Commission hereby decides to admit said claimant, Lafayette Harlin to all the rights, privileges, and franchise of Cherokee citizenship by blood.

September 14, 1880

J.B. Mayes

Clerk

Roach Young, President
William Harnage
G.W. Mayes
Asst. Comm.

Jan. 14, 1880

Case #5

MURCAN HARLIN

vs   Petition for Citizenship

Cherokee Nation

The above case continued until the September term, 1880, by the Nation. Ord. for 10th, Sept, continued until 13th.

The above claimant has been reported as having taken a reservation on the neutral lands under the Treaty of 1866, between the United States and the Cherokee Nation. The testimony shows that the father of claimant did take a reservation on said land under said Treaty.

But the Commission is of the opinion from the testimony that the claimant did not take a reservation on said land under said Treaty.

Therefore the Commission hereby decides to admit said claimant, Murcan Harlin, to all the rights, privileges, and franchise of Cherokee citizenship by blood.

Roach Young, President
William Harnage

J.B. Mayes   G.W. Mayes
    Clerk

Jan. 14, 1880
Case #6

    MRS. NANCY GUNTER & CHILDREN
    LULA H. CURTIS, AMANDA O. MARRS,
    ANN E. CHAMBER, J.T. GUNTER and
    LUCY JANE FALKNER
        vs   Petition for Citizenship
    Cherokee Nation

The evidence before the Commission in the above case shows to the satisfaction of the Commission that the said Nancy Gunter is a Cherokee by blood. Also native born. And therefore, do hereby decide to admit the said Nancy Gunter and family; to wit: Lula H. Curtis, Amanda O. Marrs, Ann E. Chandler, John T. Gunter, and Lucy Jane Falkner to all the rights and full privileges of Cherokee citizenship.

                        Roach Young, President Comm
                        Wm Harnage
J.B. Mayes   G.W. Mayes
    Clerk   Associate Comm.

Jan. 14, 1880
Case #7

    WILLIAMINA C. CLELAND
        vs   Petition for Citizenship
    Cherokee Nation

The above case continued to September term, 1880, by the Plaintiff; Continued until January term, 1881, by consent of both parties; Continued by the Cherokee Nation until the September term, 1881.

The Plaintiff failing to appear and submit the above case, the Commission continues the case until the next meeting of the Commission, Oct. 3, 1881. Jan. 10, 1882 - The above case is set to be tried on the 15th Jan, 1882, unless sooner called up by the Claimant. Jan. 19, 1882 - Solicitor for the Cher. Nat. continues the case till next term, Sept, 1882. Oct. 4, 1882 - Continued by the Commission to the January term, 1883.

Cherokee Citizenship Commission Docket Books
Tahlequah, Cherokee Nation (1880-84, 1887-89)
Volume I

And now on this the 3rd day of Jan, 1883, this cause coming on for final hearing and all the evidence in the case being read and duly considered, it is adjudged and determined by the Commission on Citizenship, that the claimant, Williamina C. Cleland, is a Cherokee by blood, and that she is entitled to all the rights and privileges of Cherokee citizenship existing in the Cherokee Nation, and that she is hereby admitted to the full and complete enjoyment of the same in all aspects as a native born Cherokee.

Thos. Tehee, President of Comm
Alex. Wolf

D.W.C. Duncan
Clerk of Commission

T.F. Thompson
Commissioners

Jan. 16, 1880
Case #8

SOFRONIA A. BIVENS, LOUISA J. COATS,
and **FRANK W. CRAIG**
vs
Cherokee Nation

Petition for Citizenship in
Cherokee Nation

Continued until the September (term), 1880, by the Cherokee Nation. Ord. on 10 Sept, continued until 15th.

It is proven to the satisfaction of the Commission, that the above named claimants to citizenship, are the relatives and the descendants of the David Harlan family - who (have) taken a reservation on the neutral land under the Treaty of 1866 between the Cherokee Nation and the United States, well known Cherokees - and that said claimants did not take a reservation on said land.

Therefore, the Commission admit the above named claimants to all the rights, privileges, and franchise of Cherokee citizenship. Sept. 15, 1880

Roach Young, Pres.

J.B. Mayes
Clerk

Wm Harnage
G.W. Mayes
Asst. Comm.

Jan. 19, 1880
Case #9

ELIZABETH E. MARION
and **FAMILY**

5

Cherokee Citizenship Commission Docket Books
Tahlequah, Cherokee Nation (1880-84, 1887-89)
Volume I

vs   Petition for Citizenship
Cherokee Nation

The above case continued until the September term, 1880, by the Cherokee Nation. Set for trial on 15 September.

The testimony before the Commission shows that the mother of claimant, Rebecca McCallister, was admitted to the rights of citizenship in the Cherokee Nation, 15 December, 1870.

The testimony further shows that the claimant is the daughter of said Rebecca McCallister. It is therefore natural that the child must take the same condition of the mother.

The Commission therefore hereby admit the above named claimant and family, to wit: Elizabeth E. Marion and children; Rebecca Emly Dooly, Wm Henry Màrtin, James Sherman Marion, and Emly Agnes Martin, to all the rights, privileges, and franchises of Cherokee citizenship by blood.

Sept, 15, 1880   Roach Young, Pres.
                                         Wm Harnage
J.B. Mayes   G.W. Mayes
        Clerk   Asst. Comm.

Jan. 19, 1880
Case #10

MARY KELL
vs   Petition for Citizenship
Cherokee Nation

The testimony on the above case is the mother of Mary Kell. Who testifies that James Kell was the natural father of claimant. The testimony of G.W. Mayes is that James Kell is a Cherokee by blood and the testimony further shows that the claimant was native born.

The Commission therefore issues this then decree readmitting the claimant Mary Kell to all the rights and privileges of Cherokee citizenship.

                                         Roach Young, President
                                         Wm Harnage
J.B. Mayes   G.W. Mayes
        Clerk   Associate Comm.

Jan. 19, 1880
Case #11

Cherokee Citizenship Commission Docket Books
Tahlequah, Cherokee Nation (1880-84, 1887-89)
Volume I

ANN BELL SHELTON, EUGENE M. SHELTON,
NORMAN SHELTON, & H.W. SHELTON
vs   Petition for Citizenship
Cherokee Nation

The evidence in the above case is conclusive beyond a doubt that the claimants are of Cherokee blood being the immediate descendants of John A. Bell, of Delaware Dist, Cherokee Nation. And that the said Ann B. Shelton is a native born Cherokee.

The Commission therefore do(sic) hereby issue this then decree admitting the above named Ann B. Shelton, Eugene M. Shelton, Norman Shelton, and H.W. Shelton to all the rights, privileges, and franchise of Cherokee citizens by blood.

	Roach Young, President
	Wm Harnage
J.B. Mayes	G.W. Mayes
Clerk Commission	Associate Comm.

Jan. 19, 1880
Case #12

JACKSON, JAMES, FANNY and
MARTIN JORDAN
vs   Petition for Citizenship
Cherokee Nation

The above case continued until the September term, 1880, by the Cherokee Nation; Continued until 21 September; Continued until January, 1881.

The above case continued by Plaintiff until September term, 1881.

The above case continued by the Commission on grounds of the Plaintiff lacking to finally close the case. Oct. 3, 1881

Jan. 17, 1882 - Submitted by the claimant.

Jan. 18, 1882 - Submitted by the Solicitor for the Nation.

Jan. 18, 1882 - And now on this the 18th day of January, A.D. 1882, this case coming on for final hearing and notice having issued to the Claimants of the coming on of said case for final hearing and all the evidence produced said case having been read and duly considered, it was adjudged by the Commission on Citizenship, that said claimants, Jackson Jordan, James Jordan, Fanny Jordan and Martin Jordan, are not Cherokees by blood and that they are not entitled to the rights and privileges of Cherokee citizenship within the Cherokee Nation; and their claim for said citizenship should be and is hereby rejected.

Thos. Tehee, President
Alex Wolfe
D.W.C. Duncan   T.F. Thompson
Clerk   Commissioners

Jan. 19, 1880
Case #13

NARCISSA CHISHOLM OWEN,
ROBT. L. OWEN, and
W.O. OWEN
vs   Petition for Citizenship
Cherokee Nation

After hearing the testimony in the above case, the Commission is thoroughly satisfied that the above named Narcissa Chisholm Owen is the daughter of Thos. Chisholm, late, of Delaware Dist, C.N; and a Cherokee by blood and is therefore entitled to all the rights and privileges of other Cherokees.

The Commission therefore hereby issues this then decree readmitting the said Narcissa Chisholm Owen and her children; to wit: Robt. L. Owen and W.O. Owen, to all the rights, privileges, and franchises of Cherokee citizenship by blood. Feb, 2, 1880

Roach Young, President Comm
William Harnage
J.B. Mayes   G.W. Mayes
Clerk Commission   Associate Comm.

Jan. 20, 1880
Case #14

JANE B. GASS
vs   Petition for Citizenship
Cherokee Nation

The evidence in the above case is conclusive beyond a doubt that the above named claimant, Jane B. Gass for citizenship, is a native born Cherokee and entitled to all the rights and privileges of Cherokee citizenship.

8

Cherokee Citizenship Commission Docket Books
Tahlequah, Cherokee Nation (1880-84, 1887-89)
Volume I

A decree is therefore hereby issued readmitting the above named Jane B. Gass and family; to wit: William Akin, Russo Akin, Minnie Akin, Ida Gass, Oscar Gass and Noah Gass; to all the rights, privileges and franchises of Cherokee citizenship by blood.

	Roach Young, President Comm.
	William Harnage
J.B. Mayes	G.W. Mayes
Clerk Commission	Associate Commissioners

Jan. 20, 1880
Case #15

GEORGE WARD	
EMMA BLACKWOOD	
vs	Petition for Citizenship
Cherokee Nation	

The above case continued until the September term by the Nation; Continued until 10 Sept;   Continued until 15th;   Submitted by both parties, 20th Sept 1880

After carefully examining the testimony in the above case, the Commission is satisfied that (they) are Cherokees by blood. Therefore, the Commission hereby admits the said George Ward, Emma Blackwood and Marjorett and Mary Blackwood to all the rights and privileges of Cherokee citizenship by blood.   Oct. 1, 1880

	Roach Young, President
	Wm Harnage
J.B. Mayes	G.W. Mayes
Clerk	Asst. Comm.

Jan. 20, 1880
Case #16

SIDNEY WILKEY & FAMILY	
vs	Petition for Citizenship
Cherokee Nation	

Trial set on the 5th February, 1880; Case continued by the Cherokee Nation until the September term, 1880; Continued until 10th Sept; Continued until 15th; Submitted by both parties 20th Sept 1880

Cherokee Citizenship Commission Docket Books
Tahlequah, Cherokee Nation (1880-84, 1887-89)
Volume I

The testimony in the above case shows beyond a doubt that the above named claimant, Sidney E. Wilkey, is of Cherokee blood being a descendant of the Welch family, noted Cherokees.

The Commission therefore hereby admits the said Sidney Wilkey and family; to wit: John M. Wilkey, Margaret Ann Lindsey, Dave W. Wilkey, George W. Wilkey, Nancy M. Wilkey, Mary I. Wilkey, Sidney E. Wilkey, Jessie W. Wilkey, John Wilkey and George H. Wilkey, Dave Martin and Minnie E. Lindsy(sic) to all the rights, privileges, and franchise of Cherokee citizenship.   Oct. 1, 1880

Roach Young, President
Wm. Harnage

J.B. Mayes   G.W. Mayes
         Clerk   Asst. Comm.

Jan. 20, 1880
Case #17

ELIZABETH and EDGAR HAYES
vs   Petition for Citizenship
Cherokee Nation

The evidence before the Commission shows the claimants, above named, to be the grandchildren of Mrs. E.C. Eblen, who was the daughter of the late Peggy Morgan of the Cherokee Nation, all Cherokees by blood.

The Commission therefore hereby issues this then decree admitting the above named claimants, Elizabeth Hayes and Edgar Hayes, to all the rights, privileges, and franchise of Cherokee citizenship by blood.

Roach Young, President Comm.
William Harnage
J.B. Mayes   G.W. Mayes
         Clerk Commission   Associate Commissioners

Jan. 20, 1880
Case #18

GEORGE HAMMER
vs   Petition for Citizenship
Cherokee Nation

The evidence in the above case of George Hammer, although colored, shows that he is a descendant on his mother's side from Cherokee ancestors

10

by blood and free born, being the descendant of the sister of the late Judge James Brown of Sequoyah Dist, C.N, a well known Cherokee by blood.

The Commission therefore hereby decides to recognize and admit the said George Hammer to all the rights, privileges, and franchise of Cherokee citizenship in the Cherokee Nation.

	Roach Young, President
	William Harnage
J.B. Mayes	G.W. Mayes
Clerk Comm.	Asst. Comm.

Jan. 21, 1880
Case #19

NELSON C. VICKERY
vs   Petition for Citizenship
Cherokee Nation

The evidence in the above case of Nelson C. Vickery, shows that the claimant is a native born Cherokee, a full blood Indian.

The Commission therefore readmits the said Nelson C. Vickery to all the rights, privileges, and franchise of Cherokee citizenship by blood.

Feb. 3, 1880

	Roach Young, President
	William Harnage
J.B. Mayes	G.W. Mayes
Clerk Comm.	Asst. Comm.

Jan. 21, 1880
Case #20

JOHN S. HARNAGE
SARAH BACON
vs   Petition for Citizenship
Cherokee Nation

The evidence in the above case of John S. Harnage and Sarah Bacon is conclusive as to their Indian blood being a descendant of the noted Starr family.

The Commission therefore issues then a decree in favor of claimants, admitting the said John S. Harnage and Sarah Bacon to all the rights, privileges, and franchise of Cherokee citizenship by blood.

Roach Young, President
William Harnage
J.B. Mayes   G.W. Mayes
Clerk Comm.   Asst. Comm.

Jan. 21, 1880
Case #21

VICTORIA SEMORE* GREENE
vs   Petition for Citizenship
Cherokee Nation

The above case continued by the consent of parties until the September term, 1880;   The above case continued until January term, 1881, by Plaintiff;   The above case continued by consent of both parties - Oct, 1881

Jan. 28, 1882 - And now this case coming on for final hearing, and all the testimony produced in the case on both sides, being carefully read and duly considered, and the fact that the claimant is a Cherokee by blood, being clearly proved by the testimony and being undisputed by the Defense, the defense being (unable to read word) wholly upon the allegation that Claimant took a reservation on the neutral land under the provisions of the Treaty of 1866, thereby parting with her rights to Cherokee citizenship; and said defense having been found to be unsustained by the evidence; it was adjudged by the Commission on Citizenship that the claimant, Victoria Sizemore* Greene, is a Cherokee by blood and that she is entitled to all the rights and privileges of Cherokee citizenship within the Cherokee Nation; and that she should be and she is hereby admitted to the full and perfect enjoyment of the same within the Cherokee Nation in all respects as completely as a native born Cherokee.

Thos. Tehee, Pres. of Comm
Alex Wolfe
D.W.C. Duncan   T.F. Thompson
Clerk   Commissioners
(* **NOTE:** Name spelled both ways.)

Jan. 22, 1880
Case #22

POLLY A. LORIN
vs   Petition for Citizenship
Cherokee Nation

The evidence on the above named case of Polly A. Lorin is satisfactory to the Commission that the claimant is a native born Cherokee by blood. The Commission therefore hereby issues this then decree readmitting the said Polly A. Lorin and children; to wit: George Lorin, Gid Lorin and Lucinda Lorin, to all the rights, privileges and franchise of Cherokee citizenship by blood. Feb. 3, 1880

	Roach Young, President
	William Harnage
J.B. Mayes	G.W. Mayes
Clerk Comm.	Asst. Comm.

Jan. 27, 1880
Case #23

LEMUEL PARIS
   vs   Petition for Citizenship
Cherokee Nation

The above case continued by the Plaintiff until the September term, 1880;   Continued until the January term, 1881, by Plaintiff.

The above case withdrawn by Plaintiff, September 15, 1881 ----- L.B. Bell, Attorney

And the papers in the case turned over to the Plaintiff or Claimant.

Jan. 27, 1880
Case #24

D.H. REAVES
   vs   Petition for Citizenship
Cherokee Nation

The above case continued by the Plaintiff until the September term, 1880;   Continued by the Commission until January term, 1881;   Continued by the Commission, Oct. 5, 1881.

February 3, 1882 - Case continued by the Commission till Sept. term. Dismissed for want of prosecution, Sept. 18, 1882.

Jan. 25, 1880
Case #25

CROSBY BEAN

13

vs   Petition for Citizenship
Cherokee Nation

Continued by the Cherokee Nation until the September term, 1880.

September 16, 1880 - The above applicant claims the right to citizenship in the Cherokee Nation under a provision of the Treaty of 1866 between the United States and Cherokee Nation, which provides for the adoption as citizens, slaves that were owned by Cherokees at the commencement of the late rebellion in the United States.

After carefully considering the character of the testimony, the Commission is of the opinion that the claimant was not a slave of any citizen of the Cherokee Nation at the commencement of said rebellion; but landed in the state of Arkansas.

We the Commission therefore hereby decide not to admit the aforesaid Crosby Bean to the rights of citizenship in the Cherokee Nation.

                                            Roach Young, President
                                            Wm Harnage
J.B. Mayes   G.W. Mayes
            Clerk   Asst. Comm.

Jan. 29, 1880
Case #26
            MARTIN FIELDS
            vs   Petition for Citizenship
            Cherokee Nation

The above case continued by Plaintiff until the September term, 1880; Set for trial on 23 Sept, continued by Plaintiff until January term, 1881; Continued by the Plaintiff, Sept. 16, 1881;   Submitted by the Cherokee Nation, Sept. 24, 1881;   The above case continued by the Commission on grounds of not being thoroughly satisfied with the evidence.   Oct. 4, 1881

Jan. 16, 1882 - And now on this the 16th day of January, A.D, 1882, this cause coming on for final hearing and claimant having been duly notified in writing of the coming on of said case for final hearing and all the testimony produced in said case on both sides being read and duly considered; it was adjudged by the Commission on Citizenship that the said claimant, Martin Fields, was not a Cherokee by blood and that he is not entitled to the rights and privileges of Cherokee citizenship within the Cherokee Nation as alleged in his petition; and that his application for citizenship should be and is hereby rejected.

	Thos. Tehee, President
	Alex Wolfe
D.W.C. Duncan	T.F. Thompson
Clerk	Commissioners

Jan. 29, 1880
Case #27

ALLEN & ANDY STILL
   vs   Petition for Citizenship
Cherokee Nation

  The above case continued by the Plaintiff until the September term, 1880 - set for trial on 23 Sept; Continued until January term, 1881, by Plaintiff; Submitted by Plaintiff, Jan. 11, 1881; Continued by the Cherokee Nation until the Sept. term, 1881; Submitted by the Plaintiff, Sept. 16, 1881; Submitted by the Cherokee Nation, Sept. 24, 1881
  The above case continued by the Commission on account of not being thoroughly satisfied with the evidence, Oct. 4, 1881; Continued by Commission till Sept term, February 3, 1882.
  And now on this the 25th day of September A.D, 1882, this case coming on for final hearing and all the evidence produced in the case on both sides being carefully read and duly considered by the Commission; it was adjudged and determined by the Commission on Citizenship that the claimants, Allen Still and Andy Still, are not Cherokees by blood, and that they are not entitled to the rights of Cherokee citizenship within the Cherokee Nation; and that their claim for the same should be and the same is hereby rejected.

	Thos. Tehee, Pres. of Comm.
D.W.C. Duncan	Alex Wolfe, Commissioner
Clerk of Comm.	T.F. Thompson, Dissenting

Transcript furnished claimants, Sept. 25, 1882   D.W.C. Duncan
                     Clerk of Comm.

Jan. 29, 1880
Case #28

   ALEX BEAN

Cherokee Citizenship Commission Docket Books
Tahlequah, Cherokee Nation (1880-84, 1887-89)
Volume I

vs   Petition for Citizenship
Cherokee Nation

The petition of the above claimant, Alex Bean, set forth his claim on the grounds of a Freedman, who left the Cherokee Nation in the spring of 1866. And went to the state of Kansas and returned to the Cherokee Nation in the year 1879, A.D; which allegation within itself denies him the right to citizenship. The treaty upon which his claim is based between the Cherokee Nation and the United States made in 1866, was proclaimed July 10, 1866, which specifies that all freedmen who were in the country at that date and all who only return within six months from that date shall be claimed citizens. This fact evidently excludes claimant. A fact of the testimony supports the above allegation and the remaining facts of the testimony is conflicting.

The Commission therefore decides not to admit claimant to the right of citizenship in the Cherokee Nation. Feb. 4, 1880

Roach Young, President
William Harnage
J.B. Mayes   G.W. Mayes
Clerk Commission   Asst. Comm.

Jan. 31, 1880
Case #29
J.T. KEYS
vs   Petition for Citizenship
Cherokee Nation

The above case continued by the Cherokee Nation until the September term, 1880;   Continued until 21 Sept, submitted by the Plaintiff Sept. 21, 1880;   Continued by the Cherokee Nation until January, 1881;   Submitted by the Cherokee Nation also, Jan. 18, 1881.

The above named claimant J.T. Keys, set forth his claim to citizenship in the Cherokee Nation on the grounds of his Cherokee blood being an immediate descendant of the Keys and Riley family of the Cherokee Nation.

The claim of the said J.T. Keys to citizenship is established to the satisfaction of the Commission beyond a doubt.

We the Commission, therefore hereby issue this our decree admitting the said J.T. Keys to all the rights, privileges and franchise of Cherokee citizenship by blood.

Roach Young, President Commission

Cherokee Citizenship Commission Docket Books
Tahlequah, Cherokee Nation (1880-84, 1887-89)
Volume I

J.B. Mayes

Clerk Commission

William Harnage
G.W. Mayes
Asst. Comm.

Convened September 6, 1880

Roach Young
President

J.B. Mayes

Clerk

Sept. 6, 1880
Case #30

ROBT. CANDY HARLAN*
vs
Cherokee Nation

Petition for Citizenship

Case submitted by both parties for trial.

The above named claimant claims his right to Cherokee citizenship by blood being a descendant of the Candy family who have long been known as Cherokees.

The testimony in the case in his favor is undisputed. The Commission feels justifiable in saying that there is no doubt as to his Cherokee blood.

Therefore as the Commission on Citizenship issue this our decree admitting the said Robt. Candy Harlin* to all the rights, privileges and franchise of Cherokee citizenship by blood.

Roach Young, President
Wm Harnage
J.B. Mayes
Clerk

G.W. Mayes
Asst. Comm.

(*NOTE: Name spelled both ways.)

Sept. 6, 1880
Case #31

JANE LAWTHER*
vs
Cherokee Nation

Petition for Citizenship

Set for trial on 20th   Submitted by both parties, 20 Sept. 1880

Cherokee Citizenship Commission Docket Books
Tahlequah, Cherokee Nation (1880-84, 1887-89)
Volume I

The Commission on Citizenship hears the complaint of the above named Jane Lowther* in accordance with the proclamation of the Principal Chief, dated 27 July 1880, in regard to doubtful citizens reported on the census roll. The testimony shows to the Commission that the rights of the above claimant to citizenship is undisputed; that she is a native born Cherokee and therefore entitled to all the rights, privileges and franchises of a Cherokee by blood; and that there was simply an error in reporting the said claimant as doubtful on the census roll.   Sept. 25, 1880

Roach Young, President
Wm Harnage

J.B. Mayes

G.W. Mayes

Clerk Commission

Asst. Comm.

(*NOTE: Name spelled both ways.)

Sept. 11, 1880
Case #32

LEMUEL WICKED and C.H. Taylor, Atty for Claimant
JOHN N. WICKED & FAMILY
vs   Petition for Citizenship
Cherokee Nation

Continued until January, 1881, by Plaintiff;   Continued by the Commission on grounds of the testimony not being closed, Oct. 5, 1881
Jan. 19, 1882 - Atty for claimant submits the case;   Solicitor for the Cher. Nat. submits the case, Jan. 19, 1882;   Case continued by the Commission till Sept. term, next, Jan. 23, 1882.
And now this case coming up for final hearing on this 7th day of September, 1882. It is ordered that the same be set for final hearing on the 25th day of September, 1882, at the present term, and that each party be allowed to introduce such further evidence as they may see fit on or before the day of final hearing.
And now on this the 25th day of September A.D, 1882, this case coming on for final hearing, and all the evidence produced in the case having been carefully read and duly considered by the Commissioners, it was adjudged and determined by the Commission on Citizenship that the claimants, Lemuel Wicked and John N. Wicked, Lenora Wicked, Laura L. Wicked, Mary Wicked, Albert Wicked, Newton Wicked, Vaden Wicked, Lafelia Wicked and Alice Wicked, are Cherokees by blood; and that they are entitled to all the rights and privileges of Cherokee citizenship within the Chero-

Cherokee Citizenship Commission Docket Books
Tahlequah, Cherokee Nation (1880-84, 1887-89)
Volume I

kee Nation; and that they are hereby admitted to the full and complete enjoyment of the same in all respects as native born Cherokees.

Thos. Tehee, Pres of Comm.
Alex Wolfe

D.W.C. Duncan   T.F. Thompson
   Clerk of Comm   Commissioners

Transcript delivered to Claimants, Sept. 25, 1882.   D.W.C. Duncan
Clerk of Comm.

Sept. 8, 1880
Case #33

A. W. HARLIN*

vs   Petition for Citizenship
Cherokee Nation

Continued until 20th next;   The above case submitted by both parties, 20 Sept 1880.

The above claimant appears before this Commission in obedience to a proclamation of the Principal Chief, dated 27 July 1880, in regard to doubtful citizens.

The facts before the Commission shows that the said claimant, A.W. Harlan*, takes a reservation on the "Neutral Land" under a provision of the Treaty of 1866, between the Cherokee Nation and the United States. Thereby forfeiting his citizenship in the Cherokee Nation and all other rights he may have been entitled to on account of his Cherokee blood. The widower shows that he has since become a citizen of the Cherokee Nation under the law regulating intermarriages with citizens of the United States.

It is therefore the opinion of the Commission that there is no doubt as to his citizenship and should not have been reported as a doubtful citizen on the census roll.

The Commission therefore recognizes the said claimant, A.W. Harlan, as a citizen of the Cherokee Nation with only the rights of other adopted citizens of the United States. Sept. 25, 1880

Roach Young, President
Wm Harnage

J.B. Mayes   G.W. Mayes
     Clerk Comm.   Asst. Comm.
        (***NOTE:** Name spelled both ways.)

Cherokee Citizenship Commission Docket Books
Tahlequah, Cherokee Nation (1880-84, 1887-89)
Volume I

Sept. 8, 1880
Case #34

> **L.P, GEORGE ANN, THOMAS** and
> **BEULA CLYDE ISABEL**
> vs   Petition for Citizenship
> Cherokee Nation

Set for 21st next.   The above case submitted by both parties, 21 Sept 1880;   Continued by the court until January, 1881, on account of the fact that there is no evidence to show that L.P. Isabel (unable to read, writing smudged) a white man

The above parties are ordered to appear before the Commission under a proclamation of the Principal Chief, dated 27 July 1880 as doubtful citizens.

The testimony before the Commission shows that L.P. Isabel is a white man and can get citizenship in the Cherokee Nation only under the law regulating intermarriages between Cherokees and citizens of the United States. The Commission leaves this matter to be accomplished by the said L.P. Isabel himself.

The testimony shows conclusively to the Commission that George Ann Isabel, Thos. Isabel and Beula Clyde Isabel, are Cherokees by blood and are therefore entitled to all the rights, privileges and franchise of Cherokee citizenship and that the late census takers committed an error in reporting the said George Ann Isabel, Thos. Isabel and Beula Clyde Isabel as intruders. The right to full citizenship is hereby admitted on grounds of their blood.
Jan. 29, 1881

	Roach Young, President Commission
	William Harnage
J.B. Mayes	G.W. Mayes
Clerk Commission	Asst. Commissioners

Sept. 8, 1880
Case #35

> **NANCY GUNTER** and **FAMILY**
> vs   Petition for Citizenship
> Cherokee Nation

Set for trial on the 11th, next.

In accordance with a proclamation of the Principal Chief dated 27 July 1880, requesting certain persons to appear before the Commission on Citi-

Cherokee Citizenship Commission Docket Books
Tahlequah, Cherokee Nation (1880-84, 1887-89)
Volume I

zenship in September, who have been reported as doubtful citizens in accordance with the late census law. The Commissioners take up the above case.

The Commission is unanimously of the opinion that the above claimants are lawful citizens of the Cherokee Nation, and ought not to have been reported as a doubtful citizen. It therefore seems that they are entitled to all the rights and privileges of any other Cherokee citizen.   Sept. 11, 1880

	Roach Young, President
	Wm Harnage
J.B. Mayes	G.W. Mayes
(Clerk)	Asst. Comm.

Sept. 8, 1880
Case #36

SETH R. & MARY HALL
vs   Petition for Citizenship
Cherokee Nation

Set for trial 10th;   Continued until 13th, next.

The above named Claimants are cited before the Commission by the Principal Chief under a proclamation dated 27 July 1880; agreeable to the Census Law passed, Dec. 3, 1879.

The Commission takes up the case in accordance with the said proclamation and Law.

The testimony shows that the said Mary Hall is a Cherokee citizen. The Commission hereby recognizes her as such; and also recognizes the said Seth R. Hall a citizen with only the rights of an adopted citizen under the marriage law. The above claimants, Seth R. Hall and Mary Hall, are hereby admitted to all the rights of Cherokee citizenship.   Sept. 15, 1880

	Roach Young, Pres.
	Wm Harnage
J.B. Mayes	G.W. Mayes
Clerk	Asst. Comm.

Sept. 9, 1880
Case #37

RICHARD W. DUNCAN
vs   Petition for Citizenship
Cherokee Nation

21

The above case continued by the Plaintiff until January term, 1881, Oct. 2, 1880; Continued by Plaintiff until January term, 1881; Continued by the Commission on account of the testimony not being close, Oct. 3, 1881; Continued by the Claimant till the next Sept. term, Jan, 1882 Dismissed for want of prosecution, Sept. 18, 1882.

Sept. 10, 1880
Case #38

W. H. & JOHN W. SHOEMAKER
vs   Petition for Citizenship
Cherokee Nation

Continued until January term, 1881, by Plaintiff; Continued by Plaintiff until September, 1881; Continued, Sept. 24, 1881.

And on this 4th day of January, 1882, Claimant by leave of the Commission files his new petition; and said case is to be terminated upon the Docket.

Case continued till Sept. term by Commission, Feb. 3, 1882; Case submitted by the Claimant, Sept. 18, 1882; Submitted by the Solicitor, Oct. 4, 1882; Continued by the Commission till the January term, 1883, October 4, 1882.

And not on this the 25th day of January A.D, 1883, this case coming on for final hearing and all the evidence introduced in the case on both sides being carefully read and duly considered by the Commission on Citizenship, it was adjudged and determined by said Commission on Citizenship that the above named W.H. Shoemaker and John W. Shoemaker, are Cherokees by blood and that they are therefore entitled to all the rights and privileges of Cherokee citizenship within the Cherokee Nation, and that they should be and they are hereby admitted to the full and complete enjoyment of the same in all aspects as native born Cherokees.

Thos. Tehee, Pres of Comm
Alex Wolfe
D.W.C. Duncan   T.F. Thompson
        Clerk of Commission   Commissioners

Sept. 11, 1880
Case #39

**THOS, REBECCA, JAMES F; EDDIE,
SHERMAN, MARY, and MARTHA JOHNSON**

Cherokee Citizenship Commission Docket Books
Tahlequah, Cherokee Nation (1880-84, 1887-89)
Volume I

vs   Petition for Citizenship

Cherokee Nation

Submitted by Plaintiff 17 Sept;   The above case submitted by both parties, 25 Sept. 1880.

The above named claimants come before the Commission in obedience to a proclamation of the Principal Chief dated 27 July A.D, 1880. Their names appearing on the census roll as doubtful citizens.

The testimony before the Commission proves to the satisfaction of the Commission that the said, Rebecca Johnson, is a native born Cherokee. Also that her children; to wit: Jas. F. Johnson, Eddie Johnson, Sherman Johnson, Mary Johnson, and Martha Johnson; are of Cherokee blood and are entitled to all the rights and privileges of Cherokee citizenship by blood. And that there was an error in the census roll in reporting them as doubtful.

The testimony further shows that, Thomas Johnson, the husband of Rebecca becomes a citizen of the Cherokee Nation under the marriage law regulations intermarriages with citizens of the Cherokee Nation and citizens of the United States; although the said Thos. Johnson is a colored man.

Their rights to citizenship is hereby fully recognized.   Sept. 25, 1880

Roach Young, President
Wm Harnage
J.B. Mayes   G.W. Mayes
Clerk Comm.   Asst. Comm.

Sept. 11, 1880
Case #40

**LEWIS, SARAH,
FRANKLIN & OMA E. LAFALIER**
vs   Petition for Citizenship

Cherokee Nation

Submitted by Plaintiff and by Cherokee Nation also, 23 Sept. 1880.

The testimony in the above case shows beyond a doubt that Sarah Lafalier, the above claimant, is one of the Shawnee tribe of Indians, embraced, numbered and enrolled and admitted to citizenship in the Cherokee Nation; under Articles of Agreement, contracted between the Cherokee Nation and said Shawnee tribe of Indians in Washington City, June 7, 1869; and approved by the President of the United States, June 9, 1869. And that Franklin Lafalier and Oma E. Lafalier are children born of her since she was admitted to Cherokee citizenship; and as there is no testimony to show that they have ever forfeited their citizenship; the Commission is of the opinion that they should not have been reported as doubtful citizens on the late census roll. The Commission hereby admits them to the full rights of Cherokee citizenship.

The said Lewis Lafalier is shown to be a Miami Indian and claims the right of citizenship by marriage.

From time in memorial there has been no law but custom regulating intermarriage between the Cherokee and other tribes of Indians; neither is there any law to this day placing any restrictions or regulating it in any manner; although it has ever been lawful for Indians of different tribes to marry among one another.

In view of these facts, the Commission hereby admits the said Lewis Lafalier to all the rights of an adopted citizen. Sept. 25, 1880

Roach Young, Pres.
Wm Harnage
J.B. Mayes   G.W. Mayes
Clerk   Asst. Comm.

Sept. 11, 1880
Case #41
NANCY WESCOLA & CHILD
vs   Petition for Citizenship
Cherokee Nation

Submitted by Plaintiff, 17th 1880;   Continued by Plaintiff until January term, 1881;   Submitted by the Cherokee Nation, 24th, 1881.

The above named Nancy Wescola appears before the Commission in obedience to a proclamation of the Principal Chief dated 27 July 1880, as a doubtful citizen reported on the late census roll.

The testimony shows that the claimant is an adopted citizen of the Cherokee Nation from the Shawnee tribe of Indians, under treaty stipulations and should not have been reported as a doubtful citizen of the Cherokee Nation.

The Commission therefore recognizes the said Nancy Wescola as citizen of the Cherokee Nation enjoying all the rights, privileges and franchise thereof.   Jan. 28, 1881

Roach Young, President Comm.
William Harnage

24

J.B. Mayes
      Clerk Comm.

G.W. Mayes
      Asst. Comm.

Sept. 13, 1880
Case #42

JOSEPH and **THOS. WATIE**
      vs   Petition for Citizenship
Cherokee Nation

Continued by Plaintiff until January term, 1880; The above case continued by the Plaintiff until September term, 1881; Submitted by the Plaintiff, Sept. 10, 1881; The above case continued by the Solicitor on account of testimony, Oct. 5, 1881; Jan. 11, 1882 - Submitted by the Cherokee Nation.

And now this the 11th day of January A.D, 1882, this case coming on for hearing, and having heard and considered all the evidence provided in the case, it is adjudged and considered by the Commission on Citizenship, that the above named applicants; to wit: Joseph Watie and Thomas Watie, are entitled to and that they are hereby admitted to the full and perfect enjoyment of Cherokee citizenship within the Cherokee Nation, as Cherokees.

                Thos [his X mark] Tehee,
                President
                Alex [his X mark] Wolfe
D.W.C. Duncan   T.F. Thompson
    Clerk   Commissioners

Copies issued to Claimants in pursuance of law, Jan. 12, 1882
                D.W.C. Duncan
                Clerk

Sept. 13, 1880
Case #43

MALINDA, PEACHES* ELLEN,
JAMES ALEXANDER, JOSEPH ASBEY
and **WM. HENRY FAGAN**
      vs   Petition for Citizenship
Cherokee Nation
              C.H. Taylor, Atty for Claimant

Cherokee Citizenship Commission Docket Books
Tahlequah, Cherokee Nation (1880-84, 1887-89)
Volume I

Continued until January term, 1881, by Plaintiff; Submitted by Plaintiff, Jan. 11, 1881; Continued by the Cherokee Nation until Sept, 1881; Sept. 5, 1881 - The above case submitted by Plaintiff; The above set for trial on 26, next; The above case continued by the attorney for the Nation, Oct. 3, 1881; Oct. 4, 1882 - Continued by Commission to January term, 1883; Continued to the Sept. term, 1883; Case submitted by Solicitor, Sept. 21, 1883.

And now on this the 28th day of September A.D, 1883, this case coming on for final hearing and all the evidence produced in the case being carefully read and duly considered; it was decided by the Commission on Citizenship, that the above named Claimants, Malinda Fagan, Peachie* Ellen Fagan, James Alexander Fagan, Joseph Asbey Fagan, and Wm Henry Fagan, are Cherokees by blood and that they are justly entitled to all the rights and privileges of Cherokee citizenship within the Cherokee Nation, and that they should be and they are hereby admitted to the full and complete enjoyment of the same in all respects as native born Cherokees.

<table>
<tr><td></td><td>Thos. Tehee, President Comm.</td></tr>
<tr><td></td><td>Alex Wolfe</td></tr>
<tr><td>Wm Eubanks</td><td>T.F. Thompson</td></tr>
<tr><td>Clerk Comm</td><td>Commissioners</td></tr>
<tr><td>A copy furnished, Sept. 3, 1884</td><td></td></tr>
</table>

C.O. Frye, Clerk
(*NOTE: Name spelled both ways.)

Oct. 13, 1880
Case #44

JAMES DANIELS
MARY A. SHERMAN
vs   Petition for Citizenship
Cherokee Nation   Benge & Lyons, Attys.

Submitted by Plaintiff, 22 Sept. 1880; Continued by the Cherokee Nation until January term, 1881; Submitted by both parties, Jan. 19, 1881.

The Commission after a careful and thorough consideration of the testimony now on file in this office, are unanimously of the opinion that the testimony fails to establish the fact of the claimants, James Daniels and Mary A. Sherman, Cherokee blood.

Cherokee Citizenship Commission Docket Books
Tahlequah, Cherokee Nation (1880-84, 1887-89)
Volume I

We the Commission therefore hereby decide that the claimants are not Cherokees by blood and are not therefore entitled to the rights of Cherokee citizenship in the Cherokee Nation.

	Roach Young, President Comm.
	William Harnage
J.B. Mayes	G.W. Mayes
Clerk	Asst. Comm.

Sept. 13, 1880
Case #45

MUSSELSHELL SA-NI COUI

vs	Petition for Citizenship
Cherokee Nation	

The above claimant claims his right under an act of the National Council passed Nov. 13, 1843, admitting certain Creek Indians to citizenship in the Cherokee Nation.

After examining the law admitting certain Creek Indians to citizenship before mentioned; the Commission is of the opinion that the above named claimant is included in the list of Creek Indians mentioned in the above mentioned law.

The Commission therefore hereby admits the above named claimant to all the rights, privileges and franchises of Cherokee citizenship.   Sept. 15, 1880.

	Roach Young, Pres.
	Wm Harnage
J.B. Mayes	G.W. Mayes
Clerk	Asst. Comm.

Sept. 15, 1880
Case #46

DAVID J. LYONS

vs	Petition for Citizenship
Cherokee Nation	

The above case comes before the Commission in obedience (to) a proclamation of the Principal Chief, dated 27 July 1880, which was issued in compliance with a law passed by the National Council approved Dec. 3,

1879. An act for taking the census of the Cherokee Nation in 1880. The above claimant is reported on said census roll as a doubtful citizen.

After examining the testimony in the case, the Commission is of the opinion that there was an error in reporting said claimant as doubtful. He being a Cherokee by blood and now a resident.

The Commission hereby admits the said claimant to all the rights, privileges and franchises of Cherokee citizenship.   Sept. 17, 1880

	Roach Young, Pres.
	Wm Harnage
J.B. Mayes	G.W. Mayes
Clerk	Asst. Comm.

Sept. 16, 1880
Case #47

ISAAC N. McDONALD, JOHN O. McDONALD, JAMES E. COATS, CHARLES F. COATS, WILLIAM COATS, ROBT. W. CRAIG and EDNA E. CRAIG

vs   Petition for Citizenship

Cherokee Nation

The above claimants show to the Commission by satisfactory testimony that they are children of Sofrina A. Bivins, Louisa J. Coats, and Frank W. Craig, who was admitted to citizenship by the Commission during this term of said Commission.

The Commission hereby therefore issues this their decree admitting the above named claimants to all the rights, privileges, and franchises of Cherokee citizenship by blood.   Sept. 17, 1880

	Roach Young, Pres.
	Wm. Harnage
J.B. Mayes	G. W. Mayes
Clerk	Asst. Comm.

Sept. 17, 1880
Case #48

CHARLES E. BETTS

vs   Petition for Citizenship

Cherokee Nation

Cherokee Citizenship Commission Docket Books
Tahlequah, Cherokee Nation (1880-84, 1887-89)
Volume I

Submitted by Plaintiff, Sept. 18, 1880, also by the Cherokee Nation; The Commission continues the above case until January, 1880, in order to sustain other facts "of his wife being admitted to citizenship by the Nation. Council which was asserted in said petition, but not proven. (NOTE: no end quotes given)

The above named claimant is a Choctaw Indian and notified to appear before this Commission under the proclamation of the Principal Chief, dated 27 July 1880, as a doubtful citizen reported on the late census roll.

The testimony before the Commission proves that the said claimant has married a Cherokee Indian and furthermore since the above case has been elected for a hearing before the Commission; an act of the National Council affirmed Nov. 27, 1880, legalizing all marriages heretofore and all after the passage of said act between the Cherokee and different tribes of the Indian Territory.

The Commission therefore hereby recognizes the said Charles E. Betts as a man entitled to all the rights of Cherokee citizenship.   Jan. 29, 1881

Roach Young, President Comm.

William Harnage

J.B. Mayes   G.W. Mayes

      Clerk Comm.   Asst. Comm.

Sept. 17, 1880
Case #49

WINNIE DAUGHERTY
and **CHILDREN**
       vs   Petition for Citizenship
Cherokee Nation

Continued by Plaintiff until January term, 1881;   Submitted by the Plaintiff, Sept. 29, 1881;   Submitted by the Solicitor, Oct. 5, 1881.

The Commission is of the opinion that the Claimant is a native born Cherokee Indian by blood.

The claimant comes before (the) Commission under a proclamation of the Principal Chief dated July, 1880, as a doubtful citizen reported as such on the late census roll.

The Commission hereby decides that there was an error in reporting said claimant as a doubtful citizen and that she is entitled to all the rights and privileges of Cherokee citizenship just the same as other native Cherokees.

Cherokee Citizenship Commission Docket Books
Tahlequah, Cherokee Nation (1880-84, 1887-89)
Volume I

Roach Young, President Comm.
William Harnage

J.B. Mayes   G.W. Mayes
    Clerk Comm.   Asst. Comm.

Sept. 17, 1880
Case #50

A. J. IVEY
vs   Petition for Citizenship
Cherokee Nation

The above case submitted by the Plaintiff, Sept. 30, 1880;   Continued by the Cherokee Nation until January term, 1881;   Continued by the Cherokee Nation until the September term, 1881;   Submitted by both parties for the action of the Commission, Sept. 6, 1881.

The evidence before the Commission shows the claimant to be an immediate relative and descendant of the Rogers and Jordan families, long known to be Cherokees by blood. The Commission is therefore of the opinion that the Petitioner's claim is well founded and that he is of (Cherokee) blood.

Therefore we the Commission on Citizenship do hereby admit the above named A.J. Ivey to all the rights, privileges and franchise of Cherokee citizenship by blood.   Sept. 18, 1881

Roach Young, President Comm
William Harnage

J.B. Mayes   G.W. Mayes
    Clerk   Asst. Comm.

Sept. 17, 1880
Case #51

**D.W, BELLE, ALONZO,
MAGGIE,** and **BENJ. IVEY**
vs   Petition for Citizenship
Cherokee Nation

Submitted by Plaintiff, Sept. 18, 1880;   Continued by the Cherokee Nation until the January term, 1881;   Continued by the Cherokee Nation until the September term, 1881;   The above case submitted by both parties for the action of the Commission, Sept. 6, 1881.

Cherokee Citizenship Commission Docket Books
Tahlequah, Cherokee Nation (1880-84, 1887-89)
Volume I

The testimony before the Commission shows conclusively that the Claimants are Cherokees by blood; being immediate descendants of the noted families of Rogers and Jordans, long known to be Cherokees by blood. The Commission on Citizenship therefore hereby admits the said claimants; D.W. Ivey, Belle Ivey, Alonzo Ivey, Maggie Ivey, and Benjamin Ivey, to all the rights and privileges of Cherokee citizenship by blood.   Sept. 18, 1881

	Roach Young, President
	William Harnage
J.B. Mayes	G.W. Mayes
Clerk Comm	Asst. Comm.

Sept. 17, 1880
Case #52

JAMES and CHARLES GARDENHIRE
vs	Petition for Citizenship
Cherokee Nation	

Submitted by Plaintiff and Defendant, Sept. 18, 1880.

The testimony in the above case shows that the father and mother were both native born Cherokees being the descendants of noted Cherokees.

The Commission therefore hereby admits the above named claimants to all the rights, privileges, and franchises of Cherokee citizenship by blood. Sept. 25, 1880

	Roach Young, Pres.
	Wm. Harnage
J.B. Mayes	G.W. Mayes
Clerk	Asst. Comm.

Sept. 20, 1880
Case #53

GEORGE W. BRADSHAW
vs	Petition for Citizenship
Cherokee Nation	

Continued by Plaintiff until January term, 1881;   Set for trial on the 27th next;   Continued by the Plaintiff on account of important testimony, Oct. 3, 1881.

Jan. 10, 1882 - Case considered and laid over till the 16th day of Jan, 1882, to be then finally disposed of unless claimant moves to take up the case before that date.

Jan. 16, 1882 - And now on this the 16th day of January A.D, 1882, this cause coming for final hearing and said claimant having been duly notified in writing of the coming on of said case for final hearing and all the testimony produced in said case on both sides being read and duly considered; it is adjudged by the Commission on Citizenship that the said claimant, George W. Bradshaw, is not a Cherokee by blood as alleged in this petition and that he is not entitled to the rights and privileges of Cherokee citizenship within the Cherokee Nation; and that his petition and claim for Cherokee citizenship should be and the same is hereby rejected.

Thos. Tehee, President
Alex Wolfe
D.W.C. Duncan   T.F. Thompson
Clerk   Commissioners

Sept. 21, 1880
Case #54

AMANDA ROSS
vs   Petition for Citizenship
Cherokee Nation

The above case withdrawn by Plaintiff and Defendant from the docket.
Sept. 22, 1880

Sept. 21, 1880
Case #55

VIC* ARMSTRONG
vs   Petition for Citizenship
Cherokee Nation   Before the Commission under the
                         Proclamation of the Principal Chief,
                         dated 27 July 1880
Continued by Plaintiff until January term, 1881;   Submitted by Plaintiff, 11th, 1881;   Submitted by the Cherokee Nation, Sept. 16, 1881.

Office Commission on Citizenship, Tahlequah, C.N. Sept. 30, 1881

Cherokee Citizenship Commission Docket Books
Tahlequah, Cherokee Nation (1880-84, 1887-89)
Volume I

The Claimant comes before the Commission under a Proclamation of the Principal Chief dated 27 July 1880, as a doubtful citizen reported as such by the late census takers.

The testimony before the Commission shows the claimant to be a Cherokee by blood being a descendant of the Kell and Owens families, well known Cherokees.

The testimony does not show that the claimant ever forfeited the right to Cherokee citizenship.

The Commission therefore decides that there was an error committed by the census takers in reporting him as a doubtful citizen. That the claimant Vick* Armstrong is now and heretofore been entitled to all the rights and privileges of Cherokee citizenship by blood.

Roach Young, President Comm.
William Harnage
G.W. Mayes
Asst. Comm.

J.B. Mayes
    Clerk Comm

(*NOTE: Name spelled both ways.)

===

Sept. 21, 1880
Case #56

    HANNA THOMPSON
        vs   Petition for Citizenship
    Cherokee Nation

The above case withdrawn by Plaintiff, Sept. 25, 1880.

===

Sept. 21, 1880
Case #57

    MINERVIA, ELIZABETH
    and **ALLISON DAVIS**
        vs   Petition for Citizenship
    Cherokee Nation

Submitted by Plaintiff, 22 Sept. 1880; Continued by the Cherokee Nation until January, 1881; Continued by the Cherokee Nation until the September term, 1881; Witness subpoenaed to appear on the 12th, next; Continued by the attorney for the nation on account of witness, Oct. 5, 1881; Jan. 21, 1882 - Case submitted by the Solicitor for the Cher. Nation.

Jan. 21, 1882 - And now this case coming on for final hearing and notice having been issued to Claimants of the coming on of said case for final hearing and all the evidence provided in the case on

both sides having been carefully read and duly considered; it was adjudged by the Commission on Citizenship that the above named claimants; to wit: Minervia Davis, Elizabeth Davis and Allison Davis, are not Cherokees by blood as alleged in their petition and that they are not entitled to the rights and privileges of Cherokee citizenship within the Cherokee Nation; and that their claim for the same should be, and therefore is hereby <u>rejected</u>.

Thos. Tehee, Pres of Comm
Alex Wolfe, Commissioner

D.W.C. Duncan   T.F. Thompson, Comm. being <u>absent</u>
       Clerk

Sept. 21, 1880
Case #58

EMMA CRITTENDEN
ANN TUCKER
vs   Petition for Citizenship
Cherokee Nation

Continued until January term, 1881, by Plaintiff;   The above case withdrawn by Plaintiff, Sept. 16, 1881.

Sept. 22, 1880
Case #59

JESS ORR
vs   Petition for Citizenship
Cherokee Nation

Continued until January term, 1881, by Plaintiff;   The above case withdrawn by Plaintiff, Sept. 16, 1881.

Sept. 22, 1880
Case #60

L. D. KEYS
vs   Petition for Citizenship
Cherokee Nation

Continued until January term, 1881, by Plaintiff; Submitted by the Plaintiff, Jan. 26, 1881; Submitted by the Cherokee Nation, Jan. 28, 1881. The testimony before the Commission shows beyond a doubt that the claimant, L. D. Keys, is an immediate descendant of the noted Keys and Riley families, who are Cherokees and are now living in the Cherokee Nation; well known Cherokees by blood.

The Commission therefore hereby admits the said L. D. Keys to all the rights, privileges and franchises of Cherokee citizenship by blood. Jan. 29, 1881

Roach Young, President Comm.

William Harnage

J.B. Mayes   G.W. Mayes

Clerk Commission   Asst. Comm.

Sept. 22, 1880
Case #61

PATTY GRIGGS

vs   Petition for Citizenship

Cherokee Nation

Submitted by Plaintiff, 23 Sept. 1880; Continued by the Cherokee Nation until January term, 1881; Continued by the Cherokee Nation to the September term, 1881; Submitted by Plaintiff, Sept. 18, 1881.

The above party claims to have been admitted by the Supreme Court. A copy of said claim introduced as testimony. The Commission continued said case on account of a portion of the parties evidence, the record of said court.

Jan. 13, 1882 - The above case set for trial on the 16th day of January, 1882. Submitted by the Cherokee Nation, Jan. 16, 1882.

Jan. 16, 1882 - And now on this the 16th day of January A.D, 1882, this case coming on for final hearing and said Claimant being duly notified in writing of the coming on of said case for final hearing and all the testimony produced in the case on both sides being read and duly considered; it is adjudged by the Commission on Citizenship, that the said Claimant, Patty Griggs, is not a Cherokee by blood; and that she is not entitled to the rights and privileges of Cherokee citizenship within the Cherokee Nation as claimed in her petition; and that her said claim for Cherokee citizenship should be and the same is hereby rejected.

Thos. Tehee, President

Alex Wolfe, Commissioner

D.W.C. Duncan   T.F. Thompson, Commissioner, Dissenting
        Clerk

Sept. 25, 1880
Case #62

ELIZA CATHERINE REDING*
vs   Petition for Citizenship
Cherokee Nation

The above case continued until January term, 1881;   Continued by the
Commission, Oct. 3, 1881;   Continued by the Commission till Sept. term,
Feb. 3, 1881;   Submitted by atty for claimant, Sept. 19, 1882;   Submitted
by the Solicitor, Sept. 19, 1882.

And now on this the 27th day of September A.D, 1882, this case coming
on for final hearing, and all the evidence produced in the case on both sides
being carefully read and duly considered by the Commission; it is adjudged
and determined by the Commission on Citizenship that the claimant, Eliza
Catherine Reeding*, is not a Cherokee by blood, and that she is not entitled
to the rights and privileges of Cherokee citizenship within the Cherokee Nation; and that her claim therefore should be and the same is hereby rejected.

                                      Thos. Tehee, Pres. of Comm.
                                      Alex Wolfe
D.W.C. Duncan   T.F. Thompson
        Clerk of Comm.   Commissioners

(***NOTE:** Name spelled both ways.)

Sept. 23, 1880
Case #63

JAMES M. COKER
LUCY A. DALE

            vs   Petition for Citizenship
        Cherokee Nation

The above case continued by Plaintiff until January term, 1881;   The
above case submitted by both parties, Sept. 24, 1881.

The testimony before the Commission of reliable witnesses shows the claimant to be of Cherokee blood; being descendant of the Ratcliff family, well known Cherokees by blood.

The Commission therefore hereby admits the said claimants, James M. Coker and Lucy A. Dale, to all the rights, privileges, and franchises of Cherokee citizenship by blood.

Roach Young, President
William Harnage
G.W. Mayes
Asst. Comm.

J.B. Mayes
    Clerk Commission

Sept. 23, 1880
Case #64

R.C. PARCKS & WIFE
vs   Petition for Citizenship
Cherokee Nation

The above case continued until January term, 1881, by Plaintiff; Submitted by Plaintiff, Jan. 25, 1881;   Submitted by the Cherokee Nation, Feb. 2, 1881.

The testimony in the above case shows that the claimant, R.C. Parcks is an Indian by blood.

The Commission therefore hereby admits the said R.C. Parcks to all the rights, privileges and franchises of Cherokee citizenship.   Feb. 2, 1881.

Roach Young, President
William Harnage
G.W. Mayes
Asst. Comm.

J.B. Mayes
    Clerk

Sept. 25, 1880
Case #65

RUTH McCLURE
ALICE LEE McCLURE

vs   Petition for Citizenship
Cherokee Nation

The above case continued by the Plaintiff, 30th Sept. 1880;   Continued by the Cherokee Nation until January term, 1881;   Submitted by the Cherokee Nation also, Jan. 11, 1881.

The testimony in the above case proves to the satisfaction of the Commission that the above claimants are Cherokee by blood and entitled to all the rights and privileges of Cherokee citizenship.

The Commission therefore hereby issues this their decree admitting the above named claimants to all rights, privileges, and franchises of Cherokee citizenship by blood.   Jan. 12, 1881

Roach Young, Pres. Commission
William Harnage

J.B. Mayes
    Clerk

G.W. Mayes
Asst. Comm.

Oct. 5, 1880
Case #66

HENRY C. ROGERS and WIFE

vs	Petition for Citizenship
Cherokee Nation	Atty for Pltffs. C.H. Taylor

Continued by Plaintiff until January, 1881;   Continued by the Plaintiff, Oct. 3, 1881;   Jan. 14, 1882 - Submitted by claimant;   Jan. 30, 1881 - Submitted by the Solicitor for the Cher. Nation.

Jan. 23, 1882 - And now on this the 23rd day of January A.D, 1882, this case coming on for final hearing and all the testimony produced in the case on both sides being carefully read and duly considered, it was adjudged by the Commission on Citizenship that the above named claimants, to wit: Henry C. Rogers and Louisa J. Rogers, claimant's wife, are Cherokees by blood, and that they are entitled to all the rights and privileges of Cherokee citizenship within the Cherokee Nation; and that they should be and they are hereby admitted to the full and perfect enjoyment of the same as native born Cherokees.

Thos. Tehee, Pres, Dissenting
Alex Wolfe

D.W.C. Duncan
    Clerk

T.F. Thompson
Commissioners

Certificate of admission issued to claimants in pursuance (of) law, Jan. 23, 1882.

D.W.C. Duncan, Clerk

Oct. 5, 1880
Case #67

JULIA A. SPENCER
LOUISA REYNOLDS
      vs   Petition for Citizenship
Cherokee Nation

The above case continued by Plaintiff until January, 1881;   The above case withdrawn by Plaintiff, 18 Sept. 1881.

Oct. 5, 1881
Case #68
        J.C. GATES
        FRANK GATES
           vs   Petition for Citizenship
        Cherokee Nation

The above case continued until January, 1881, by Plaintiff.
The above case withdrawn by Plaintiff, Sept. 16, 1881.

Oct. 5, 1880
Case #69
        RACHEL F. NIX and FAMILY
           vs   Petition for Citizenship
        Cherokee Nation   C.H. Taylor, Atty for Claimant

The above case continued until January, 1881;   Continued by Plaintiff, Oct. 3, 1881;   Case continued by Commission till Sept. term, Feb. 3, 1882; Submitted by the claimant and the Solicitor, Sept. 28, 1882.
    And now on this the 28th day of September A.D, 1882, this case coming on for final hearing and all the evidence produced in the case on both sides having carefully read and duly considered by the Commission; it is adjudged and determined by the Commission on Citizenship that said claimants Rachel F. Nix, Wm M. Nix, F.M. Nix, M.B. Nix, John C. Nix, and Sooz L. Nix; are not a(sic) Cherokee by blood and that they are not entitled to the rights and privileges of Cherokee citizenship within the Cherokee Nation and that their claim therefore should be and the same is hereby rejected.

                                    Thos. Tehee, Pres. of Comm
                                      Alex Wolfe
D.W.C. Duncan   T.F. Thompson
        Clerk of Comm   Commissioners

Cherokee Citizenship Commission Docket Books
Tahlequah, Cherokee Nation (1880-84, 1887-89)
Volume I

Oct. 7, 1880
Case #70

ISAAC ROGERS
vs   Petition for Citizenship
Cherokee Nation

Continued by the Plaintiff, Oct. 3, 1881;   Feb. 3, 1882 - continued by
Commission till Sept. term;   Dismissed for want of prosecution, Sept. 18,
1882.

Convened at Tahlequah, Cherokee Nation in accordance with laws for
the United States of America, on the 3rd day of January, 1881.
Roach Young, Presiding Judge

Jan. 12, 1881
Case #71

WILLIAM P, JAMES S; JOHN R,
and MARY E. ARCHER
vs   Petition for Citizenship
Cherokee Nation

The above case continued by the Plaintiff until the Sept. term, 1881;
The case withdrawn by Plaintiff, Sept. 16, 1881.

Jan. 13, 1881
Case #72

GEORGE W, EMILY JANE, ORVILLE E,
and ARCHIE AUGUSTUS THORNTON
vs   Petition for Citizenship
Cherokee Nation   I.M. Bryan Atty for Claimant

The above case submitted by the Plaintiff, Sept. 17, 1881;   Continued
by the Cherokee Nation, Oct. 3, 1881;   Case continued by Commission till
Sept. term, Feb. 3, 1882;   Submitted by the Claimant's Atty and by the Solicitor, Sept. 22, 1882.
And now on this the 25th day of September A.D, 1882, this case coming
on for final hearing and all the evidence produced in the case on both sides

being carefully read and duly considered by the Commission; it was adjudged and determined by the Commission on Citizenship that the said
claimants, George W. Thornton, Emily Jane Thornton, Orville E.
Thornton, and Archie Augustus Thornton, are Cherokees by blood, and that they are
entitled to all the rights and privileges of Cherokee citizenship within the
Cherokee Nation; and that they should be and are hereby admitted to the full
and complete enjoyment of the same within the Cherokee Nation in all aspects as native born Cherokees.

                                        Thos. Tehee, Pres of Comm.
                                        Alex Wolfe
D.W.C. Duncan   T.F. Thompson
        Clerk   Commissioners

Transcript furnished claimant, Sept. 25, 1882.
                                        D.W.C. Duncan, Clerk

Jan. 17, 1881
Case #73

THOS. & ADIE HUBBARD
            vs   Petition for Citizenship
    Cherokee Nation   Atty for Pltf, C.H. Taylor

     The above case submitted by the Plaintiff, Jan. 28, 1881;   Continued
by the Cherokee Nation till the Sept. term, 1881;   Continued by the Solicitor for the Nation on account of testimony, Oct. 3, 1881;   Jan. 13, 1882 -
Continued by the Commission until the next term, in Sept, 1882, and on motion of Claimant, the above continuance is rescinded and the case taken up of
trial. Case set for trial on Jan. 16, 1882.

     Jan. 17, 1882 - And not on this the 17th day of January A.D, 1882, this
cause coming on for final hearing and said claimants having due notice issued to them that said cause was coming on for final hearing; and all the testimony produced in said case by both parties having been carefully read and
duly considered; it is adjudged by the Commission on Citizenship that the
above named claimants; Thomas Hubbard and Adie Hubbare are not Cherokees by blood and that they are not entitled to the rights and privileges of
Cherokee citizenship within the Cherokee Nation as claimed in their petition;
and that their said claim for Cherokee citizenship should be and the same is
hereby rejected.

                                        Thos. Tehee, President

                           41

Alex Wolfe
D.W.C. Duncan   T.F. Thompson
              Clerk   Commissioners

Jan. 18, 1881
Case #74

JACKSON RANDOLF
              vs   Petition for Citizenship
Cherokee Nation

The above case continued until September term, 1881, by Plaintiff; Submitted by Plaintiff, Sept. 23, 1881;   Submitted by the Nation, Oct. 3, 1881.

The claimant, Jackson Randolf, asks to be admitted to Cherokee citizenship on account of his Cherokee blood; being a descendant of John Randolf of Roanoke. The Cherokee Indians have never acknowledged John Randolf as a Cherokee. If he was an Indian, he certainly belonged to another tribe. The testimony fails to prove the claimant to be a Cherokee by blood.

The Commission therefore decides not to admit the said claimant, Jackson Randolf to Cherokee citizenship.

                    Roach Young, President
                    William Harnage
J.B. Mayes   G.W. Mayes
         Clerk Commission   Asst. Comm.

Jan. 19, 1881
Case #75

SALLY LUMPKIN* & FAMILY   Appear per se
              vs   Petition for Citizenship
Cherokee Nation   M.O. Ghormly & E.C. Boudinott
                                   Attys for Claimant

Continued by the Commission, Oct. 3, 1881;   Continued by Commission till Sept. term, Feb. 3, 1882;   Continued on motion of claimant till the Jan. term, 1883, Sept. 30, 1882.

And not on this the 9th day of January A.D, 1883, this case coming on for final hearing and all the evidence introduced in the case being carefully read and duly considered by the Commission, it was adjudged and determined by the Commission on Citizenship, that the claimants, Sally Lumpkins*, Jefferson Lumpkins, Charles Lumpkins, Patty Lumpkins, Elizabeth Lumpkins, and Frank Lumpkins, are not Cherokees by blood nor by adoption and that they are not entitled to the right and privilege of Cherokee citizenship within the Cherokee Nation and that their claim therefore should be, and the same is hereby rejected.

Thomas Tehee, President
Alex Wolfe

D.W.C. Duncan

Clerk Commission

T.F. Thompson

Commissioners

(*NOTE: Name spelled both ways.)

Transcript delivered to Claimant; but Claimant refused to accept the same, Jan. 13, 1883

D.W.C. Duncan, Clerk of Comm.

Jan. 25, 1881
Case #76

**MARGARET, ELLA, DORA, &
OKLA SPRADLING**

vs

Petition for Citizenship

Cherokee Nation

The above case submitted by the Plaintiff, Jan. 25, 1881;   Submitted by the Cherokees also, Jan. 27, 1881.

The above claimant, Margaret Spradling, has shown to the satisfaction of the Commission that she is a native born Cherokee but married a white man and lived in the state of Ark. and now asks to be readmitted to citizenship in the Cherokee Nation under provisions of the Constitution.

The Commission therefore hereby readmits the said Margaret Spradling and her children; to wit: Ella, Dora, and Okla Spradling, to all the rights and privileges of Cherokee citizenship by blood.

Jan. 31, 1881.

Roach Young, President Comm.

William Harnage

J.B. Mayes

Clerk Commission

G.W. Mayes

Asst. Comm.

Jan. 26, 1881
Case #77

MARY J. CASS

vs	Petition for Citizenship
Cherokee Nation	

The above case continued by the Plaintiff until Sept. term, 1881;   Continues by the Commission, Oct. 3, 1881;   Feb. 3, 1882 - Continued by the Commission till Sept. term;   Dismissed for want of prosecution, Sept. 18, 1882.

Jan. 26, 1881
Case #78

ALICE, ROBT. OTWAY, JANE, WILLIAM, CHARLES, OWEN, & ALACE OWEN

vs	Petition for Citizenship
Cherokee Nation	

The above case submitted by both parties, Jan. 27, 1881.

The above parties claim to be Cherokees by blood. The testimony shows that Alice Owen is a native born Cherokee, a descendant of the native Chisholm family; and was educated and partly raised in Virginia; married there, and is the mother of the children mentioned in petition; to wit: Robt. Otway Owen, Jane Owen, William Owen, Charles Owen, Owen Owen, and Alace Owen.

The Commission therefore feels justified in making a decision in favor of the above named claimants, admitting them to all the rights and privileges of Cherokee citizenship by blood. Jan. 31, 1881.

                                        Roach Young, President Comm.
                                        William Harnage
J.B. Mayes   G.W. Mayes
          Clerk Comm.   Asst. Comm.

Jan. 26, 1881
Case #79

C.L, MARTHA J, CHARLES, DAVID R, JOHN A, & BETTY J. KEYS

vs	Petition for Citizenship
Cherokee Nation	

The above case submitted by the Plaintiff, Jan. 26, 1881;   Submitted by the Cherokee Nation, also, Jan. 31, 1881.

Cherokee Citizenship Commission Docket Books
Tahlequah, Cherokee Nation (1880-84, 1887-89)
Volume I

The testimony before the Commission proves to its satisfaction that the above claimant, C.L. Keys, is a descendant of the Keys and Riley family of the Cherokee Nation, all Cherokees by blood.

The Commission hereby decides that the claimants; C.L. Keys and children are Cherokees by blood and are therefore entitled to all the rights and privileges of Cherokee citizenship by blood.

And his wife, Martha J. Keys, is entitled to all the rights of an adopted citizen of the Cherokee Nation being a white woman. Jan. 31, 1881

	Roach Young, President
	William Harnage
J.B. Mayes	G.W. Mayes
(Clerk)	Asst. Comm.

Transcript furnished, Sept. 27, 1883

Wm Eubanks, Clerk Comm.

Jan. 27, 1881
Case #80

FRANCES A. WARD
vs   Petition for Citizenship
Cherokee Nation

The above case submitted by the Plaintiff, Jan. 27, 1881;   Continued to the September term, 1881, by the Cherokee Nation;   Submitted by the Cherokee Nation for the action of the Commission, Sept. 13, 1881.

The testimony before the Commission proves to their satisfaction that the claimant is a descendant of the noted Welch family, who have long been known to be of Cherokee blood.

The Commission on Citizenship, therefore decides that the claimant is a Cherokee and hereby admits the said Frances A. Ward to all the rights and privileges of Cherokee citizenship by blood.

Sept. 13, 1881   Roach Young, President
                                    William Harnage
J.B. Mayes   G.W. Mayes
          Clerk Comm.   Asst. Comm.

Jan. 27, 1881
Case #81

W.L. & MARY V. CARR

vs   Petition for Citizenship
Cherokee Nation

The above case submitted by both parties after hearing the testimony, Jan. 31, 1881.

The above named Mary V. Carr, is a native born Cherokee daughter of J.G. Harnage, an acknowledged Cherokee by blood. This fact is established by ample proof.

The Commission therefore admits the said Mary V. Carr to all the rights and privileges of Cherokee citizenship by blood.

The claimant, W.L. Carr, is a white man, citizen of the United States and his admission into the Cherokee Nation as a citizen must be under the marriage law regulating intermarriages between citizens of the Cherokee Nation and citizens of the United States. His citizenship must therefore be assigned in part by his own actions; simply complying with the requirements of said law. Jan. 31, 1881.   Roach Young, President
                                                    William Harnage
J.B. Mayes   G.W. Mayes
          Clerk Commission   Asst. Comm.

Jan. 27, 1881
Case #82

J. G. & EMILY W. HARNAGE
vs   Petition for Citizenship
Cherokee Nation

The above case submitted by both parties after taking the testimony, Jan. 31, 1881.

The testimony shows to the satisfaction of the Commission that the above names claimants, J.G. Harnage and Emily W. Harnage, are native born Cherokees but have resided in the state of Texas for a number of years, becoming a citizen of that state, but now desire to return to their native country.

The Commission therefore admits them to all the rights, privileges and franchises of Cherokee citizenship by blood. Jan. 31, 1881
                                                    Roach Young, President
                                                    William Harnage
J.B. Mayes   G.W. Mayes
          Clerk Comm.   Asst. Comm.

Cherokee Citizenship Commission Docket Books
Tahlequah, Cherokee Nation (1880-84, 1887-89)
Volume I

Transcript furnished this Sept. 29, 81   C.O. Frye, Clk, Comm. on Citizenship

Jan. 27, 1881
Case #83

MOLLIE PHESANT
             vs   Petition for Citizenship
Cherokee Nation

The above case submitted by Plaintiff, Jan. 27, 1881;   Continued by the Cherokee Nation to Sept. term, 1881;   Submitted by the Cherokee Nation, 25 Sept. 1881.

The claimant comes before the Commission under a proclamation of the Principal Chief dated 27 July 1880, as a doubtful citizen.

The Commission is of the opinion that the claimant is of Cherokee blood, being a daughter (of) Ki-ya-nu Phesant, a full-blood Cherokee.

The Commission hereby admits said Mollie Phesant to all the rights and privileges of Cherokee citizenship by blood.

                                  Roach Young, President Commission
                                   William Harnage
J.B. Mayes   G.W. Mayes
         Clerk, Comm.   Asst. Comm.

Jan. 29, 1881
Case #84

**SARAH MAYFIELD, WILLIAM W. HARNAGE,
W. H. STILL, JESSIE CORA MURPHY, ROBT.
D. WYCH, JOHN W. WYCH, BETTY ORA WYCH,**
and **SILLAR SUSAN WYCH**
             vs   Petition for Citizenship
Cherokee Nation

The above case submitted by both parties, Feb. 2, 1881.

The testimony in the above case shows that the above named claimants, Sarah Mayfield, William W. Harnage, W.H. Still, Jessie Cora Murphy, Robt. D. Wych, John W. Wych, Betty Ora Wych, and Sillar Susan Wych, are Cherokees by blood.

The Commission therefore hereby admits the said claimants to all the rights, privileges, and franchises of Cherokee citizenship by blood.

Cherokee Citizenship Commission Docket Books
Tahlequah, Cherokee Nation (1880-84, 1887-89)
Volume I

Roach Young, President
Wm Harnage
J.B. Mayes   G.W. Mayes
Clerk Comm.   Asst. Comm.

Jan. 29, 1881
Case #85

SUBINA BEASON
vs   Petition for Citizenship
Cherokee Nation

The above case submitted by both parties after hearing the testimony, Jan. 31, 1881.

The testimony of William Harnage shows that the claimant is his niece and a Cherokee by blood.

The Commission therefore hereby issues this then decree admitting the said Subina Beason to all the rights, privileges, and franchises of Cherokee citizenship by blood. Jan. 31, 1881

Roach Young, President
William Harnage
J.B. Mayes   G.W. Mayes
Clerk Commission   Asst. Comm.

Jan. 29, 1881
Case #86

NANCY HARNAGE
vs   Petition for Citizenship
Cherokee Nation

The above case submitted by both parties after hearing the testimony, Jan. 31, 1881.

The testimony of reliable witnesses shows to the satisfaction of the Commission that the claimant, Nancy Harnage, is a native born Cherokee by blood, but has lived in the state of Texas for a number of years and now wishes to return to the Cherokee and live among her people.

The Commission therefore admits the above named claimant to all the rights, privileges, and franchises of Cherokee citizenship by blood.   Jan. 31, 1881   Roach Young, President

Cherokee Citizenship Commission Docket Books
Tahlequah, Cherokee Nation (1880-84, 1887-89)
Volume I

J.B. Mayes	William Harnage
	G. W. Mayes
Clerk Commission	Asst. Comm.

Feb. 2, 1881
Case #87

VICTORY GALLOWAY*
vs   Petition for Citizenship
Cherokee Nation

The above case submitted by both parties, Feb. 2, 1881.
The testimony of Judge J.T. Adair and Wm Harnage (shows) that the above named applicant is a Cherokee by blood.
Therefore it is ordered by the Commission on Citizenship that the said Victory Galoway* be admitted to all the rights, privileges and immunities of Cherokee citizenship by blood. Feb. 4, 1881

Roach Young, Pres. Comm.
Wm Harnage, Member Comm.
W.A. Reese, Clerk   G.W. Mayes, Member Comm.
(***NOTE:** Name spelled both ways.)

Feb. 3, 1881
Case #88

JOHN W. VANN
vs   Petition for Citizenship
Cherokee Nation   Atty for Pltf, C.H. Taylor

Submitted by the Plaintiff, Feb. 4, 1881;   Continued by the Cherokee Nation to September term, 1881;   Continued by the attorney for the Nation on account of witnesses, Oct. 3, 1881;   Case continued by Commission till Sept. term, Feb. 3, 1882;   Submitted by the Solicitor, September 7, 1882.
And now on this the 7th day of September A.D, 1882, this case coming on for final hearing and all the evidence in the case being duly considered; it is adjudged by the Commission on Citizenship, that the claimant, John W. Vann, is not a Cherokee by blood, as claimed in his petition, and that he is not entitled to the rights of Cherokee citizenship within the Cherokee Nation, and that his said claim should be and the same is hereby rejected.

Thos. Tehee, Pres of Comm.
Alex Wolfe

Cherokee Citizenship Commission Docket Books
Tahlequah, Cherokee Nation (1880-84, 1887-89)
Volume I

D.W.C. Duncan
  Clerk of Commission

T.F. Thompson
  Commissioners

Copy furnished claimant, Sept. 7, 1882
  D.W.C. Duncan, Clerk of Comm.

Feb. 4, 1881
Case #89

CHARLOTTE VICKERY, LIDA PAGET,
EMER PAGET, MARY PAGET, and
ELLA LOVENA PAGET
    vs
  Cherokee Nation

Petition for Citizenship
Atty. for Pltf, C.H. Taylor

Continued by the Commission on account of the testimony not being closed, Oct. 3, 1881; Continued by Commission till Sept. term, Feb. 3, 1881; Submitted by claimants and Solicitor, Sept. 18, 1882.

And now on this the 19th day of September, 1882; this case coming on for final hearing; and there being no evidence produced in the case by either side, it is ordered by the court that said case be, and the same is hereby dismissed without victorial adjudication.

    Thos. Tehee, President of Commission
    Alex Wolfe
D.W.C. Duncan   T.F. Thompson
  Clerk of Commission   Commissioners

And now on this the 10th day of Sept, 1883, on motion of the Claimant, the above case is reinstated on the Docket and planned for trial.
  Submitted by claimant, Sept. 14, 1883; Submitted by Solicitor, Sept. 19, 1883.

And now on this the 25th day of September A.D, 1883, this case coming on for final hearing and all the evidence produced in the case on both sides being carefully read and only considered by the Commission on Citizenship, it was adjudged by said Commission that the above named claimants, Charlotte Vickery, Lida Paget, Emer Paget, Mary Paget, and Ella Lovena Paget, are Cherokees by blood and that they are justly entitled to all the rights and privileges of Cherokee citizenship in the Cherokee Nation, and that they should be and are hereby admitted to the full and complete enjoyment of the same in all respects as native born Cherokees.

	Alex Wolfe
Wm Eubanks	T.F. Thompson
Clerk Comm.	Commissioners
Pro Tem.	

Transcript furnished, Sept. 26, 1883.

Feb. 4, 1881
Case #90

BEN & HOWELL* COBB
vs   Petition for Citizenship
Cherokee Nation   Atty. for Pltf. C.H. Taylor

Continued by the Commission on account of the testimony not being submitted by the Plaintiff, Oct. 3, 1881;   Jan. 11, 1882 - Claimant, Ben Cobb, now appears before the Commission and claiming to and for his brother, Howel* Cobb, asks leave to withdraw their application for Cherokee citizenship, where upon said request was granted, and said application was withdrawn.

	Thos. Tehee, President
	Alex Wolfe
D.W.C. Duncan	T.F. Thompson
Clerk	Commissioners

(***NOTE:** Name spelled both ways.)

Convened at Tahlequah, C.N., September 1, 1881, in accordance with law.

	Roach Young, President
	G.W. Mayes
J.B. Mayes	William Harnage
Clerk	Asst. Commissioners

Sept. 5, 1881
Case #91

**ALEXANDER G, LOUISA J, THOS. A,
ELONZO I, JOSEPH S, HATTIE J,**

Cherokee Citizenship Commission Docket Books
Tahlequah, Cherokee Nation (1880-84, 1887-89)
Volume I

ROBT. D, and OLLIE C. SLOAN
vs   Petition for Citizenship
Cherokee Nation

The Plaintiff introduced the testimony of D.W.W. Campbell; and submitted it to the court for decision;   Submitted also by the Cherokee Nation, Sept. 7, 1881.

The testimony before the Commission shows that Alex. G. Sloan, is a native born Cherokee, but moved to the state if Texas when a small boy and has remained there ever since.

The Commission therefore, hereby readmits the said Alex G. Sloan, to all the rights and privileges of Cherokee citizenship by blood.

The Commission also admits to all the rights and privileges of Cherokee citizenship the following named persons as the family of the said Alex G. Sloan; to wit: Louisa J. Sloan, Thos. A. Sloan, Elonzo I. Sloan, Joseph S. Sloan, Hattie J. Sloan, Robt. D. Sloan, and Ollie C. Sloan. Sept. 13, 1881.

Roach Young, President
William Harnage

J.B. Mayes   G.W. Mayes
       Clerk Comm   Asst. Comm.

Sept. 6, 1881
Case #92

A. H. TANKSLEY
vs   (Petition for Citizenship)
Cherokee Nation

The Plaintiff submitted the above case on a decision of the Supreme Court which he claims denied him citizenship;   Continued by the attorney of the Nation on account of witnesses, Oct. 3, 1881.

The above case dismissed from further hearing on the ground that said case has been already adjudicated and decided in favor of Claimant - as appears from the following showing.

Thos. Tehee President
Alex Wolfe
T.F. Thompson   Commissioners

Cherokee Citizenship Commission Docket Books
Tahlequah, Cherokee Nation (1880-84, 1887-89)
Volume I

Case of CHEROKEE NATION

vs

A.H. Tankesly* claiming Cherokee rights by blood

Taken up and from the evidence adduced before the court, they are convinced o the validity of the
claim and make the following decision, to wit: That the claimant, A.H. Tankesly is of a Cherokee by blood which entitles him to all the rights and privileges as such. Dated April 7, 1871(sic).

I hereby certify that the above decision is a true copy of the original on file in this office.

Given under my hand, seal of office, Jan. 9, 1882.

Mark Bean
Clerk of Supreme Court, C.N.

(*NOTE: Name spelled both ways.)

Sept. 17, 1881
Case #93

A.C, MARY, IDA, ADA, &
OMER E. k-KENNISON

vs   (Petition for Citizenship)

Cherokee Nation

Before the Commission on Citizenship under a proclamation of the Principal Chief, dated Aug. 24, 1881; Submitted by Plaintiff and also by the Cherokee Nation, Sept. 17, 1881

The Claimant comes before the Commission under the proclamation of the Principal Chief as (a) doubtful citizen.

There is before the Commission an act of the National Council admitting the said A.C. Kennison and family to citizenship. The Commission recognizes the act as valid, and that the rights to Cherokee citizenship is undisputed.

The Claimants are therefore entitled to all the rights and privileges of Cherokee citizenship by blood.

Roach Young, President Commission
William Harnage
J.B. Mayes   G.W. Mayes
Clerk Comm.   Asst. Comm.

53

Sept. 14, 1881
Case #94

THOS. N. GIVINS

vs   Petition for Citizenship

Cherokee Nation

Submitted by both parties, Sept. 12, 1881.

The testimony before the Commission shows the Claimant to be a native born Cherokee and that he never did forfeit his right to citizenship as provided by the Constitution.

It is proven to the satisfaction of the Commission that the claimant is of Cherokee blood, being a grandson of Nelson Harlin, a well known Cherokee by blood.

The Commission therefore hereby decides that the claimant is entitled to all the rights and privileges of Cherokee citizenship by blood.

         Roach Young, President Comm
          William Harnage
J.B. Mayes   G.W. Mayes
   Clerk Comm.   Asst. Comm.

Sept. 19, 1881
Case #95

MARY, RICHARD, DANIEL, EASTER, & THOS. MARTIN

vs   Petition for Citizenship

Cherokee Nation   C.H. Taylor, Atty for Claimant

Continued by the Plaintiff on account of witnesses, Oct. 3, 1881; Jan. 23, 1882 - Continued by Claimant till Sept. term, next; Submitted by the Claimants and the Solicitor, Sept. 18, 1882.

And now on this the 25th day of September A.D, 1882, this case coming on for final hearing and all the evidence in the case on both sides being carefully read and duly considered by the Commission; it is adjudged and determined by the Commission on Citizenship, that the Claimants; Mary Martin, Richard Martin, Daniel Martin, Easter Martin, and Thomas Martin; are Cherokees by blood and that they are entitled to all the rights and privileges of Cherokee citizenship within the Cherokee Nation; and that they should be and are hereby admitted to the full and complete enjoyment of the same in all respects as native born Cherokees.

Thos. Tehee, Pres. of Commission
Alex Wolfe

D.W.C. Duncan   T.F. Thompson
     Clerk of Comm.   Commissioners

Transcript furnished Claimants, Sept. 25, 1882

D.W.C. Duncan, Clerk of Commission

Sept. 20, 1881
Case #96

T. J. AYERS
vs   (Petition for Citizenship)
Cherokee Nation

Before the Commission on Citizenship under a proclamation of the Principal Chief, as doubtful citizen.

Submitted by the Plaintiff, Sept. 20, 1881;   Continued on account of absent witnesses by the Cherokee Nation, Oct. 3, 1881;   Submitted by the Cherokee Nation, Jan. 28, 1882

Jan. 28, 1882 - And now on this the 28th day of January A.D, 1882, this case coming on for final hearing, and all the testimony produced in the case by both sides, having been read and duly considered; it was adjudged by the Commission on Citizenship that the above named Claimants; to wit: T.J. Ayers, is entitled to all the rights and privileges of Cherokee citizenship by virtue of his marriage with the said Virginia Frazier, as alleged in his petition, because there is completed and sufficient evidence produced to prove that Virginia Frazier, is a Cherokee by blood, and otherwise entitled to the rights and privileges of a Cherokee citizen within the Cherokee Nation; and that Claimant's claim for citizenship should therefore be, and the same is hereby allowed and that he should be and he is hereby admitted as a citizen of the Cherokee Nation.

Thos. Tehee, Pres. of Comm.
Alex Wolfe

D.W.C. Duncan   T.F. Thompson
     Clerk   Commissioners

Copy issued to Claimant in pursuance of law, Jan. 28, 1882.

D.W.C. Duncan, Clerk

Sept. 21, 1881
Case #97

JASPER CHANEY
vs   (Petition for Citizenship)
Cherokee Nation

Before the Commission on Citizenship under proclamation of the Principal Chief, Aug. 24, 1881, as a doubtful citizen;   The above case submitted by the Plaintiff, Sept. 21, 1881;   Continued by the Cherokee Nation on account of witnesses, Oct. 3, 1881.

Jan. 17, 1882 - And now on this the 17th day of January A.D, 1882, this case coming on for hearing and all the testimony produced in the case on both sides having been read and duly considered; it is adjudged by the Commission on Citizenship, that the above named Claimant, Jasper Chaney, is entitled by his intermarriage with a Cherokee woman, who is a citizen of the Cherokee Nation, to all the rights and privileges of an adopted citizen within the Cherokee Nation.

Thos. Tehee, President
Alex Wolfe

D.W.C. Duncan   T.F. Thompson
    Clerk   Commissioners
Certificate of citizenship issued to Claimant as provided by law.

D.W.C. Duncan, Clerk

Sept. 21, 1881
Case #98

NANCY ANN KEEN
Wm ANDERSON KEEN
vs   Petition for Citizenship
Cherokee Nation

Continued by Plaintiff on account of witnesses, Oct. 3, 1881;   Jan. 13, 1881 - The above case continued by the Cherokee Nation till Sept. term; Submitted by the Solicitor and the Atty for Claimant, Sept. 31, 1882.

And now on the 25th day of September A.D, 1882, this case coming on for final hearing and all the evidence produced in the case on both sides being read carefully and duly considered by the Commission; it is adjudged and determined by the Commission on Citizenship, that the claimants; Nancy

Cherokee Citizenship Commission Docket Books
Tahlequah, Cherokee Nation (1880-84, 1887-89)
Volume I

Ann Keen and Wm. Anderson Keen, are Cherokees by blood and that they are entitled to all the rights and privileges of Cherokee citizenship within the Cherokee Nation; and that they should be and are hereby admitted to the full and complete enjoyment of the same in all respects as native born Cherokees.

Thos. Tehee, Pres. of Comm.
Alex Wolfe
D.W.C. Duncan   T.F. Thompson
Clerk of Comm.   Commissioners

Transcript delivered to Claimants, Sept. 25, 1882.
D.W.C. Duncan, Clerk of Comm.

Sept. 22, 1881
Case #99
EMILY CONNELLY
vs   Petition for Citizenship
Cherokee Nation   Atty. for Pltf, C.H. Taylor

The above case submitted by Plaintiff, Sept. 22, 1881;   Continued by the Cherokee Nation, Oct. 3, 1881.
Jan. 14, 1882 - And now on this the 14th day of January A.D, 1882, this case coming on for hearing and all the testimony produced in the case having been read and duly considered; it is adjudged by the Commission on Citizenship, that the claimant, Emily J. Connelly, is entitled to and she is hereby admitted to the full and perfect enjoyment of all the rights and privileges of Cherokee citizenship with the Cherokee Nation in all respects as a native born Cherokee.

Alex Wolfe, Acting President
T.F. Thompson, Commissioner
D.W.C. Duncan
Clerk   Thos. Tehee, President, being absent

Copy issued to Claimant as required by law, Jan. 14, 1882
D.W.C. Duncan, Clerk

Sept. 22, 1881
Case #100
SAVANA, SALLY, MACK,

and FILO OLIVER

vs   Petition for Citizenship

Cherokee Nation

The above case submitted by Plaintiff, Sept. 22, 1881;   Continued by the Cherokee Nation, Oct. 3, 1881.

Jan. 14, 1882 - And now on this the 14th day of January A.D, 1882, this case coming on for trial, and all the testimony in the case being read and duly considered; it is adjudged by the Commission on Citizenship that the Claimants; Savana Oliver, Sally Oliver, Mack Oliver, and Filo Oliver, are entitled to and they are hereby admitted to the full and perfect enjoyment of all the rights and privileges of Cherokee citizenship within the Cherokee Nation in all respects as native born Cherokees.

Alex Wolfe, Acting President

T.F. Thompson, Commissioner

D.W.C. Duncan

Clerk   Thos. Tehee, President, being absent

Copy issued to Claimant as required by law. D.W.C. Duncan, Clerk

Sept. 22, 1881
Case #101

JOSEPH HARRIS

vs   Petition for Citizenship

Cherokee Nation   Atty. for Pltf, C.H. Taylor

The above case submitted by the Plaintiff, Sept. 22, 1881;   Continued by the Cherokee Nation, Oct. 3, 1881.

Jan. 14, 1882 - And now on this the 14th day of January A.D, 1882, this case coming on for trial and all the testimony produced in the case having been read and duly considered, it is adjudged by the Commission on Citizenship that the Claimant, Joseph Harris, is entitled to and he is hereby admitted to the full and perfect enjoyment of all the rights and privileges of Cherokee citizenship in all respects as a native born Cherokee, within the Cherokee Nation.

Alex Wolfe, Acting President

D.W.C. Duncan   T.F. Thompson, Commissioner

Clerk   Thomas Tehee, President, being absent

Cherokee Citizenship Commission Docket Books
Tahlequah, Cherokee Nation (1880-84, 1887-89)
Volume I

Copy issued to Claimant as required by law.

D.W.C. Duncan, Clerk

Sept. 22, 1881

Case #102

JACK, MARY SUSAN, ALLEN P,
SARAH JANE, CRISTINA, &
ALBERT C. JONES

vs   Petition for Citizenship

Cherokee Nation   C.H. Taylor, Atty for Claimant

The above case submitted and testimony closed on part of the Plaintiff, Oct. 1, 1881; Continued by the Cherokee Nation, Oct. 3, 1881; Jan. 13, 1882 - Case continued by the Cherokee Nation till the Sept. term; Oct. 4, 1882 - Continued by Commission till January term, 1883; Continued till September term, 1883; Case submitted by the Solicitor, Sept. 7, 1883; Case submitted by the Solicitor, Sept. 21, 1883.

And now on this the 27th day of September A.D, 1883, this case coming on for final hearing and all the evidence produced in the case having (been) carefully read and duly considered; it was decided by the Commission on Citizenship that the above named Claimants; Jack Jones, Mary Susan Jones, Allen P. Jones, Sarah Jane Jones, Cristina Jones, and Albert C. Jones are Cherokees by blood and that they are justly entitled to all the rights and privileges of Cherokee citizenship within the Cherokee Nation, and that they should be and they are hereby admitted to the full and complete enjoyment of the same in all respects as native born Cherokees.

Thos. Tehee, Pres.

T.F. Thompson

Wm Eubanks   Alex Wolfe

Clerk Comm, Pro Tem   Commissioners

Transcript furnished Sept. 29, 1883

Sept. 22, 1881

Case #103

EMILINE T, JAMES A, DEDRIC T,
JOHN E, LANDON C, CAPITOLIA,
and WILLIAM GARFIELD SMITH

vs   Petition for Citizenship

Cherokee Nation
The above case submitted by the Plaintiff, Oct. 1, 1881;   Continued by the Cherokee Nation, Oct. 3, 1881;   The above case continued by the Cherokee Nation till Se[t. term, Jan. 13, 1882;   Submitted by the Atty for the Claimant, Sept. 22, 1882;   Continued to the January term, 1883, by Commission, Oct. 4, 1882;   Continued till Sept. term, 1883;   Submitted by the Solicitor, Sept. 7, 1883;   Submitted by the Solicitor, Sept. 21, 1883.

And now on this the 27th day of September, 1883, this case coming on for final hearing and all the testimony in the case on both sides being carefully read and duly considered; it was decided by the Commission on Citizenship, that the above named Claimants; Emiline T. Smith, James A. Smith, Dedric T. Smith, John E. Smith, Landon C. Smith, Capitolia Smith and Wm Garfield Smith, are not Cherokees by blood and are not entitled to citizenship in the Cherokee Nation.

Thos. Tehee, Pres of Comm.
Alex Wolfe
T.F. Thompson
Commissioners

Wm Eubanks
Clerk, Pro Tem

Sept. 22, 1881
Case #104

ROBBY, EDNEY, &
ZULAR AUSTON
vs   Petition for Citizenship
Cherokee Nation

The above case submitted by the Plaintiff, Sept. 22, 1881;   Continued, Oct. 3, 1881, by the Cherokee Nation until the next meeting of the Commission;   Continued by the Commission till Sept. term, Feb. 3, 1882; Submitted by the Solicitor, Sept. 29, 1882.

And now on this the 29th day of September A.D, 1882, this case coming on for final hearing, and all the evidence in the case being carefully and duly considered by the Commission; it was adjudged and determined by the Commission on Citizenship that the above named Claimants; Robby Auston, Edney Auston and Zular Auston, are Cherokees by blood and that they are entitled to all the rights and privileges of Cherokee citizenship within the Cherokee Nation and that they should be and are hereby admitted to the full and complete enjoyment of the same within the Cherokee Nation in all respects as native born Cherokees.

Thos. Tehee, Pres of Commission
Alex Wolfe
D.W.C. Duncan   T.F. Thompson
        Clerk of Comm   Commissioners

Transcript furnished Claimants, Sept. 29, 1882
                    D.W.C. Duncan, Clerk

Sept. 22, 1881
Case #105

ISAAC H, MARY M, LELAR MAGNOLIA,
JOSEPH M, ISAAC H, Jr, and
REJOINER MAYFIELD
                vs   Petition for Citizenship
        Cherokee Nation

The above case submitted by the Plaintiff, Sept. 23, 1881;   Continued
by the Cherokee Nation, Oct. 3, 1881.
        Jan. 13, 1882 - And now on this the 13th day of January A.D, 1882, this
case coming on for trial and all the evidence in the case being read and duly
considered; it is adjudged that the Claimants; to wit: Isaac H. Mayfield,
Mary M. Mayfield, Lelar Magnolia Mayfield, Joseph M. Mayfield, Isaac H.
Mayfield, Jr, and Rejoiner Mayfield; are entitled to and are hereby admitted
to the full and perfect enjoyment of all the rights and privileges of Cherokee
citizenship within the Cherokee Nation, in all respects as native born Cherokees.
                                    Thos. Tehee, President
                                    Alex Wolfe
D.W.C. Duncan   T.F. Thompson
        Clerk   Commissioners
Copy of decision issued to Claimants as provided by law.
                            D.W.C. Duncan, Clerk

Sept. 23, 1881
Case #106

        ADISON F. McCALEB
                vs   Petition for Citizenship
        Cherokee Nation

Cherokee Citizenship Commission Docket Books
Tahlequah, Cherokee Nation (1880-84, 1887-89)
Volume I

Submitted by Plaintiff, Oct. 1, 1881;   Continued by the Cherokee Nation until next term, Oct. 3, 1881;   Continued by Commission till Sept term, Feb. 3, 1882;   Submitted by the Solicitor, Sept. 27, 1882.

And now on this the 26th day of September A.D, 1882, this case coming on for final hearing and all the evidence produced in the case on both sides being carefully read and duly considered by the Commission; it was adjudged and determined by the Commission on Citizenship that the said Claimant, Adison F. McCaleb, is a Cherokee by blood, and that he is entitled to all the rights and privileges of Cherokee citizenship within the Cherokee Nation and that he should be, and is hereby admitted to the full and complete enjoyment of the same in all respects as a native born Cherokee.

Thos Tehee, Pres. of Commission

Alex Wolfe

D.W.C. Duncan   T.F. Thompson

    Clerk of Commission   Commissioners

Transcript furnished Claimant, Sept. 26, 1882.

D.W.C. Duncan, Clerk of Comm.

Sept. 23, 1881

Case #107

CHARLES MANIS

            vs   (Petition for Citizenship)

    Cherokee Nation   Atty for Pltf, C.H. Taylor

Before the Commission under a proclamation of the Principal Chief, dating 24 Aug. 1881.

Continued by the Cherokee Nation, Oct. 3, 1881

Feb. 1, 1882 - And on this the 1st day of February A.D, 1882, this case coming on for final hearing, and all the evidence produced n the case having been carefully read and duly considered, and Claimant having relied for his rights to Cherokee citizenship upon his marriage with a woman by the name of Alice Johnson, and Claimant having failed to establish the fact that said Alice Johnson was a Cherokee by blood or otherwise entitled to the rights and privileges of Cherokee citizenship within the Cherokee Nation.

Therefore, it was adjudged by the Commission on Citizenship that the claim of said Charles Manis for Cherokee citizenship was not sustained by the proof, and that the same should be, and is hereby rejected.

Thos. Tehee, Pres of Comm.

Alex Wolfe

62

Cherokee Citizenship Commission Docket Books
Tahlequah, Cherokee Nation (1880-84, 1887-89)
Volume I

D.W.C. Duncan   T.F. Thompson
    Clerk   Commissioners
Copy issued in accordance with the requirements of law.
                  D.W.C. Duncan, Clerk

Sept. 24, 1881
Case #108

> **ROBT, ELBERT, JASPER, JOHN,**
> **JOSEPHINE, JOSEPH, JANE, MOLLY,**
> **WILBRON, JAMES,** and **RIAL DAWSON**
>   vs   Petition for Citizenship
> Cherokee Nation

Continued by the Plaintiff, Oct. 3, 1881; Submitted by Claimants and the Solicitor, Jan. 11, 1883; Jan. 13, 1882 - The above case continued by the Cherokee Nation till Sept term; Agreed by the parties that the above case shall not be taken up for final disposition before the 4th day of Oct, 1882; Oct. 4, 1882 - It is agreed by the parties that this shall be finally disposed of at the next January term, if the Claimant is present and ending the same; if not, the case shall be there continued to the September term, 1883.

On this agreement, Commission continues the case till the next January term; to wit: January, 1883.

And not on this 11th day of January A.D, 1883, this case coming on for final hearing and all the evidence produced in the case being carefully read and duly considered by the Commission; it was adjudged and determined by the Commission on Citizenship that the Claimants, Robert Dawson, F.M. Dawson, Elbert Dawson, Jasper Dawson, John Dawson, Josephine Dawson, Joseph Dawson, Jane Dawson, Molly Dawson, Wilbron Dawson, James Dawson, and Rial Dawson; are Cherokees by blood and that they are entitled to all the rights and privileges of Cherokee citizenship within the Cherokee Nation, and that they should be, and they are, hereby admitted to the full and complete enjoyment of the same in all respects as native born Cherokees.

                Thos. Tehee, President of Comm.
                Alex Wolfe
D.W.C. Duncan   T.F. Thompson
    Clerk   Commissioner
Transcript issued to Claimants, January 11, 1883.
              D.W.C. Duncan, Clerk

Sept. 24, 1881
Case #109   Attys for Pltf.
      COOSE BALDRIDGE   J.M. Bryan & C.H. Taylor
           vs   Petition for Citizenship
     Cherokee Nation

Continued by Plaintiff, Oct. 3, 1881;   Continued by the Commission till Sept. term, Feb. 3, 1882;   Submitted by the Claimant and the Solicitor, Sept. 26, 1882.

And now on this the 26th day of September A.D, 1882, this case coming on for final hearing and all the evidence in the case produced on both sides being carefully read and duly considered by the Commission, and said Claimant being a colored person who was held as a slave in the states by an owner, or owners, who was a white person, or persons, not a citizen, or citizens, of the Cherokee Nation at the time of the commencement of the late war of the Rebellion; and said Claimant not being of that class of freedmen who were allowed citizenship within the Cherokee Nation by the Treaty of 1866, on condition that they should return to the Cherokee Nation within six months from the 19th day of July, 1866.

It was adjudged and determined by the Commission on Citizenship that the Claimant is not entitled to the rights and privileges of Cherokee citizenship within the Cherokee Nation and that his claim therefore should be and the same is hereby rejected.

                         Thos. Tehee, Pres of Comm.
                         Alex Wolfe
D.W.C. Duncan   T.F. Thompson
     Clerk of Comm.   Commissioners
Copy furnished Claimant, Sept. 26, 1882.
               D.W.C. Duncan, Clerk of Commission

Sept. 24, 1881
Case #110   J.M. Bryan & C.H. Taylor
     POSE & AMARETTA GIBSON   Attys for Claimants
           vs   Petition for Citizenship
     Cherokee Nation

Cherokee Citizenship Commission Docket Books
Tahlequah, Cherokee Nation (1880-84, 1887-89)
Volume I

Submitted by Plaintiff, Oct. 1, 1881; Continued by the Cherokee Nation, Oct. 3, 1881; Continued by Commission till Sept. term, Feb. 3, 1882; Submitted by the Solicitor, Sept. 30, 1882.

And now on this the 26th day of September A.D, 1882, this case coming on (for) final hearing and all the evidence produced in the case on both sides being carefully and duly considered by the Commission; it was adjudged by the Commission on Citizenship that the Claimants, Pose Gibson and Amaretta Gibson, are not Cherokees by blood, and that said claimants being colored persons who were free and residing in the Cherokee Nation at the commencement of the war of Rebellion, and who being absent from the limits of said nation at the ratification of the Treaty of 1866, failed to return thereto within "six months from the 19th day of July, 1866", are not entitled to the rights and privileges of Cherokee citizenship within the Cherokee Nation; and that their claim therefore should be, and the same is hereby rejected.

Thos Tehee, Pres of Comm.
Alex Wolfe

D.W.C. Duncan   T.F. Thompson, Dissenting
      Clerk of Comm   Commissioners

Transcript furnished claimants, Sept. 26, 1882
           D.W.C. Duncan, Clerk of Commission

Sept. 24, 1881
Case #111

        CALLIS ISAACS
            vs   (Petition for Citizenship)
        Cherokee Nation

Before the Commission under the proclamation of the Principal Chief as a doubtful citizen, dated August 24, 1881.

The case continued by Plaintiff until next term of the Commission on account of a marriage license which is important in this case, Sept. 24, 1881; Continued by the Commission till Sept term, Feb. 3, 1882; Dismissed for want of prosecution, Sept. 18, 1882.

Sept. 26, 1881
Case #112

        MARY, ELIZA, JANE, BESSY,

65

Cherokee Citizenship Commission Docket Books
Tahlequah, Cherokee Nation (1880-84, 1887-89)
Volume I

LYDIA, ANGELINA, & MARY STOVER
vs   Petition for Citizenship

Cherokee Nation   J.M. Bryan, Atty for Claimants

Continued by the Plaintiff, Oct. 3, 1881;   Continued by Commission till Sept term, Feb. 3, 1882;   Submitted by the Claimant, Sept. 20, 1882; Submitted by the Solicitor, Sept. 28, 1882.

And now on this the 28th day of September A.D, 1882, this cause coming on for final hearing and all the evidence in the cawe being read and duly considered by the Commission; it was adjudged and determined by the Commission on Citizenship that the Claimants, being colored persons and having failed to return to the Cherokee Nation within six months from the 19th day of July 1866, as provided by the Treaty of 1866, are not entitled to the rights and privileges of Cherokee citizenship within the Cherokee Nation, and that their claim therefore should be and the same is hereby rejected; said Claimants being the above named Mary Stover, Eliza Stover, Jane Stover, Bessy Stover, Lydia Stover, Angelina Stover, and Mary Stover.

Thos. Tehee, Pres of Comm.

Alex Wolfe, Comm.

D.W.C. Duncan, Clerk   T.F. Thompson, Comm. Dissenting

Sept. 26, 1881
Case #113

STEVE, PEGGY, DOVE,
and CHANY LOONY
vs   Petition for Citizenship

Cherokee Nation

Continued by Plaintiff, Oct. 3, 1881;   Continued by Commission till Sept. term, Feb. 3, 1882;   Dismissed for want of Prosecution, Sept. 18, 1882.

Sept. 28, 1881
Case #114

JOHN SWAIN
vs   (Petition for Citizenship)

Cherokee Nation

Cherokee Citizenship Commission Docket Books
Tahlequah, Cherokee Nation (1880-84, 1887-89)
Volume I

Before the Commission under a proclamation of the Principal Chief, dated Aug. 24, 1881, as a doubtful citizen. Submitted by Plaintiff, Oct. 1, 1881;   Continued by the Cherokee Nation, Oct. 3, 1881.

Jan. 12, 1882 - And now on this the 12th day of January A.D, 1882, this case coming on for hearing and all the testimony produced in the case having been heard and duly considered; it was adjudged by the Commission on Citizenship that the above named Claimant, John Swain, is entitled to and that he is hereby admitted to the full and perfect enjoyment of all the rights and privileges of Cherokee citizenship within the Cherokee Nation as a Cherokee.

Thos. Tehee, President
Alex Wolfe

D.W.C. Duncan   Thos. F. Thompson
      Clerk   Commissioners

Copy issued in pursuance of law to Claimant, Jan. 12, 1882
D.W.C. Duncan, Clerk

Sept. 30, 1881
Case #115

        SARAH, J.A, JASPER,
        W.M, & LELA GIBSON
             vs   Petition for Citizenship
        Cherokee Nation

Continued by Plaintiff, Oct. 3, 1881;   Continued till the next term on motion of the Claimant, Jan. 30, 1882;   It is ordered by the court that the above case be postponed till noon on next Friday, this being the 22nd day of September, 1882.

And now on this the 22nd day of Sept, 1882, this case coming on for hearing, and it appearing that no evidence has been produced to support Claimant's claim as alleged in her petition; and Claimant having failed to appear and prosecute her said claim, therefore said case is dismissed from the docket.

Jan. 3, 1882
Case #116

        WILLIAM, THERESSA, FRANK,
        MARY, JOSEPH, WILLIAM, Jr,
        and **RACHEL LITTLE**

(vs)   Petition for Citizenship
(Cherokee Nation)

Jan. 30, 1882 - And not on this the 30th day of January A.D, 1882, this case coming on for final hearing and all the evidence produced in said case being carefully read and duly considered; and there being no evidence produced in the case showing that the Claimant, William Little, being a white man, has ever complied with the requirements of Chapter 12, Article 15 of the Compiled Laws of the Cherokee Nation, in reference to intermarriage between citizens of the Cherokee Nation and citizens of the United States, it was adjudged by the Commission on Citizenship, that the said Claimants; to wit: Theressa Little, Frank Little, Mary Little, Joseph Little, William Little, Jr, and Rachel Little, are Cherokees by blood, and that they are entitled to all the rights and privileges of Cherokee citizenship within the Cherokee Nation, and that they should be and they are hereby admitted to the full and perfect enjoyment of the same in all respects as completely as native born Cherokees; and it is further adjudged that the claim of William Little, Sr, husband of Theressa Little, should be and the same is hereby rejected.

        Thos. Tehee, Pres. of Comm.
        Alex Wolfe
D.W.C. Duncan   T.F. Thompson
  Clerk   Commissioners

Jan. 9, 1882
Case #117   Lem Sanders & Wm. F. Rasmus,
  M.L, R, ANN, J.A, LUE, A, S.E, Attys. for Claimants
  JULIE, WILLIE, JESSE, & ROLLIE HOOD
    vs   Petition for Citizenship
  Cherokee Nation

Continued by the Commission, till Sept. term, Feb. 3, 1882; Submitted by the Claimant, Sept. 28, 1882; Submitted by the Solicitor, Oct. 3, 1882.

And now on this the 3rd day of October A.D, 1882, this case coming for final hearing; and all the evidence produced in the case and both sides being carefully read and duly considered by the Commission on Citizenship.

It was adjudged and determined by the Commission on Citizenship, that the above named Claimants, M.L. Hood, R. Hood, Ann Hood, J.A. Hood, Lue Hood, A. Hood, S.E. Hood, Julie Hood, Willie Hood, Jesse Hood, and Rollie Hood, are not Cherokees by blood and that they are not entitled to the rights and privileges of Cherokee citizenship within the Cherokee Nation, and that their claim therefore should be and the same is hereby rejected.

Thos. Tehee, Pres. of Comm.
Alex Wolfe
D.W.C. Duncan   T.F. Thompson
Clerk   Commissioners

Jan. 9, 1882
Case #118

SARAH J, A. V, MARY E, ANDORA A,   C.H. Taylor,
MARTHA J, & NANCY M. MORELAND   Atty. for Claimants
     vs   (Petition for Citizenship)
Cherokee Nation

And now on this the 11th day of January A.D, 1882, this case coming on for hearing and having heard and considered all the testimony produced; it was adjudged by the Commission on Citizenship, that the above named Claimants, to wit: Sarah J. Moreland, A.V. Moreland, Mary E. Moreland, Andora A. Moreland, Martha J. Moreland, and Nancy M. Moreland, are entitled to and that they are hereby admitted to the full and perfect enjoyment of all the rights and privileges of Cherokee citizenship within the Cherokee Nation, as Cherokees.

Thos. Tehee, President

Alex Wolfe
D.W.C. Duncan   T.F. Thompson
Clerk   Commissioners
Certificates delivered to Claimants, Jan. 12, 1882.
D.W.C. Duncan, Clerk of Commission

Jan. 9, 1882
Case #119

GEORGE W, SARAH E, L.V, ENNA, L.R,
Wm. C, and ORA B. McDONALD
     vs   (Petition for Citizenship)
Cherokee Nation

And now on this the 11th day of January A.D, 1882, this case coming on for hearing and having heard and considered all the testimony produced in the case; it was adjudged by the Commission on Citizenship that the above named Claimants, to wit: George W. McDonald, Sarah E. McDonald, L.V. McDon-

69

ald, Enna McDonald, L.R. McDonald, Wm. C. McDonald, and Ora B. McDonald, are entitled to and that they are hereby admitted to the full and perfect enjoyment of all the rights and privileges of Cherokee citizenship within the Cherokee Nation, as Cherokees.

Thos. Tehee, President
Alex Wolfe

D.W.C. Duncan   T.F. Thompson
    Clerk   Commissioners

Certificates delivered to Claimants, Jan. 13, 1882.

D.W.C. Duncan, Clerk of Comm.

Jan. 9, 1882
Case #120

            JAMES M, MARY E, L.G, Z.E,   Lew Sanders,
            J.S, & CHARLES W. TRUETT   Atty.   for
Claimant

                   vs   (Petition for Citizenship)
            Cherokee Nation

Continued by Claimant till the January term, 1881, Sept. 28, 1882; Motion for Continuance filed by Claimant Jan. 6, 1883; Continued by the Claimant till the Sept term, 1883.

    Case continued till January, 1885, by cousin of parties.

Jan. 10, 1882
Case #121

            EMILY MEASLES, THOMAS M. MEASLES,
            JOHN M. BECK, & JOHN E. FREENY
                 vs   (Petition for Citizenship)
            Cherokee Nation

And now on this 11th day of January A.D, 1882, the above case coming on for hearing and after hearing and considering the evidence produced; it was considered and adjudged by the Commission of Citizenship that said Claimants, Emily Measles, Thomas M. Measles (husband), John M. Beck, and John E. Freeny, are entitled to and they are hereby admitted to the enjoyment of all the rights and privileges of Cherokees within the Cherokee Nation, including the right of Cherokee citizenship.

Thos. Tehee, President

Cherokee Citizenship Commission Docket Books
Tahlequah, Cherokee Nation (1880-84, 1887-89)
Volume I

	Alex Wolfe
D.W.C. Duncan	T.F. Thompson
Clerk	Commissioners

Certificate delivered to Claimants, Jan. 12, 1882.

D.W.C. Duncan, Clerk of Commission

Jan. 14, 1882
Case #122

MICAJAH P. HAYNES
vs   (Petition for Citizenship)
Cherokee Nation

Petition filed Jan. 14, 1882;   Continued by Commission till Sept. term, Feb. 3, 1882
Dismissed for want of prosecution, Sept. 29, 1882.

Jan. 19, 1882
Case #123

RUTH COLEMAN
vs   Petition for Citizenship
Cherokee Nation

Case submitted by the Solicitor on part of the Cher. Nation.

And now on this the 19th day of January A.D, 1992, this case coming on for final hearing and all the testimony produced in the case having been read and duly considered; it was adjudged by the Commission on Citizenship that the above named Claimant, Ruth Colemen, is a Cherokee by blood and that she is entitled to all the rights and privileges of Cherokee citizenship within the Cherokee Nation, and that she should be and is hereby admitted to the full and perfect enjoyment of the same as a native born Cherokee.

Thos. Tehee, Pres. of Comm.

Alex Wolfe

	T.F. Thompson
D.W.C. Duncan	
Clerk	Commissioners

Copy of decision issued to Claimant as provided by law.

D.W.C. Duncan, Clerk

Jan. 19, 1882
Case #124

JOSEPH M, NANCY D, JULIA L,
ROBERT S, BENJ. F.L, & WILLIAM F.   Lem Sanders
LITTLE, and W. L. JACKSON   Atty for Claimants
      vs   (Petition for Citizenship)
Cherokee Nation

Case continued by the Commission till Sept. term, Feb. 3, 1882;   Dismissed for want of prosecution, Sept. 29, 1882.

Jan. 21, 1882
Case #125

MARY J, THOMAS J, JOSEPH M,
FRANCES B, WARREN L, WILLIAM L,
and **CHARLES N. FOWLER**
      vs   (Petition for Citizenship)
Cherokee Nation

Continued till Sept. term, 1882;   Dismissed for want of prosecution, Sept. 29, 1882.

Jan. 24, 1882
Case #126

JULIA A. DAVIS
      vs   (Petition for Citizenship)
Cherokee Nation

Continued till Sept. term by Commission, Feb. 3, 1882;   Case continued by the Commission till the January term, and not to be taken up for final hearing till the 15th of January, 1883.

And now this the 15th day of January, 1883, this case being taken for final action; and the Commission being made aware of the fact that the Claimant has deceased since the commencement of this action; it was ordered by the Commission that the same should be discontinued and stricken from the docket.

      D.W.C. Duncan
          Clerk of Commission

Jan. 27, 1882
Case #127

Cherokee Citizenship Commission Docket Books
Tahlequah, Cherokee Nation (1880-84, 1887-89)
Volume I

H.H, ELIZABETH, ELIZA,
RACHEL & ALICE A. HAMPTON
(vs)   (Petition for Citizenship)
(Cherokee Nation)

Jan. 30, 1882 - Be it known that on the 27ᵗʰ day of January, 1882, that the above named Claimant, H.H. Hampton, filed his petition in the above entitled case, and asked the court orrally(sic) that the default heretofore entered against him in this court be opened, and that he be granted a hearing upon the

merits of his case; and be it further known that now on this the 30ᵗʰ day of January, 1882, this case coming on for hearing upon Claimant's motion to open said default; it was adjudged by the court that whereas there is no provision found in the law creating the Commission on Citizenship, authorizing said Commission to entertain such a motion; and whereas the jurisdiction and power of said Commission is as specifically defined in said law.

Therefore, it was adjudged that the Commission on Citizenship has no jurisdiction over the question caused by said motion, and that the hear said motion and to offer said default, and grant to Claimant a new hearing upon his case would be transcending the limits of judicial power vested in the Commission by law.

Thos Tehee, Pres. of Comm
Alex Wolfe, Approving

D.W.C. Duncan   T.F. Thompson, Dissenting
    Clerk   Commissioners
Copy issued according to law to Claimant, H.H. Hampton, Feb. 2, 1882.
D.W.C. Duncan, Clerk

Jan. 27, 1882
Case #128

A. B. NICHOLS
vs   (Petition for Citizenship)
Cherokee Nation

Continued by Commission till Sept. term, Feb. 3, 1882;   Dismissed for want of prosecution, Sept. 29, 1882;   And on this the 5ᵗʰ day of Sept, 1883, on motion of Claimant, this case is reinstated upon the docket for trial;   Case submitted by the claimant and Solicitor, Sept. 11, 1883.

And now on this the 11ᵗʰ day of September A.D, 1883, this case coming on for final hearing and all the evidence produced in the case on both sides being carefully read and duly considered; it was adjudged by the Commission on Citizenship, that the above named claimant, A.B. Nichols, is a Cherokee by blood and that he is thereby justly entitled to all the rights and privileges of Cherokee citizenship within the Cherokee Nation, and that he should be and he is hereby admitted to the full and complete enjoyment of the same in all respects as a native born Cherokee.

	Thos. Tehee, Pres. of Comm
	Alex Wolfe
D.W.C. Duncan	T.F. Thompson
Clerk of Comm.	Commissioners

Jan. 31, 1882
Case #129

SARAH E, MARY E, JAMES H,
TILLMAN H, & ELROY HUFFMAN
vs   (Petition for Citizenship)
Cherokee Nation

Continued by the Commission till Sept. term, 1882, Feb. 3, 1882; Dismissed for want of prosecution, Sept. 29, 1882;   And now on this day the 31st of Sept. 1883, on motion of Claimant, the above case is reinstated upon the docket and set for trial;   Case submitted by Claimant and Solicitor, Sept. 22, 1883.

And now on this the 2nd day of October A.D, 1883, this case coming on for final hearing and all the evidence produced in the case on both sides being carefully read and duly considered; it was decided by the Commission on Citizenship that the Claimants, Sarah E. Huffman, Mary E. Huffman, James H. Huffman, Tillman H. Huffman and Elroy Huffman, are not Cherokees by blood and are therefore not entitled to Cherokee citizenship within the Cherokee Nation.

	Thos. Tehee, Pres. Comm
	Alex Wolfe
Wm Eubanks,	T.F. Thompson
Clerk, Pro Tem.	Commissioners

Jan. 31, 1882
Case #130

MARGARETT, HENRY M, LAURA,
ANDREW S, & GEORGE WASHINGTON PUFFEN

Cherokee Citizenship Commission Docket Books
Tahlequah, Cherokee Nation (1880-84, 1887-89)
Volume I

vs   (Petition for Citizenship)
(Cherokee Nation)

Continued by Commission till Sept. term, Feb. 3, 1882;   Dismissed for
want of prosecution, Sept. 29, 1882.

September Term A.D, 1883

Thomas Tehee, President of the Commission
Alex Wolf(sic), Commissioner
T.F. Thompson, Commissioner
C.W. Reese, Interpreter
Wilson Sanders, Solicitor
D.W.C. Duncan, Clerk
Jesse Crittenden, Bailiff

Sept. 4, 1882
Case #131   E.C. Boudinot, G.O. Butler,
MARY C, JAMES L, ANNIE B,   C.H. Taylor,
& HENRY B. SMITH   Attys. for Claimants
vs   (Petition for Citizenship)
Cherokee Nation

Case submitted by Attys. for Claimants and Solicitor, Sept. 4, 1882.
And now on this 6th day of September A.D, 1882, this case coming on for
final hearing and all the evidence produced in said case having been duly examined and considered by the Commission and there being no evidence produced in the case showing that the Claimant, James L. Smith, being a white
man, has ever complied with the requirements of Chapter 12, Article 15, of the
Compiled Laws of the Cherokee Nation in reference to intermarriage between
citizens of the United States and citizens of the Cherokee Nation. It was adjudged by the Commission on Citizenship, that the said Claimants, Mary C.
Smith, Annie B. Smith, and Henry B. Smith, are Cherokees by blood and that
they are entitled to all the rights and privileges of Cherokee citizenship within
the Cherokee Nation, and that they should be and that they are hereby admitted
to the full and perfect enjoyment of the same in all respects as completely as
native born Cherokees; and it is further adjudged that the claim of James L.

Smith, husband of said Mary C. Smith, should be and the same is hereby re‑
jected.

Thomas Tehee, President of Comm

Alex Wolf

D.W.C. Duncan   T.F. Thompson

Clerk of Commission   Commissioners

Transcript issued to Claimants, Sept. 6, 1882

D.W.C. Duncan, Clerk

Sept. 5, 1882

Case #132

PATRICK, LAURA A, HUGH B, PATRICK Jr, E.C. Boudinot, Jr.
THOMAS B, MYRA, GIBBS, ALBERT G,   C.H. Taylor,
and **MARIE HENRY**   Attys. for Claim‑
ants

vs   (Petition for Citizenship)

Cherokee Nation

Submitted by the Claimant and Solicitor, Sept. 6, 1882.

And now on this the 7th day of September A.D, 1882, this case coming on
for final hearing and all the evidence produced in said case having been duly
examined and considered by the Commission, and the evidence showing that
Laura A. Henry, is a white woman and duly married to the Claimant, Patrick
Henry. It was adjudged by the Commission on Citizenship that the said Claim‑
ant, Patrick Henry and his children, Hugh B. Henry, Patrick Henry, Jr, Thomas
B. Henry, Myra Henry, Gibbs Henry, Albert G. Henry, and Marie Henry, are
Cherokees by blood and that they are entitled to all the rights and privileges of
Cherokee citizenship within the Cherokee Nation; and that they should be and
that they are hereby admitted to the full and perfect enjoyment in all respects as
completely as native born Cherokees. And it is further adjudged that the
Claimant, Laura A. Henry, wife of said Patrick Henry, is entitled to and is
hereby admitted to the full and complete enjoyment of all the rights and privi‑
leges of an adopted citizen within the Cherokee Nation.

Alex Wolf, Commissioner

T.F. Thompson, Commissioner

D.W.C. Duncan   Thos. Tehee, President, Dissenting

Clerk of Commission

Transcript issued, Sept. 7, 1882

D.W.C. Duncan, Clerk of the Commission

Cherokee Citizenship Commission Docket Books
Tahlequah, Cherokee Nation (1880-84, 1887-89)
Volume I

Sept. 5, 1882
Case #133   E.C. Boudinott, Wm T. Rasmus,
        WILLIAM A. LEWIS   Geo O. Butler, Attys. for Claimant
                vs   (Petition for Citizenship)
        Cherokee Nation
Submitted by the Attys. for Claimant Sept. 18, 1882;   Submitted by the
Solicitor, Oct. 4, 1882;   Continued till the January term, 1883, Oct. 4, 1882.
And now on this the 30th day of January A.D, 1883, this case coming on
for final hearing and all the evidence produced in the case being carefully read
and duly considered; it was adjudged and determined by the Commission on
Citizenship that the above named Claimant, William A. Lewis, is not a Cherokee by Blood, nor by adoption, and that he is not entitled to the rights and privileges of Cherokee citizenship within the Cherokee Nation and that his claim
therefore should be and is hereby rejected.
                        Thos. Tehee, President of Comm.
                        Alex Wolf

D.W.C. Duncan   T.F. Thompson
        Clerk of Comm   Commissioners

Sept. 6, 1882
Case #134
        HARRIETT, KATE, JAMES, ANN,   C.H. Taylor,
        JOHN, & ALBERT CHILDERS   Atty for Claimants
                vs   (Petition for Citizenship)
        Cherokee Nation

Dismissed for want of prosecution, Sept. 29, 1882;   Jan. 26, 1883, motion by Claimant to reinstate case, and upon said motion, ordered by the court
to defer the docketing of said case till Claimant is ready with his testimony and
presents himself ready to proceed with the trial;   And now on this the 5th day
of Sept, 1883, the above case in pursuance of the proceeding order, and on motion of Claimants, is ordered to be reinstated upon the docket and put upon the
calendar for trial;   Submitted by both parties, Sept. 19, 1884.
And now on this the 19th day of September, 1884, comes this case for final hearing and all the evidence in the case having been read and considered by
the Commission on Citizenship; it was decided by said Commission that the

77

above Claimants are not Cherokees in any sense, and are therefore, not entitled
to citizenship in the Cherokee Nation.

Eli Spears, Pres.

John Lee

John L. Adair   Andrew Young
   Clk Comm.   Comm.

Sept. 9, 1882
Case #135

      WM. & ANN STEPHENS   C.H. Taylor, Atty for Claimant
            vs   (Petition for Citizenship)
      Cherokee Nation

    Commission grants Claimant permission to withdraw the above case and
to take the testimony from the files, to be duly certified by the Clerk;   Case is
accordingly withdrawn;   Case reinstated on the docket, Jan. 23, 1883;   Case
continued till Sept. term, 1883;   Case submitted by the Claimant and the Solicitor, Sept. 6, 1883;   Case transferred to page 205 on docket.

Sept. 9, 1882
Case #136

      JESSE, POLLY, MARTIN, MARTHA
      JACKSON & THOMAS RAPER
            vs   (Petition for Citizenship)
      Cherokee Nation

    Submitted by the Solicitor, Sept. 11, 1882.
    And now on this the 11th of September A.D, 1882, this case having been
submitted by the Solicitor on part of the Cherokee Nation, and coming on for
final hearing and all the evidence produced in said case having been carefully
examined and considered by the Commission, and the evidence showing that
the Claimant, Jesse Raper, being a white man, has never complied with the requirements of Chapter 12, Art. 15, of the Compiled Laws of the Cherokee Nation in reference to intermarriage with United States citizens and citizens of the
Cherokee Nation.
    It was adjudged by the Commission on Citizenship, that the said Claim-
ants, Polly Raper, Martin Raper, Martha Raper, Jackson Raper, and Thomas
Raper are Cherokees by blood and that they are entitled to all the rights and
privileges of Cherokee citizenship within the Cherokee Nation; and that they

should be and that they are hereby admitted to the full and perfect enjoyment of the same in all respects as completely as native born Cherokees. And it is further adjudged that the claim of Jesse Raper, the husband of the said Polly Raper, should be and the same is hereby rejected.

	Thos. Tehee, Pres. Comm.
	Alex Wolfe
Wm Eubanks	T.F. Thompson
Clerk, Pro Tem.	Commissioners

Sept. 9, 1882	E.C. Boudinot, E.S. Sanders, &
Case #137	G.O. Butler, Attys for Claimant
Wm BURGES, Jr.	
vs	(Petition for Citizenship)
Cherokee Nation	

Continued by consent of parties till the January term, 1883, Oct. 2, 1882; Continued on motion of Claimant till the September term, 1883;   Case withdrawn, Sept. 27, 1883.

Wm Eubanks,
Clerk Comm, Pro Tem.

Sept. 12, 1882
Case #138

DAVID, MATILDA, MANDA, JAMES,	
JULEY, CLERCY, OWEN, and	C.H. Taylor, Atty for
FRONAH BALES	Claimant
vs	(Petition for Citizenship)
Cherokee Nation	

Continued till the January term, 1883;   Submitted by the Claimants, Jan. 10, 1883;   Submitted by the Solicitor, Jan. 11, 1883.

And now on this the 11th day of January A.D, 1883, this case coming on for final hearing and all the evidence produced in the case being carefully read and duly considered by the Commission on Citizenship; it was adjudged and determined by the Commission on Citizenship that the above named Claimants; David Bales, Matilda Bales, Manda Bales, James Bales, Juley Bales, Clercy Bales, Owen Bales, and Fronah Bales, are not Cherokees by blood, not by adoption, and that they are not entitled to the rights and privileges of Cherokee citizenship within the Cherokee Nation and that their claim therefore

Cherokee Citizenship Commission Docket Books
Tahlequah, Cherokee Nation (1880-84, 1887-89)
Volume I

should be and the same is, hereby <u>rejected</u>.   Thos.   Tehee,   President   of
Comm.

	Alex Wolfe
D.W.C. Duncan	T.F. Thompson
Clerk	Commissioners

Sept. 19, 1882
Case #139

**ELIZABETH GILLIS, ANTOINE GILLIS,
ANNALIZA* SHOEMAKE, ALLIS SHOEMAKE,
and MATILDA GILLIS**
vs   (Petition for Citizenship)
Cherokee Nation

Wilson Sanders, Solicitor, and E.C. Boudinot - For the Nation / C.H. Taylor,
Atty. for Claimants

Continued by consent of parties to the January term, 1883;   Continued
on motion of Claimants, Jan. 23, 1883;   Case submitted by Claimant and Solicitor, Sept. 26, 1883.

And now on this the 1st day of October A.D, 1883, this case coming on
for final hearing and all the evidence in the case on both sides being carefully
read and duly considered; it was decided by the Commission on Citizenship
that the claimants, Elizabeth Gillis, Antoine Gillis, Analiza* Shoemake, Allis
Shoemake, and Matilda Gillis, are not Cherokees by blood and are therefore
not entitled to Cherokee citizenship within the Cherokee Nation.

Thos. Tehee, Pres. Comm.
Alex Wolfe

Wm Eubanks   T.F. Thompson
Clerk Comm, Pro Tem.   Commissioners
(***NOTE:** Name spelled both ways.)

Sept. 19, 1992
Case #140

L.M. WHIDDEN &   C.H. Taylor, Atty. for Claimants
J.W. STOKES
vs   (Petition for Citizenship)
Cherokee Nation

80

Continued by consent of parties till the January term, 1883; On motion filed this day by Claimants, this case is continued till the Sept. term, Jan. 15, 1883; Continued till Sept. term, 1884, C.O. Frye, Clerk; Pass till Jan. term, 1885.

Sept. 31, 1882
Case #141

> Cherokee Nation
>   vs   (Unknown)
> **J. N. SMITH**

Continued by the Commission till Jan. term, 1883. L.B. Bell, Esqr, appears as Attorney for Defendant, Jan. 3, 1883. Messrs. Boudinott and Butler, appeared for the Defendant, Jan. 4, 1883. And now on this the 5th day of January, 1883, the above case is continued by the Commission on its own motion to the Sept. term, 1883.

Papers in the above case drawn from the files by R.L. Owen, Esqr, Atty. for the Nation.

On motion of the Deft, case set for hearing on the 24th day of Sept, 1883, the present term, Sept. 4, 1883.

And now on this the 29th day of September A.D, 1883, this case coming on for final hearing and all the evidence produced in the case being carefully read and duly considered; it was decided by the Commission on Citizenship, that the above named Defendant, J. N. Smith, in the case of Cherokee Nation vs J.N. Smith, is an adopted citizen of the Cherokee Nation and entitled to all the rights and privileges of an adopted Cherokee citizen within the Cherokee Nation.

	Thos. Tehee, President
	Alex Wolfe
Wm. Eubanks	T.F. Thompson
Clerk, Pro Tem.	Commissioners

Sept. 22, 1882
Case #142

> **CHARLES, JANE, JOHN M,**   C.H. Taylor, Atty for Claimant
> **ANNA E. & ELLEN L. COATS**
>   vs   (Petition for Citizenship)
> Cherokee Nation

And now on this the 28th day of September A.D, 1882, this case coming on for final hearing and all the evidence produced in the case on both sides being carefully read and duly considered by the Commission; it is adjudged and determined by the Commission on Citizenship that the Claimants; Charles Coats, Jane Coats, Anna E. Coats, John M. Coats, and Ellen L. Coats, are Cherokees by blood and that they are entitled to all the rights and privileges of Cherokee citizenship; and that they should be and are hereby admitted to the full and complete enjoyment of the same in all respects as native born Cherokees.

Thos. Tehee, Pres. of Comm.
Alex Wolfe

D.W.C. Duncan   T.F. Thompson
        Clerk of Comm.   Commissioners

Copy furnished Claimants, Sept. 22, 1882.
                                        D.W.C. Duncan, Clerk of Comm.

Sept. 29, 1882
Case #143

JOHN KIMBROUGH   M.O. Gormley, Atty for Claimant

                  vs   (Petition for Citizenship)
        Cherokee Nation

Submitted by the Claimant and the Solicitor, Sept. 29, 1882.

And now this case on this the 29th day of September A.D, 1882, coming on for final hearing and all the evidence produced in the case on both sides being carefully read and duly considered by the Commission; it was adjudged and determined by the Commission on Citizenship, that the above named Claimant, John Kimbrough, is a Cherokee by blood and that he is entitled to all the rights and privileges of Cherokee citizenship within the Cherokee Nation and that he should be and is hereby admitted to the full and complete enjoyment of the same within the Cherokee Nation in all respects as a native born Cherokee.

                                        Thos. Tehee, Pres of Comm.
                                        Alex Wolfe
D.W.C. Duncan   T.F. Thompson
        Clerk Comm.   Commissioners

Oct. 4, 1882

Cherokee Citizenship Commission Docket Books
Tahlequah, Cherokee Nation (1880-84, 1887-89)
Volume I

Case #144

LUCK RIDER	J.M. Bryan, Atty. for Claimant
vs	(Petition for Citizenship)
Cherokee Nation	

Submitted by Claimant, Oct. 4, 1882.

And now on this the 4th day of October A.D, 1882, this case coming on for final hearing, and all the evidence produced in the case being carefully read and duly considered by the Commission; it was adjudged and determined by the Commission on Citizenship that the Claimant, Luck Rider, is a Cherokee by blood; and that he is entitled to all the rights and privileges of Cherokee citizenship within the Cherokee Nation, and that he should be and is hereby admitted to the full and complete enjoyment of the same in all respects as a native born Cherokee.

Thos. Tehee, Pres of Comm.
Alex Wolfe

D.W.C. Duncan	T.F. Thompson
Clerk of Comm.	Commissioners

Transcript furnished Claimant, Oct. 21, 1882.

D.W.C. Duncan, Clerk of Comm.

Jan. 1, 1883
Case #145

A. W. MARTIN	Robt. L. Owens, Atty. for Claimant
vs	(Petition for Citizenship)
Cherokee Nation	

Case continued till Sept. term, 1883;   Case withdrawn by Claimant, Sept. 6, 1883.

Jan. 3, 1883
Case #146

JENNY WILLIAMS Robt. L. Owens, Atty. for Claimant	
vs	(Petition for Citizenship)
Cherokee Nation	

Case continued till Sept. term, 1883;   Submitted by Claimant, Sept. 10, 1883;   Submitted by the Solicitor, Sept. 19, 1883.

And now on this the 30th day of September, 1883, this case coming on for final hearing and all the evidence produced in the case on both sides being carefully read and duly considered, it was decided by the Commission on Citizenship, that the above named Claimant, Jenny Williams, is a Cherokee by blood, and that she is thereby entitled to all the rights and privileges of Cherokee citizenship within the Cherokee Nation and that she should be, and she is hereby, admitted to the full and complete enjoyment of the same in all respects as a native born Cherokee.

                                    Thos. Tehee, Pres. of Comm.
                                    Alex Wolfe, Commissioner
D.W.C. Duncan   T.F. Thompson, being absent,
not voting
        Clerk of Comm.
Transcript furnished Claimant, Sept. 24, 1883
                D.W.C. Duncan, Clerk of Comm

Jan. 5, 1883
Case #147
        J. J. & MARY E. FORD   C.H. Taylor, Atty. for Claim-
ant

            vs   (Petition for Citizenship)
        Cherokee Nation

        Case submitted by the Claimant, Jan. 16, 1883;   Case submitted by the Solicitor, Jan. 24, 1883.
        And now this the 24th day of January A.D, 1883, this case coming on for final hearing and all the evidence in the case being carefully read and duly considered; it was adjudged and determined by the Commission on Citizenship, that the applicant, Mary E. Ford, above mentioned is a Cherokee by blood and that she is entitled to all the rights and privileges of Cherokee citizenship within the Cherokee Nation, and that she should be and she is hereby admitted to the full and complete enjoyment of the same in all respects as a native born Cherokee.

                                    Thos. Tehee, Pres. of Comm.
                                    Alex Wolfe
D.W.C. Duncan   T.F. Thompson
        Clerk of Comm.   Commissioners

Jan. 5, 1883

Cherokee Citizenship Commission Docket Books
Tahlequah, Cherokee Nation (1880-84, 1887-89)
Volume I

Case #148

GENUINA CREASE
vs   (Petition for Citizenship)
Cherokee Nation

Privilege granted claimant to continue the case till Sept. term for the introduction of testimony if found necessary;   Case set for taken testimony on the morning of the 13th of Jan, 1883;   Case continued till Sept. term, 1883; Case continued till Jan. term, 1884, this Sept. 10, 1883.

Jan. 6, 1883
Case #149

J.N. GUINN, ASA GUINN, J.L. GUINN,   M.O.Ghormley,
MARY WEBB, JOHN GUINN, JOSEPH   Atty. for Claimants
WEBB, & CHARLES W. WEBB
vs   (Petition for Citizenship)
Cherokee Nation

The above case submitted by the Claimant, Jan. 9, 1883;   The above submission is withdrawn by person of Court, Jan. 9, 1883;   Case continued till Sept. term, 1883.

And now on this the 1st day of October A.D, 1883, this case coming on for final hearing and all the evidence produced in the case being carefully read and duly considered; it was decided by the Commission on Citizenship that the Claimants above named; to wit: J.N. Guinn, Asa Guinn, J.L. Guinn, Mary Webb, John Guinn, Joseph Webb, and Charles Webb, are not Cherokees by blood and are not therefore, entitled to Cherokee citizenship within the Cherokee Nation.

Thos. Tehee, Pres. Comm.
Alex Wolfe
Wm. Eubanks,   T.F. Thompson
Clerk Comm, Pro Tem   Commissioners

Jan. 8, 1883
Case #150

JAMES, MAHALAH, ELSEY,   C.H. Taylor, Atty. for Claimant

JOHN, & ADA MISSA RICH
vs   (Petition for Citizenship)
Cherokee Nation

Cherokee Citizenship Commission Docket Books
Tahlequah, Cherokee Nation (1880-84, 1887-89)
Volume I

Submitted by the Claimant, Jan. 25, 1883; Continued till Sept. term, 1883; Continued till Sept. 1884; Resubmitted Sept. 2, 1884; Called Sept. 10, 1884, passed to the 20th; Passed to Sept. 25, 1884.

Jan. 9, 1883
Case #151   Boudinot & Butler, Attys. for Claimant
        WILLIAM J. ALLISON
            vs   (Petition for Citizenship)
        Cherokee Nation

Submitted by the Claimant, Jan. 22, 1883; Submitted by the Solicitor, Jan. 25, 1883.

And now on this the 25th day of January A.D, 1883, this case coming on for final hearing and all the evidence produced in the case being carefully read and duly considered; it was adjudged and determined by the Commission on Citizenship, that the above named Claimant, William J. Allison, is a Cherokee by blood and that he is entitled to all the rights and privileges of Cherokee citizenship within the Cherokee Nation, and that he should be and he is hereby admitted to the full and complete enjoyment of the same in all respects as a native born Cherokee.

                    Alex Wolfe, Acting Pres. of Comm.
D.W.C. Duncan   T.F. Thompson, Commissioner
        Clerk of Comm
            Thos. Tehee, Pres. of Comm, absent and not voting

Jan. 9, 1883
Case #152   Boudinot & Butler, Attys. for Claimant
        GEORGE HORNE
            vs   (Petition for Citizenship)
        Cherokee Nation

Submitted by the Claimant and the Solicitor, Jan. 10, 1883.

And now on this the 11th day of January A.D, 1883, this case coming on for final hearing and all the evidence introduced in the case being carefully read and duly considered by the Commission; it was adjudged and determined by the Commission on Citizenship that the above named Claimant, George Horne, is a Cherokee by blood and is entitled to all the rights of Cherokee citizenship within the Cherokee Nation; and that he should be and is hereby ad-

Cherokee Citizenship Commission Docket Books
Tahlequah, Cherokee Nation (1880-84, 1887-89)
Volume I

mitted to the full and complete enjoyment of the same in all respects as a native born Cherokee.

	Thos. Tehee, Pres. of Comm.
	Alex Wolfe
D.W.C. Duncan	T.F. Thompson
Clerk of Comm.	Commissioners

Jan. 10, 1883
Case #153   Boudinot & Butler, Attys. for Claimant
JAMES ALLEN THOMPSON, Jr.
                   vs   (Petition for Citizenship)
Cherokee Nation
Submitted by the Claimant and the Solicitor, Jan. 19, 1882.
And now on this the 30th day of January A.D, 1883, this cause coming on for final hearing and all the evidence produced in the case being carefully read and duly considered by the Commission; it is adjudged and determined by the Commission on Citizenship that the above named Claimant, James Allen Thompson, (Jr.); is a Cherokee by blood and that he is entitled to all the rights and privileges of Cherokee citizenship within the Cherokee Nation and that he should be and is hereby admitted to the full and complete enjoyment of the same in all respects as a native born Cherokee.

	Thos. Tehee, President of Comm.
	Alex Wolfe
D.W.C. Duncan	T.F. Thompson
Clerk of Comm	Commissioners

Transcript delivered to Claimant, Jan. 30, 1883
                          D.W.C. Duncan, Clerk

Jan. 10, 1883
Case #154

          CYNTHIA HORNE Boudinot & Butler, Attys. for Claimant
          CAROLINE McNEIL
                   vs   (Petition for Citizenship)
          Cherokee Nation

Case submitted by the Claimants and the Solicitor, Jan. 12, 1883.
And now on this the 12th day of Jan, 1883, this case coming on for final hearing; and all the evidence produced in the case being carefully read and duly considered by the Commission; it was adjudged and determined by the

Commission on Citizenship that the above named Claimants, Cynthia Horne and Caroline McNeil, are Cherokees by blood and that they are entitled to all the rights and privileges of Cherokee citizenship within the Cherokee Nation and that they should be and are hereby admitted to the full and complete enjoyment of the same in all respects as native born Cherokees.

Thos. Tehee, Pres. of Comm.
Alex Wolfe
D.W.C. Duncan   T.F. Thompson
Clerk of Commission   Commissioners
Transcript delivered to Claimants, Jan. 12, 1883.
D.W.C. Duncan, Clerk

Jan. 10, 1883
Case #155

CHARLES WESLEY, BARBARA, &   Boudinot & Butler,
Attys.

THOMAS LEE HORNE   for Claimants

vs   (Petition for Citizenship)
Cherokee Nation

Case submitted by Claimant and Solicitor, Jan. 12, 1883.
And now on this the 12th day of January A.D, 1883, this case coming on for final hearing, and all the evidence produced in the case being carefully read and duly considered by the Commission; it was adjudged and determined by the Commission on Citizenship that the above named Claimants, Charles Wesley Horne, Barbara Horne, and Thomas Lee Horne, are Cherokees by blood and that they are entitled to all the rights and privileges of Cherokee citizenship within the Cherokee Nation and that they should be and they are hereby admitted to the full and complete enjoyment of the same in all respects as native born Cherokees.

Thos. Tehee, President of Comm.
Alex Wolfe
D.W.C. Duncan   T.F. Thompson
Clerk   Commissioners
Transcript delivered to Claimants, Jan. 12, 1883.
D.W.C. Duncan, Clerk of Comm.

Jan. 11, 1883

Cherokee Citizenship Commission Docket Books
Tahlequah, Cherokee Nation (1880-84, 1887-89)
Volume I

Case #156

RUTH E, W.J, L.Z, M.C, C.E,	Boudinot & Butler, Attys. for
G.W, R.C, & M.T. MARTIN	Claimants
vs	(Petition for Citizenship)
Cherokee Nation	

It is ordered by the Commission that the evidence on file in the cases of Chas. Wesley Horne, [#155] and Cynthia Horne, [#154], be accepted and used as competent evidence in the above entitled case

Case submitted by Claimants and Solicitor, Jan. 12, 1883.'

And now on this the 12th day of January A.D, 1883, this case coming on for final hearing and all the evidence in the case being carefully read and duly considered by the Commission; it was adjudged and determined by the Commission on Citizenship that the above named Claimants, Ruth E. Martin, W.J. Martin, L.Z. Martin, M.C. Martin, C.E. Martin, G.W. Martin, R.C. Martin, and M.T. Martin, are Cherokees by blood and that they are entitled to all the rights and privileges of Cherokee citizenship within the Cherokee Nation and that they should be and they are hereby admitted to the full and complete enjoyment of the same in all respects as native born Cherokees.

Thos. Tehee, President of Comm
Alex Wolfe

D.W.C. Duncan   T.F. Thompson
   Clerk of Comm.   Commissioners
Transcript delivered to Claimants, Jan. 12, 1883
D.W.C. Duncan, Clerk

Jan. 12, 1883

Case #157

MARGARET*, JOHN W, SUSAN L,	
ALICE C, W.G.C, LOUISA F,	Butler & Boudinot, Attys.
LAWRENCE R, & ALETHIA F. HORNE	for Claimants
vs	(Petition for Citizenship)
Cherokee Nation	

Case submitted by the Claimants and the Solicitor, Jan. 12, 1883.
And now on this the 12th day of January AD, 1883, this case coming on for final hearing and all the

evidence produced in the case being duly read and considered by the Commission; it was adjudged and determined by the Commission on Citizenship that the above named Claimants, Margarett* Horne, John W. Horne, Susan Horne, Alice Horne, W.G.C. Horne, Louisa F. Horne, Lawrence R. Horne, and Alethia F. Horne, are Cherokees by blood and that they are entitled to all the rights and privileges of Cherokee citizenship within the Cherokee Nation and that they should be and they are, hereby admitted to the full and complete enjoyment of the same in all respects as native born Cherokees.

Thos. Tehee, Pres. of Comm.
Alex Wolfe

D.W.C. Duncan   T.F. Thompson
    Clerk of Comm.   Commissioners

Transcript delivered to Claimants, Jan. 12, 1883.

D.W.C. Duncan, Clerk
(*NOTE: Name spelled both ways.)

Jan. 16, 1883   C.H. Taylor, Sept. 19, 1884
Case #158

    MARTHA CAROLINE, FRANK L, Butler & Boudinot, Attys.
    and **ROMULUS N. VAUGHN**   for Claimants
         vs   (Petition for Citizenship)
    Cherokee Nation

Case continued till Sept. term, 1883;   Passed till June term, 1885.

Jan. 18, 1883
Case #159

    JUBER PHILPOT Boudinot & Butler, Attys. for Claimant
         vs   (Petition for Citizenship)
    Cherokee Nation

Certificate of Citizenship issued to Nuvana Mitchell by John S. Vann, dated Nov. 1, 1871, submitted as evidence to the consideration of the Commission.

    Case continued till Sept. term, 1883.

Jan. 23, 1883
Case #160   Pro Se Atty. (for himself, in one's own behalf)

Cherokee Citizenship Commission Docket Books
Tahlequah, Cherokee Nation (1880-84, 1887-89)
Volume I

G.W.C. SHAW
vs
(Petition for Citizenship)
Cherokee Nation

Continued till Sept. term, 1883; Case submitted by the Claimant, Sept. 17, 1883; Case submitted by the Solicitor, Sept. 21, 1883. And now on this the 25th day of Sept, 1883, this case coming on for final hearing and all the evidence produced on both sides in said case having been read and carefully considered; it was adjudged by the Commission on Citizenship that said Claimant, G.W.C. Shaw, is not a Cherokee by blood and that

he is not entitled to the rights and privileges of Cherokee citizenship within the Cherokee Nation; and that his claim for said citizenship should be and the same is hereby rejected.

	Thos. Tehee, Pres. of Comm.
	Alex Wolfe
Wm Eubanks	T.F. Thompson
Clerk Comm. Pro Tem	Commissioners

Jan. 25, 1883
Case #161

MISSOURI, WILLIAM, PERRY,   C.H. Taylor,
JULIA, ALFREDM, & VIOLA DOWNING Atty. for Claimants

vs   (Petition for Citizenship)
Cherokee Nation

Case continued till Sept. term, 1883; Continued to Sept. term of Commission, 1884; Withdrawn Sept. 24, 1884, by Claimants' Atty.

Jan. 30, 1883
Case #162

W.H. SHOEMAKE   **J.W. SHOEMAKE**
For his children: For his children:
**JESSE, HUGH, RICHARD, JAMES, WILLIAM, HARMAN*,
CHARLES, THOMAS, RHODA, JOHN, JODA ALICE,
MATTIE, LULU, & MARY SHOEMAKE, HENRY CLAY,
MINNIE MAY, & CALVIN SHOEMAKE**
vs

Cherokee Citizenship Commission Docket Books
Tahlequah, Cherokee Nation (1880-84, 1887-89)
Volume I

Cherokee Nation

Case submitted by Claimants and Solicitor, Jan. 30, 1883.

And now on this the 30th day of January A.D, 1883, this case coming on for final hearing and all the evidence produced in the case being carefully read and duly considered; it was adjudged and determined by the Commission on Citizenship, that the above named children of W.H. Shoemake, to wit: Jesse Shoemake, Hugh Shoemake, Richard Shoemake, Charles Shoemake, Thomas Shoemake, Rhoda Shoemake, Lulu Shoemake, Mary Shoemake; and also the above named children of J.W. Shoemake, to wit: James Shoemake, William Shoemake, Harmon* Shoemake, John Shoemake, Joda Alice Shoemake, Mattie Shoemake, Henry Clay Shoemake, Minnie May Shoemake and Calvin Shoemake, are Cherokees by blood and that they are entitled to all the rights of Cherokee citizenship within the Cherokee Nation and that they should be and are hereby admitted to the full and complete enjoyment of the same in all respects as native born Cherokees.

Thos. Tehee, President of Comm.

Alex Wolfe

D.W.C. Duncan   T.F. Thompson

    Clerk of Comm.   Commissioners

(***NOTE:** Name spelled both ways.)

Jan. 30, 1883
Case #163

J.W. SHOEMAKE
For his grand-children
MARY J, WILLIAM LEE,   C.H. Taylor, Atty. for Claim-
ant

THOMAS ELLIS, and
FELIX L. COLLINS
      vs   (Petition for Citizenship)
Cherokee Nation

Case submitted by the Claimants, Jan. 30, 1883;   Continued till Sept. term, 1883;   Case submitted by the Solicitor, Sept. 6, 1883.

And now on this the 11th day of September A.D, 1883, this case coming on for final hearing and all the evidence produced in the case on both sides being carefully read and duly considered by the Commission on Citizenship; it was adjudged by said Commission that the above named Claimants, Mary J.

Collins, William Lee Collins, Thomas Ellis Collins, and Felix L. Collins, are Cherokees by blood and that they are thereby justly entitled to all the rights and privileges of Cherokee citizenship within the Cherokee Nation, and that they should be and they are hereby admitted to the full and complete enjoyment of the same in all respects as native born Cherokees.

Thos. Tehee, Pres. of Comm.
Alex. Wolfe
D.W.C. Duncan   T.F. Thompson
    Clerk of Comm.   Commissioners

Sept. 3, 1883
Case #164

**GILBERT TAYLOR, JOSEPHINE A,
ALLISON, ERNEST, MILTON,**   Geo. O. Butler,
JAMES, CLEO, and **GILBERT TAYLOR, Jr,** Atty. for Claimant
THOMPSON
      vs   (Petition for Citizenship)
Cherokee Nation

Case submitted by Claimant and Solicitor, Sept. 4, 1883.

And now on this the 7th day of September A.D, 1883, this case coming on for final hearing, and all the evidence produced in the case on both sides having been carefully read and duly considered by the Commission on Citizenship; it was adjudged and determined by said Commission, that the above named Claimants, Gilbert Taylor Thompson, Allison Thompson, Ernest Thompson, Milton Thompson, James Thompson, Cleo Thompson, and Gilbert Taylor Thompson, Jr, are Cherokees by blood and they are by virtue thereof entitled (to) all the rights and privileges of Cherokee citizenship within the Cherokee Nation, and that they should be, and they are hereby admitted to the full and complete enjoyment of the same in all respects as native born Cherokees.

Thos. Tehee, President of Comm.
Alex Wolfe
D.W.C. Duncan   T.F. Thompson
    Clerk of Comm.   Commissioners
Transcripts furnished Claimant, Sept. 11, 1883.
D.W.C. Duncan, Clerk of Comm.

Sept. 3, 1883
Case #165   E.C. Boudinot & Geo. O. Butler,

Cherokee Citizenship Commission Docket Books
Tahlequah, Cherokee Nation (1880-84, 1887-89)
Volume I

PAULINA E, JAMES A, EMMA,   Attys.
for Claimants
ROSA, MARTHA, & ARTHUR HERRIN
        vs   (Petition for Citizenship)
Cherokee Nation

    Case submitted by Claimant and Solicitor, Sept. 6, 1883.

    And now on this the 7th day of September A.D, 1883, this case coming on for final hearing, and all the evidence produced in the case on both sides, having been carefully read and duly considered by the Commission on Citizenship; it was adjudged and determined by said Commission that the said Claimants, Paulina E. Herrin, James A. Herrin, Emma Herrin, Rosa Herrin, Martha Herrin, and Arthur Herrin, are Cherokees by blood, and that they are by virtue thereof entitled to all the rights and privileges of Cherokee citizenship within the Cherokee Nation, and that they should be and they are hereby admitted to the full and complete enjoyment of the same in all respects as native born Cherokees.

                              Thos. Tehee, Pres. of Comm
                              Alex Wolfe
D.W.C. Duncan   T.F. Thompson
        Clerk of Commission   Commissioners
Transcript furnished Claimant, Sept. 11, 1883.
        D.W.C. Duncan, Clk.

Sept. 3, 1883
Case #166   Geo. O. Butler, Atty. for Claimant
A.B. & OLIVE ISABELL ALLEN
        vs   (Petition for Citizenship)
Cherokee Nation

    Case submitted by Claimants, Sept. 8, 1883;   Case submitted by Solicitor, Sept. 10, 1883.

    And now on this the 10th day of September A.D, 1883, this case coming on for final hearing and all the evidence produced in the case on both sides being carefully read and duly considered by the Commission on Citizenship; it was adjudged by said Commission that the above named Claimants, A.B. Allen and Olive Isabell Allen, are Cherokees by blood, and that they are thereby justly entitled to all the rights and privileges of Cherokee citizenship within the Cherokee Nation, and that they should be and they are hereby admitted to the

full and complete enjoyment of the same in all respects as native born Cherokees.

Thos. Tehee, Pres. of Comm.
Alex Wolfe

D.W.C. Duncan   T.F. Thompson
      Clerk   Commissioners

Transcript furnished Claimants, Sept. 11, 1883.

D.W.C. Duncan, Clerk

Sept. 3, 1883
Case #167   Geo. O. Butler, Atty. of Claimant
      THOMAS & MURTA ALLEN
           vs   (Petition for Citizenship)
      Cherokee Nation

Case submitted by Claimants, Sept. 8, 1883; Case submitted by Solicitor, Sept. 10, 1883.

And now on this the 10th day of September A.D, 1883, this case coming on for final hearing and all the evidence produced in the case on both sides being carefully read and duly considered by the Commission on Citizenship; it was adjudged by said Commission, that the above named Claimants, Thomas Allen and Murta Allen, are Cherokees by blood and that they are thereby justly entitled to all the rights and privileges of Cherokee citizenship in the Cherokee Nation, and that they should be and they are hereby admitted to the full and complete enjoyment of the same in all respects as native born Cherokees.

Thos. Tehee, Pres of Comm
Alex Wolfe

D.W.C. Duncan   T.F. Thompson
      Clerk   Commissioners

Transcript furnished Claimants, Sept. 11, 1883.

D.W.C. Duncan, Clerk

Sept. 3, 1883
Case #168   Geo. O. Butler, Atty for Claimant
      W.B. ALLEN
           vs   (Petition for Citizenship)
      Cherokee Nation

Submitted by the Claimants, Sept. 8, 1883;   Submitted by the Solicitor, Sept. 10, 1883.

And now on this the 10th day of September A.D, 1883, this case coming on for final hearing and all the evidence produced in the case on both sides having been carefully read and duly considered by the Commission on Citizenship; it was adjudged by said Commission that the above named Claimant, W.B. Allen, is a Cherokee by blood and that he is thereby entitled to all the rights and privileges of Cherokee Citizenship within the Cherokee Nation and that he should be and he is hereby admitted to the full and complete enjoyment of the same in all respects as a native born Cherokee.

Thos. Tehee, Pres of Comm.
Alex Wolfe

D.W.C. Duncan   T.F. Thompson
Clerk   Commissioners

Transcript furnished Claimant, Sept. 11, 1883.

D.W.C. Duncan, Clerk

Sept. 3, 1883
Case #169

ELIZABETH, S.E, L.J,
FLORA, DOLLIE, AGNES,   J.E. Welch, Atty. for Claimant
& FREDRIC GARLAND
vs   (Petition for Citizenship)
Cherokee Nation

Submitted on part of Claimant, Sept. 4, 1883;   Submitted by Solicitor, Sept. 5, 1883.

And now on this 7th day of September A.D, 1883, this case coming on for final hearing and all the evidence produced in the case having been carefully read and duly considered by the Commission on Citizenship, it was adjudged and determined by said Commission, that the above named Claimants, Elizabeth Garland, S.E. Garland, L.J. Garland, Flora Garland, Dollie Garland, Agnes Garland, and Fredric Garland, are Cherokees by blood, and that by virtue thereof, they are entitled to all the rights and privileges of Cherokee citizenship within the Cherokee Nation, and that they should be and they are hereby admitted to the full and complete enjoyment of this same in all respects as native born Cherokees.

Thos. Tehee, Pres. of Comm.
Alex Wolfe

Cherokee Citizenship Commission Docket Books
Tahlequah, Cherokee Nation (1880-84, 1887-89)
Volume I

D.W.C. Duncan   T.F. Thompson
       Clerk   Commissioners
Transcript furnished Claimants, Sept. 11, 1883.
               D.W.C. Duncan, Clerk of Comm.

Sept. 3, 1883
Case #170   J.E. Welch, Atty. for Claimant
         L.R. & L.E. DAWES
            vs   (Petition for Citizenship)
         Cherokee Nation

Submitted by the Claimant, Sept. 4, 1883;   Submitted by the Solicitor, Sept. 5, 1883.

And now on this 7th day of September A.D, 1883, this case coming on for final hearing, and all the evidence produced in the case on both sides having been carefully read and duly considered by the Commission on Citizenship; it was adjudged and determined by said Commission that the above named Claimants, L.R. Dawes and L.E. Dawes, are Cherokees by blood, and that they are entitled to all the rights and privileges of Cherokee citizenship within the Cherokee Nation, and that they should be and they are hereby admitted to the full and complete enjoyment of the same in all respects as native born Cherokees.

                   Thos. Tehee, Pres. of Comm.
                   Alex Wolfe
D.W.C. Duncan   T.F. Thompson
       Clerk   Commissioners
Transcript furnished Claimants, Sept. 11, 1883.
              D.W.C. Duncan, Clerk of Comm.

Sept. 4, 1883
Case #171   C.H. Taylor, Atty. for Claimant
         PERMELIA WEST
            vs   (Petition for Citizenship)
         Cherokee Nation

Continued to September term, 1884;   Withdrawn by Claimant's Atty, Sept. 25, 1884.

Sept. 4, 1883

Cherokee Citizenship Commission Docket Books
Tahlequah, Cherokee Nation (1880-84, 1887-89)
Volume I

Case #172

MARGARETT ANN &   J.L. Springston, Atty for Claimant
REBECCA C. WARD
vs   (Petition for Citizenship)
Cherokee Nation

Submitted by the Claimant and the Solicitor, Sept. 11, 1883.

And now on this the 11th day of September A.D, 1883, this case coming on for final hearing and all the evidence produced in the case on both sides being carefully read and duly considered by the Commission on Citizenship; it was adjudged by said Commission that the above named Margarett Ann Ward and Rebecca C. Ward, are Cherokees by blood and that they are thereby justly entitled to all the rights and privileges of Cherokee citizenship within the Cherokee Nation; and that they should be and they are hereby admitted to the full and complete enjoyment of the same in all respects as native born Cherokees.

Thos. Tehee, Pres. of Comm
Alex Wolfe

D.W.C. Duncan   T.F. Thompson
Clerk Comm.   Commissioners
Transcript furnished Claimants, Sept. 11, 1883
D.W.C. Duncan, Clerk

Sept. 4, 1883
Case #173

KATE SOUTH   Lem Walker, Atty for Claimant
vs   (Petition for Citizenship)
Cherokee Nation

Case submitted by the Claimant, Sept. 12, 1883;   Jan. 3rd - Case taken up and the evidence of T.M. Warren produced on the part of Claimant

The Commission after examining the transactions of the late Commission, find that Mrs. Kate South was admitted to all the rights and privileges of a Cherokee by blood and it was so adjudged by the Commission.

Ely Spears, President

C.O. Frye, Clerk of Commission

Cherokee Citizenship Commission Docket Books
Tahlequah, Cherokee Nation (1880-84, 1887-89)
Volume I

And now on this the 5th day of Sept, 1883, on motion of the Solicitor, J.E. Welch was appointed to act as Solicitor for the Cherokee Nation, the Solicitor, Wilson Sanders, being called away by sickness in his family. Mr. J.E. Welch was qualified by taking the oath of office in open court.

	Thos. Tehee, Pres. of Comm.
	Alex Wolfe
D.W.C. Duncan	T.F. Thompson
Clerk of Comm	Commissioners

Sept. 5, 1883
Case #174   Micajah P. Haynes, Atty. for Claimant
     SARAH C. HAYNES
        vs   (Petition for Citizenship)
     Cherokee Nation

Submitted by Claimant, Sept. 7, 1883; Submitted by Claimant, Sept. 11, 1883.

And now on this the 11th day of September A.D, 1883, this case coming on for final hearing and all the evidence produced in the case on both sides being carefully read and duly considered by the Commission on Citizenship; it was adjudged by said Commission that the above named Claimant, Sarah C. Haynes is a Cherokee by blood, and that she is thereby justly entitled to all the rights and privileges of Cherokee citizenship within the Cherokee Nation and that she should be and she is hereby admitted to the full and complete enjoyment of the same in all respects as a native born Cherokee.

	Thos. Tehee, Pres. of Comm.
	Alex Wolfe
D.W.C. Duncan	T.F. Thompson
Clerk of Comm.	Commissioners

Transcript furnished Claimant, Sept. 13, 1883
        D.W.C. Duncan, Clerk

Sept. 6, 1883
Case #175   Geo. O. Butler, Atty for Claimant
     LAURA, A.B, J.G, and
     O.F. COOPER
        vs   (Petition for Citizenship)
     Cherokee Nation

Cherokee Citizenship Commission Docket Books
Tahlequah, Cherokee Nation (1880-84, 1887-89)
Volume I

Submitted by the Claimant and the Solicitor, Sept. 12, 1883.

And now on this the 25th day of September A.D, 1883, this case coming on for final hearing and all the evidence produced in the case on both sides being carefully read and duly considered by the Commission on Citizenship; it was adjudged by said Commission that the above named Claimants, Laura Cooper, A.B. Cooper, J.G. Cooper, and O.F. Cooper, are Cherokees by blood, and that they are hereby justly entitled to all the rights and privileges of Cherokee citizenship within the Cherokee Nation and that they should be and they are hereby, admitted to the full and complete enjoyment of the same in all respects as native born Cherokees.

Thos. Tehee, Pres. of Comm.

Alex Wolfe

Wm Eubanks   T.F. Thompson
     Clerk of Comm, Pro Tem   Commissioners
Transcript furnished Oct. 1, 1883
           Wm Eubanks, Clerk Comm. Pro Tem

Sept. 6, 1883
Case #176   C.H. Taylor, Atty. for Claimants
       MARGARETT SHIVALLEY
          vs   (Petition for Citizenship)
       Cherokee Nation

Continued Jan. 22, 1884, to Sept, 1884, by Petitioner;   Withdrawn by Claimant's Atty, Sept. 24, 1884.

Sept. 6, 1883
Case #177

       IDA, FRANCES, & George O. Butler, Atty. for Claimant
       DAISY MILHARLON
          vs   (Petition for Citizenship)
       Cherokee Nation

Submitted by the Claimant and the Solicitor, Sept. 12, 1883.

And now on this the 25th day of September A.D, 1883, this case coming on for final hearing and all the evidence produced in the case on both sides being read and carefully considered by the Commission on Citizenship; it was adjudged by said Commission that the above named Claimants, Ida Milharlon, Frances Milharlon, and Daisy Milharlon, are Cherokee by blood, and that they are thereby justly entitled to all the rights and privileges of Cherokee citizenship within the Cherokee Nation and that they should be and they are hereby admitted to the full and complete enjoyment of the same in all respects as native born Cherokees.

Thos. Tehee, Pres. of Comm.
A. Wolfe

Wm. Eubanks   T.F. Thompson
        Clerk Comm Pro Tem.   Commissioners
Transcript furnished Oct. 1, 1883.
        Wm Eubanks, Clerk Comm

Sept. 12, 1883
Case #178

THOMAS A, WILLIAM H, &   C.H. Taylor, Atty. for Claim.
THOMAS O. WOODSIDES
        vs   (Petition for Citizenship)
Cherokee Nation
        Case continued June 22, 1884, to Sept, 1884, by Petitioner;   Withdrawn by Claimants Atty.

Sept. 13, 1883
Case #179

SARAH J, JAMES A, MARY E, JOHN A,
GEORGE W, BESSIE B, ARCHIE B,   C.H. Taylor, Atty.
LIGNOR J, & SPENCER E. COPPLE   for Claimant
LIGNOR J, & SPENCER E. COPPLE
        vs   (Petition for Citizenship)
Cherokee Nation

        Case continued Jan. 22, 1884, to Sept, 1884;   Withdrawn by Atty. for Claimant, Sept. 27, 1884.

Sept. 13, 1883
Case #180

RICHARD L, ED VANN ROSS, RICHARD H.H,
        For himself
TOM KEMP, JAMES PARSHALL, SARAH ELLEN,
EVA MAY, ORA CHEROKEE NICHOLSON
        vs   (Petition for Citizenship)
Cherokee Nation

Cherokee Citizenship Commission Docket Books
Tahlequah, Cherokee Nation (1880-84, 1887-89)
Volume I

Case submitted by Claimant, Sept. 12, 1883;   Case submitted by Solicitor, Sept. 13, 1883.

And now on this the 13th day of September A.D, 1883, this case coming on (for) final hearing and all the evidence in the case produced on both sides being carefully read and duly considered by the Commission on Citizenship; it was adjudged by said Commission that the above named Claimants, Richard L. Nicholson, Ed Vann Nicholson, Richard H.H. Nicholson, Tom Kemp Nicholson, James Parshall Nicholson, Sarah Ellen Nicholson, Eva May Nicholson, and Ora Cherokee Nicholson, are Cherokees by blood, and that they are thereby justly entitled to all the rights and privileges of Cherokee citizenship within the Cherokee Nation and that they should be and they are hereby admitted to the full and complete enjoyment of the same in all respects as native born Cherokees.

	Thos. Tehee, Pres. of Comm.
	Alex Wolfe
D.W.C. Duncan	T.F. Thompson
Clerk of Comm	Commissioners

September 14, 1883

George W. Reese being called away by the sickness in his family, William Eubanks, Esqr, was duly appointed by the Commission on Citizenship to act as Interpreter pro tem. Wm Eubanks appeared and was duly qualified by taking the oath of office in open court before entering upon the duties of Interpreter.

	Thos. Tehee, Pres. of Comm.
	Alex Wolfe
D.W.C. Duncan	T.F. Thompson
Clerk of Comm.	Commissioners

Sept. 14, 1883
Case #181

E. DAWSON
For his grand-children: C.H. Taylor, Atty for Claim.
LULA & DALLAS DAUTHITT
        vs   (Petition for Citizenship)
Cherokee Nation

Case submitted by Claimant, Sept. 14, 1883;   Case submitted by Solicitor, Sept. 19, 1883;   Continued by Petitioner, Jan. 22, 1884, to Sept, 1884; Resubmitted Sept. 2, 1884, by Atty. Taylor;   Submitted by Defense, Sept. 9, 1884.

And now on this the 13th day of Sept, 1884, comes this case for final hearing, and all the evidence in the case having been carefully read and considered by the Commission on Citizenship; it has been decided by the Commission that the above named Lula Dauthitt and Dallas Dauthitt are Cherokees by blood and that they are entitled to all the rights and privileges of Cherokee citizenship in the Cherokee Nation, and that they should be and are hereby admitted to the full and complete enjoyment of the same in all respects as native born Cherokees.

Eli Spears, Pres.
John Lee
John L. Adair   Andrew Young
          Clerk Comm.   Commission on Citizenship

Sept. 14, 1883
Case #182

JAMES, ELLA, W.A, MALVINA,*
& MISSOURIA DAWSON
               vs   (Petition for Citizenship)
Cherokee Nation

Case submitted by Claimants, Sept. 14, 1883;   Submitted by Solicitor, Sept. 19, 1883;   Continued from the January term to the Sept. term, 1884; Resubmitted by the Atty. C.H. Taylor, Sept. 2, 1884;   Submitted by Defense, Sept. 9, 1884.

And now on this the 9th day of Sept, 1884, this case coming on for final hearing and all the evidence appertaining thereto having been carefully read and duly considered by the Commission on Citizenship; it was decided by said Commission that the above named Claimants, James Dawson, Ella Dawson, W.A. Dawson, Malinda* Dawson, and Missouria Dawson, are Cherokees by blood and that by virtue thereof they are justly entitled to all the rights and privileges of Cherokee citizenship in the Cherokee Nation and that they should be and are hereby admitted to the full and complete enjoyment of the same in all respects as native born Cherokees.   Eli Spears, Pres.
                                              John Lee
John L. Adair   Andrew Young

103

Cherokee Citizenship Commission Docket Books
Tahlequah, Cherokee Nation (1880-84, 1887-89)
Volume I

Clerk, Pro tem.	Comm.

Transcript furnished Claimant, Sept. 10, 1884.

(***NOTE:** Both names given.)

Sept. 19, 1883

Case #183   E.C. Boudinot & Capt. J.L. Smith
ANNIE BURTON HENRY   Attys. for Claimant
vs   (Petition for Citizenship)
Cherokee Nation

Case submitted by Claimant, Sept. 19, 1883.

And now on this the 22nd day of September A.D, 1883, this case coming on for final hearing and all the evidence in the case being carefully read and duly considered; it was decided by the Commission on Citizenship that the above named Claimant, Annie Burton Henry, is a Cherokee by blood and that she is thereby justly entitled to all rights and privileges of Cherokee citizenship within the Cherokee Nation, and that she should be and she is hereby admitted to the full and complete enjoyment of the same in all respects as a native born Cherokee.

Alex Wolfe, Acting Pres.

T.F. Thompson, Commissioner

D.W.C. Duncan   Thos. Tehee, Pres. (absent, not voting)
Clerk of Comm

Sept. 19, 1883

Case #184   E.C. Boudinot, Atty. for Claim.
LUCY FLEETWOOD
vs   (Petition for Citizenship)
Cherokee Nation

Submitted by Plaintiff, Jan. 11, 1884;   Set for final hearing, Jan. 19, 1884;   Continued to Feb, 1884;   Continued to Sept. term, 1884;   Submitted by both parties, Sept. 29, 1884.

And now on this the 29th day of September A.D, 1884, this case coming on for final hearing and all the evidence in the case being carefully read and duly considered; it was decided by the Commission on Citizenship that the above named claimant, Lucy Fleetwood, is not a Cherokee Indian by blood, and the said Lucy Fleetwood is hereby legally and duly <u>rejected</u>.

Eli Spears, President

104

Cherokee Citizenship Commission Docket Books
Tahlequah, Cherokee Nation (1880-84, 1887-89)
Volume I

Attest, C.O. Frye   Andrew Young, Comm.
    Clerk Comm.

Sept. 20, 1883
Case #185   E.C. Boudinot, Atty for Claimant
     DORA & RUSH WILSON
        vs   (Petition for Citizenship)
     Cherokee Nation

    Case submitted by the Claimant, Sept. 20, 1883;   Submitted by the Solicitor, Sept. 21, 1883.
    And now on this the 21st day of September A.D, 1883, this cause coming on for final hearing and all the evidence produced in the case being carefully read and duly considered; it was decided by the Commission on Citizenship that the Claimants, Dora Wilson and Rush Wilson, are Cherokees by blood and that they are thereby justly entitled to all the rights and privileges of Cherokee citizenship within the Cherokee Nation, and that they should be and they are hereby admitted to the full and complete enjoyment of the same in all respects as native born Cherokees.

                           Thos. Tehee, Pres. of Comm
                           Alex Wolfe
D.W.C. Duncan   T.F. Thompson
    Clerk of Comm.   Commissioners

Sept. 20, 1883
Case #186

    MARTHA J, JOSEPH A, HARRIET A,   C.H. Taylor, Atty
    JOHN J.H, & ELIZABETH GILLIS   for Claimant
        vs   (Petition for Citizenship)
    Cherokee Nation

    Case submitted by Claimant and Solicitor, Sept. 26, 1883.
    And now on this the 1st day of October A.D, 1883, this case coming on for final hearing and all the evidence produced in the case on both sides being carefully read and duly cnsidered; it was decided by the Commission on Citizenship that the Claimants, Martha J. Gillis, Joseph A. Gillis, Harriet A. Gillis, John J.H. Gillis, and Elizabeth Gillis, are not Cherokees by blood and therefore are not entitled to Cherokee citizenship within the Cherokee Nation.

                           Thos. Tehee, Pres. Comm.

Cherokee Citizenship Commission Docket Books
Tahlequah, Cherokee Nation (1880-84, 1887-89)
Volume I

	Alex Wolfe
Wm Eubanks	T.F. Thompson
Clerk Comm Pro Tem.	Commissioners

Sept. 24, 1883
Case #187

JOHN R, CHARLES W, JAMES J,   E.C. Boudinot, Atty. for
EMMA, ALICE, MARY, JOHN, GORDON,   Claimant
FREDRIC, LILLIE, & ELLA GEE
vs   (Petition for Citizenship)
Cherokee Nation

The above case being continued from Sept, 1883, to Jan, 1884;   Case opened Jan. 7, 1884;   Case submitted by Plaintiff, Jan. 10, 1884;   Case decided by the Commission on Citizenship, Jan. 13, 1884.

And now on this the 15th day of January, 1884, this case coming on (for) final hearing and all the evidence in the case being produced on both sides, the same being examined and considered by the Commission and there being no evidence produced in the case showing that the said Claimants, John R. Gee, Chas. W. Gee, James J. Gee, Emma Gee, Alice Gee, Mary Gee, John Gee, Jr, Gordon Gee, Frederic Gee, Lillie Gee, and Ella Gee, were Cherokee Indians by blood and there being no evidence in the case showing that Louis Stowers and from whom the evidence and petition show that the Claimants claim to have derived there(sic) Cherokee blood ever lived in the Cherokee Nation and that he was ever recognized to be a Cherokee Indian by virtue of his Cherokee blood. Therefore, the Commission on Citizenship hereby adjudged and decided that the said Claimants have failed on their part to produce evidence sufficient to satisfy the minds of the Commission that they the Claimants were Cherokee Indians by blood and therefore the petition filed before the Commission applying for admission into citizenship in the Cherokee Nation is hereby rejected and that the said Claimants should not be allowed to enjoy the privilege of citizenship in the Cherokee Nation and it is so decided by the Commission.

	Eli Spears, Pres.
	John Lee
C.O. Frye	Andrew Young
Clerk	Asst. Comm.

Transcript furnished, Jan. 18, 1884.

Sept. 24, 1883
Case #188   J.M. Keys & L.B. Bell
                                      - E.C. Boudinot, Jr.
MARY F, WILLIS, GEORGE W,   Attys. for Claimants
& MINNIE O. BATTELLE
          vs   (Petition for Citizenship)
Cherokee Nation

Case submitted by Claimant and by Cherokee Nation, Jan. 15, 1884.
And now on this the 16th day of January, 1884, this case coming on (for) final hearing and all the evidence in the case being produced on both sides and the same being duly examined and considered by the Commission and there being no evidence produced in the case showing that said Mary F. Battelle, Willis Battelle, George W. Battelle, and Minnie O. Battelle, were Cherokee Indians by blood, and there being no evidence in the case showing that Louis and Susen Stowers were ever recognized to be Cherokee Indians by the citizens of the Cherokee Nation and from whom the said Claimants claim to have derived their Cherokee blood. Therefore the Commission on Citizenship adjudged that the said Claimants had failed on their part to produce sufficient evidence to establish their right to Cherokee citizenship within the limits of the Cherokee Nation and it was decided by the Commission that they were not and should not be allowed the privilege of citizenship in the Cherokee Nation. And it was so decided by the Commission and therefore the petition asking for admission to citizenship within the limits of the Cherokee Nation is hereby rejected.

                                      Eli Spears, Pres.
                                      John Lee
C.O. Frye   Andrew Young
    Clerk   Commissioners

Sept. 24, 1883
Case #189   For himself
          MONROE BANE
          vs   (Petition for Citizenship)
Cherokee Nation

Submitted by the Claimant, Sept. 24, 1883;   Submitted by the Solicitor, Sept. 25, 1883.
And now on this the 25th day of September A.D, 1883, this case coming on for final hearing and all the evidence produced in the case being carefully

read and duly considered; it was decided by the Commission on Citizenship that the above Claimant, Monroe Bane, is a Cherokee by blood and that he is hereby justly entitled to all the rights and privileges of Cherokee citizenship within the Cherokee Nation and that he should be and he is hereby admitted to the full and complete enjoyment of the same in all respects as native born Cherokees.

	Alex Wolfe
Wm. Eubanks	T.F. Thompson
Clerk, Pro Tem.	Commissioners

Sept. 25, 1883

Case #190   J.M. Bryan, Attorney for Claimant
    Wm. P. ARCHER
        vs   (Petition for Citizenship)
    Cherokee Nation

Case submitted by Plaintiff, Jan. 10, 1884;   Case submitted by the Cherokee, Jan. 16, 1884.

And now on this the 16th day of January, 1884, this case coming on (for) final hearing and all the evidence in the case being produced and the same being duly examined and considered by the Commission on Citizenship and while Commission is satisfied beyond a reasonable doubt that the said William P. Archer is a Cherokee Indian by virtue of his Cherokee blood, it is held by the Commission that the said William P. Archer is not entitled to and should not be allowed to enjoy the rights and privileges of citizenship in the Cherokee Nation and for ground of such decision, it is held by the Commission that the evidence produced by Claimant shows periodically that his mother took advantage of Article 19 of the Treaty concluded July 19, 1866, between the United States and the Cherokee Nation.

Which provides that any person who shall elect to remain on the said lands mentioned in the said Treaty of July 19, 1866, shall receive a patent in fee simple for three-hundred and twenty acres of land and thereby <u>he</u> and <u>his family</u> shall cease to be <u>members</u> of the Cherokee Nation. And therefore the petition applying for citizenship in the Cherokee Nation is hereby <u>rejected</u>.

Given from under our hands on this the day and date above written.

	Eli Spears, Pres.
	John Lee
Attest C.O. Frye	Andrew Young
Clerk	Commissioners

Cherokee Citizenship Commission Docket Books
Tahlequah, Cherokee Nation (1880-84, 1887-89)
Volume I

Sept. 26, 1883
Case #191
                                    John E. Welch, Atty.
      THOMAS E. BANHAM
        vs   (Petition for Citizenship)
      Cherokee Nation

Passed to Jan. term, 1884.

Sept. 26, 1883
Case #192
      SERENA JONES, WILEY JONES,
      CHASER JONES, & MARY WEBSTER
        vs   (Petition for Citizenship)
      Cherokee Nation

Withdrawn or dismissed.

Sept. 27, 1883
Case #193
      LEWIS A. MARTIN
        vs   (Petition for Citizenship)
      Cherokee Nation

Case submitted by Claimant and Solicitor, Sept. 27, 1883.
And now on this the 27th day of September A.D, 1883, this case coming on for final hearing and all the evidence produced in the case being carefully read and duly considered; it was decided by the Commission on Citizenship that the above named Claimant, Lewis A. Martin, is a Cherokee by blood and that he is hereby justly entitled to all the rights and privileges of Cherokee citizenship within the Cherokee Nation, and that he should be and he is hereby admitted to the full and complete enjoyment of the same in all respects as a native born Cherokee.

                      Thos. Tehee, Pres. of Comm.
                      Alex Wolfe
Wm Eubanks   T.F. Thompson
      Clerk, Pro tem.   Commissioners

Cherokee Citizenship Commission Docket Books
Tahlequah, Cherokee Nation (1880-84, 1887-89)
Volume I

January 1, 1884

Commission on Citizenship

Ely Spears, President
Andrew Young
John Lee   C.O. Frye, Clerk
　　Commissioners   Samuel H. Downing, Interpreter
　　　　　　　　　　　　　　Commission on Citizenship

Jan. 7, 1884
Case #187
　　　　　JOHN R, CHAS. W, JAMES J,　　　E.C. Boudinot, Jr,
　　　　　EMMA, ALICE, MARY, JOHN,　　　Atty. for Claimants
　　　　　GORDON, FREDRICK, LILLIE,
　　　　　& ELLA GEE
　　　　　　　　(vs)　　　　　　　　　(Petition for Citizenship)
　　　　　(Cherokee Nation)
Petition filed before the new Commission, Jan. 7, 1884.
Rejected, January 15 A.D, 1884

　　　　　(**NOTE**) Case transferred from page 142 Docket of 1882.
Sept. 9, 1882
Case #135　　　　　　　T.E. Beavert, Atty for Claimants
　　　　　Wm. & ANN STEPHENS
　　　　　　　vs　　　　　　　　　　(Petition for Citizenship)
　　　　　Cherokee Nation

　　　Petition filed Sept. 9, 1882;　　Commission grants Claimants permission
to withdraw the above case and to take the testimony from the files to be duly
certified by the clerk;　　Case is accordingly withdrawn;　　Case reinstated on
the Docket, Jan. 23, 1883;　　Case continued to Sept, 1883;　　Submitted by the
Claimant and Solicitor, Sept. 6, 1883;　　On motion of Solicitor Smith, the
above case was set for Jan. 26, 1884;　　On motion, the above case was postponed to the Sept, 1884;　　Submitted by both parties, Sept. 8, 1884.
　　　And now on this day, Sept. 8, 1884, comes this case for final hearing and
all the evidence pro et con the case having been carefully read and considered
by the Commission on Citizenship; it is adjudged by the Commission that the

above mentioned Claimant, William Stephens, is not in any degree a Cherokee Indian, and not being such Indian in any degree, he is not, and is so pronounced by the Commission, entitled to the rights and privileges of native born Cherokees.

	Eli Spears, Pres.
	John Lee
John L. Adair	Andrew Young
Clerk	Comm.

(NOTE) This case was transferred from page - by new Comm. It appearing that the old Comm. failed to render decision thereon.

Jan. 8, 1884

Case #182   T.E. Beavert, Atty. for Claimants
JAMES, ELLA, W.A, MALVINA,
& MISSOURIA DAWSON
                 vs   (Petition for Citizenship)
Cherokee Nation

Submitted by Claimant, Jan. 8, 1884.

On motion of Mr. Solicitor Smith, the case was set for hearing on the 24th of Jan, 1884.

See decision of Comm. on page (76 of this book).

Jan. 9, 1884

Case #194   E.C. Boudinot, Atty. for Claimant
MARY B. CHURCH
                 vs   Application for Citizenship
Cherokee Nation

Petition filed Jan. 9, 1884;   Case submitted by Claimant, Jan. 9, 1884; Case submitted by Solicitor, Jan. 10, 1884;   Case argned pro & con, Jan. 10, 1884;   Decision rendered on Jan. 12, 1884.

And now on this day this case coming on final hearing and all the evidence in the case produced on both sides being carefully read and duly considered by the Commission on Citizenship; It was adjudged by said Commission that the above named Claimant, Mary B. Church, is a Cherokee by blood and that she is justly entitled to all the rights of Cherokee citizenship within the limits of the Cherokee Nation, and that she should be and is hereby admitted to all the rights and full and complete enjoyment of the same in all respects as a native Cherokee.

Ely Spears, Pres.
John Lee
C.O. Frye   Andrew Young
Clerk   Commissioners

Jan. 9, 1884
Case #195   E.C. Boudinot, Jr, Atty. for Claimant
      FRANK BOUDINOT
          vs   Application for Citizenship
      Cherokee Nation

      Case submitted by Claimant, Jan. 9, 1884;   Case submitted by Solicitor, Jan. 10, 1884;   Case argned pro & con, Jan. 10, 1884;   Decision rendered, Jan. 12, 1884.

      And now on this day this case coming on final hearing and all the evidence on both sides being produced and carefully read and duly considered by the Commission on Citizenship; It was adjudged by said Commission that the above named Claimant, Frank Boudinot, is a Cherokee by blood and that he is justly entitled to all the rights of Cherokee citizenship in the Cherokee Nation and that he should be and is hereby admitted to all the rights and privileges as a native born Cherokee.

Ely Spears, Pres.
John Lee
C.O. Frye   Andrew Young
     Clerk   Commissioners

Jan. 15, 1884
Case #120   Lem Sanders & E.C. Boudinot, Jr, Attys.
      JAMES M, MARY C, F.Y,
      Z.E, J.S, & CHARLES W. TRUETT
          vs   (Petition for Citizenship)
      Cherokee Nation

      Sept. 28, 1882 - Continued by the Claimant till Jan. term, 1883;   Motion for continuance filed by Claimant, Jan. 6, 1883;   Continued by Claimant till the Sept. term, 1883;   Jan. 15, 1884 - Case continued from Docket of January, 1882, page (51 of this book).

Jan. 17, 1884
Case #196

P.G, G.A, MARTHA F, JESSE T, ARLY E, & JASPER T. RUSSELL*

vs   Application for Citizenship

Cherokee Nation

Petition filed Jan. 18, 1884;   Set for Jan. 29, 1884;   Continued to Sept. 8, 1884;   Submitted by Atty, Sept. 16, 1884;   Passed to Sept. 24, 1884;   Submitted by both parties, Sept. 24, 1884.

And now on this the 26th day of September, 1884, this case coming on for final hearing and all the evidence in the case being read and after being duly considered; It was adjudged by the Commission on Citizenship that said P.G. Russel* is not a Cherokee by blood and consequently not entitled to the rights of citizenship in the Cherokee Nation as set forth in the application. And he, the said P.G. Russel, is clearly and legally rejected this the 26th day of September, 1884.

                        Eli Spears, Pres.

Attest, C.O. Frye   Andrew Young, Comm.

     Clerk of Comm.

       (***NOTE:** Name spelled both ways.)

Jan. 19, 1884
Case #197

JOSEPH P. SUMMERS

vs   Application for Citizenship

Cherokee Nation

Petition filed Jan. 19, 1884;   Submitted by Plaintiff and Solicitor, Jan. 19, 1884;   Case decided, Jan. 19, 1884.

And now on this the 19th day of Jan, 1884, this case coming on final hearing and all the evidence in the case being produced and the same being duly examined and considered by the Commission on Citizenship; It was adjudged and decided by the Commission that the said, Joseph P. Summers, is a Cherokee by blood and should be and is hereby admitted to enjoy the rights and privileges of Cherokee citizenship within the limits of the Cherokee Nation and the Commission has so decided. This the 19th day of Jan, 1884.

                        Ely Spears, Pres.

Cherokee Citizenship Commission Docket Books
Tahlequah, Cherokee Nation (1880-84, 1887-89)
Volume I

Andrew Young

Attest, C.O. Frye   John Lee
        Clerk   Commissioners
Transcript furnished Claimant, Jan. 19, 1884.

C.O. Frye, Clerk

Jan. 17, 1884
Case #198   T.E. Beavert, Atty.
MARGRATE JANE TAYLER
            vs   Application for Citizenship
    Cherokee Nation

Petition filed Jan. 17, 1884;   Continued to Sept. term, 1884; Withdrawn, Sept, 1884,

---

Jan. 25, 1884
Case #199
    CORNELIA CUNNEL

            vs   Application for Citizenship
    Cherokee Nation

Case submitted by Claimant and Solicitor, Jan. 28, 1884.

And now on this the 28th day of January, 1884, this case coming on final hearing and all the evidence in the case being produced and the same being carefully read and duly considered; It was adjudged and determined by the Commission on Citizenship that said applicant, Cornelia Cunnel, is a Cherokee by blood and is equally entitled to and is hereby admitted to the full and free enjoyment of all the rights and privileges of Cherokee citizenship within the limits of the Cherokee Nation as other native Cherokees and Commission has so decided.

Given from under our hands on this the day and date above written.

Ely Spears, Pres.
Andrew Young
Attest, C.O. Frye   John Lee
        Clerk   Commissioners
Copy decision furnished, Jan. 28, 1884
        C.O. Frye, Clerk

Jan. 25, 1884
Case #200   Blue Alberty, Atty for Claimant
    NORA, EUGENE, LILLY, &
    GRACE OWENS
        vs   Application for Citizenship
    Cherokee Nation

Submitted by Claimant, Jan. 25, 1884;   Submitted by Solicitor, Jan. 26, 1884.

And now on this the 26th day of Jan, 1884, this case coming on final hearing and all the evidence in the case being produced and the same being carefully read and duly considered; It was adjudged and determined by the Commission on Citizenship that said Applicants, Nora Owens, Eugene Owens, Lilly Owens, and Grace Owens, are Cherokee by blood and are equally entitled to all the rights and privileges of Cherokee citizenship in the Cherokee Nation as other Cherokee Indians and they are hereby admitted to the full enjoyment of the same as other native Cherokees.

Given from under our hands this the 26th day of Jan. 1884.

                      Ely Spears, Pres.
                      John Lee
Attest, C.O. Frye   Andrew Young
    Clerk   Commissioners

Jan. 26, 1884
Case #201

    WILLIAM, SARAH E, R.C, ELIZABETH,   Lem Sanders &
    SHROWDER, MARY, JAMES, and   E.C. Boudinot,
    JOHN BURGESS   Attys. for Petitioners
        vs   Application for Citizenship
    Cherokee Nation

Submitted by Solicitor;   Passed till Monday, 2 o'clock, this Sept. 27, 1884.

2 o'clock P.M, Sept. 29, 1884 - The above case coming on for final hearing and all the evidence in the case being produced on both sides and after being duly considered by the Commission on Citizenship; It was adjudged by the Commission on Citizenship that said Wm Burgess, Sarah Burgess, R.C. Burgess, Elizabeth Burgess, Shrowder Burgess, Mary Burgess, James Burgess, and John Burgess, are not Cherokee Indians by blood and that they failed to sub-

stantiate the allegations set forth in the petition for citizenship filed before the Commission on Citizenship, Jan. 26, 1884. And that they are hereby legally rejected. This the 29th day of September A.D, 1884.

Eli Spears, President
John Lee
Andrew Young
Commissioners

Attest, C.O. Frye
            Clerk

Cases Defaulted before Court of Commission

Known as the Cherokees Court and reopened.

June 12, 1884
Case #1

**JAMES, MARY JANE, SELLERS,
& JAMES WHITE**

(No other information given.)

June 27, 1884
Case #2

**JOHN, WILLIAM, &
CALDONA BRADSHAW**

(No other information given.)

July 2, 1884
Case #3

NANCY BRADSHAW

(No other information given.)

July 20, 1884
Case #4

J.T, T.M, & ELIZAB. MAYFIELD

(No other information given.)

Aug. 10, 1884
Case #5

LEWIS WRIGHT and **MOTHER**

(No other information given.)

Aug. 13, 1884
Case #6

H. H. HAMPTON
vs
Cherokee Nation

Application filed and other papers in the case filed Sept. 12, 1884;   Papers withdrawn, Sept. 18, 1884, by Applicant himself.

Aug. 20, 1884
Case #7

**REUBEN, AMANDA, MARY, HARISON,
DELIAH, SOLLOMAN, ANDREW, DIANNAH,
JANE, RUTHA, ELIZA, KIZA, ROSANNA,
& SARAH JOHNSON**

(No other information given.)

Aug. 21, 1884
Case #8

JELFREY(sic) **HOLT**

(No other information given.)

Aug. 22, 1884
Case #9

WILSE(sic)**, ANN, DICK,
& LUCINDA TOWERS**

(No other information given.)

Aug. 27, 1884
Case #10

SOLOMON FOREMAN

vs

C.N.

(No other information given.)

Cases Docketed September Term, 1884

Sept. 1, 1884

Case #1   E.C. Boudinot, Jr, Atty.

JOHN F. WILSON

vs   (Application for Citizenship)

Cherokee Nation

Case submitted on part of the Claimant and by Solicitor, Sept. 4, 1884.

And now on this the 5th day of Sept, 1884, all the evidence in the case being produced and after being first read and duly considered by the Commission on Citizenship; It was decided by the Commission that said Applicant, John F. Wilson, was a Cherokee Indian by blood and he is and should be admitted to all the rights and privileges as other native Cherokees within the limits of the Cherokee Nation. And that he is hereby admitted to the full and complete enjoyment of the same within the limits of the Cherokee Nation.

Ely Spears, Pres.

John Lee

Attest, C.O. Frye   Andrew Young

Clrk   Comm.

Sept. 1, 1884

Case #2

ISABELLA, JOHN D, MINNIE O,

LELIA M, JINOBIA H, and   E.C. Boudinot, Jr, Atty.

ALTHA B. WARD

vs   Application for Citizenship

Cherokee Nation

Case submitted by Claimant and Nation's Solicitor, Sept. 9, 1884.

And now on this the 9th day of Sept. A.D, 1884, coming on for final hearing, this case and all the evidence in the case having been carefully read and considered by the Commission on Citizenship; It was adjudged by the Commission that the above named Claimants, Isabella Ward, John D. Ward, Minnie

O. Ward; Lelia M. Ward, Jinobia H. Ward, and Aletha B. Ward, are Cherokees by blood and by virtue thereof are entitled to all the rights and privileges of Cherokee citizenship in the Cherokee Nation, and that they should be and are hereby admitted to the full and complete enjoyment of the same in the Cherokee Nation in all respects as native born Cherokees.

Eli Spears, Pres
John Lee

John L. Adair   Andrew Young
    Clerk, Pro tem.   Commissioners
Transcript furnished Applicants, Sept. 11, 1884.

Sept. 1, 1884
Case #3   E.C. Boudinot, Jr, Atty.
JOHN WATKINS
      vs   Application for Citizenship
Cherokee Nation

Passed to the 20th, 1884;   Submitted by Claimant and Solicitor, Sept. 23, 1884.

This case coming on final hearing on this the 25th day of Sept, 1884, and all the evidence in the case being read and duly considered; It was adjudged by the Commission on Citizenship that said John Watkins is a Cherokee Indian by blood. And is entitled to all the rights and citizenship of the Cherokee Nation as other native Cherokees. And he is hereby admitted to all the rights and privileges of other native Cherokees within the limits of the Cherokee Nation.

Given from under my hand and seal, this the 25th day of Sept, 1884.

Eli Spears, Pres.

Attest, C.O. Frye, Clerk   Andrew Young, Commissioner
Transcript furnished this Sept. 25, 1884.

Sept. 1, 1884
Case #4   E.C. Boudinot, Jr, Atty.
HARRIET C. LARKINS
      vs   Application for Citizenship
Cherokee Nation

Passed till Sept. 26, 1884.

Sept. 1, 1884

Case #5   R.B. Harris, Atty
    JACKSON & AUGUSTA ROGERS
        vs   Application for Citizenship
    Cherokee Nation

Passed, Sept. 4;   Submitted by both parties, Sept. 26, 1884.
In the above case it appearing to the satisfaction of the Commission that said Jackson Rogers and child, Augusta Rogers, and George Rogers, Ida Rogers, Iola Rogers, Jennie Rogers, W.S. Rogers, Beattris Rogers, Minni Rogers, George Rogers, and Ed Rogers, are Cherokees by blood and are hereby admitted to the full and complete enjoyment of the same.

                                    Eli Spears, Pres.
Attest, C.O. Frye, Clerk   Andrew Young, Comm.

Sept. 1, 1884
Case #6   R.B. Harris, Atty. for Claimant
    GEORGE, IDA, IOLA, JENNIE, W.S,
    BEATTRIS, MINERVA, & GEORGE ROGERS

        (vs)   Application for Citizenship
    (Cherokee Nation)

Passed, Sept. 4;   Submitted by both parties, Sept. 26, 1884;   Admitted Sept. 26, 1884. See (Previous case #5) for decision.

Sept. 1, 1884
Case #7

    ED ROGERS
        vs   Application for Citizenship
    Cherokee Nation

Passed, Sept. 4;   Submitted by both parties, Sept. 26, 1884;   See (Case #5) for decision.

Sept. 1, 1884
Case #8   T.E. Beavert, Atty.
    A.J, SARAH JANE, MATTIE,
    & VICTORIA MARTIN
        vs   Application for Citizenship

Cherokee Nation

Passed, Sept. 4;   Case submitted Sept. 5, 1884, by Claimants.
And now on this the 10th day of September A.D, 1884, comes this case for final hearing and all the evidence in the case having been carefully read and considered by the Commission on Citizenship; It is unanimously decided that the above parties, A.J. Martin, Sarah Jane Martin, and Victoria Martin, are not in any degree Cherokee Indians by blood, and are not entitled to the rights and privileges of Cherokee citizenship in the Cherokee Nation.

	Eli Spears, Pres.
	John Lee
John L. Adair	Andrew Young
Clerk Comm.	Comm.

Sept. 2, 1884
Case #9

JERRY, REBECCA, THOMAS, MARY,   T.E. Beavert, Atty.
SYLVESTER, THOMAS, WILLIAM,
& JOHN RICH
                 vs   Application for Citizenship
(Cherokee Nation)

Passed, Sept. 4; Continued till January, 1885.

Sept. 2, 1884
Case #10

OLIVE HEATH
             (vs)   Application for Citizenship
(Cherokee Nation)

Passed, Sept. 4;   Submitted Sept. 10, 1884.
And now on this day the 10th day of September A.D, 1884, comes this case for final hearing and all the evidence in the case having been carefully read and considered by the Commission on Citizenship; It was unanimously decided by said Commission that the above named Claimant, Olive Heath, is a Cherokee by blood and as such is entitled to all the rights and privileges of Cherokee citizenship in the Cherokee Nation, and that she should and is hereby

admitted to a full and complete enjoyment of the same in all respects as a native born Cherokee.

John L. Adair
Clerk

Eli Spears, Pres.
John Lee
Andrew Young
Comm.

Cases referred to the Citizenship Commission by the National Council.

Sept. 16, 1884
Case #11

EMMA WHITFIELD*
and **FAMILY**
                vs   Application for Citizenship
Cherokee Nation

And now on this the 17th day of September, 1884, comes this case for final hearing, and all the evidence in relation thereto, having been read and considered by the Commission on Citizenship; It was decided that the above Claimant, Emma Whitefield*, is a Cherokee by Blood, she being the daughter of Elizabeth Hildebrand, a known Cherokee and the same who, when a child was given to George Butler, U.S. Indian Agent for the Cherokees, at the beginning of the late war. She and her children are therefore, entitled to all the rights and privileges of citizenship in the Cherokee Nation, and should be and are hereby admitted to the full enjoyment of the same in all respects, as native born Cherokees.

John L. Adair
Clerk

Eli Spears, Pres.
John Lee
Andrew Young
Comm.
(***NOTE:** Name spelled both ways.)

Sept. 2, 1884
Case #12

RICHARD L. NICKOLSON
For minor children:
RICHARD R. & EDWARD E. NICKOLSON*
                (vs)   Application for Citizenship

Cherokee Citizenship Commission Docket Books
Tahlequah, Cherokee Nation (1880-84, 1887-89)
Volume I

(Cherokee Nation)

Submitted by Solicitor, Sept. 15, 1884.

And now on this the 16th day of September, 1884, comes this case for final hearing, and all the evidence in relation thereto having been read and considered by the Commission on Citizenship; It was unanimously decided by said Commission that the above Applicants, Richard R. Nicholson* and Edward E. Nicholson, are Cherokees by blood, they being descendants of Ed Gunter Nicholson, and are hereby admitted to the full enjoyment of all the rights and privileges of citizenship in the Cherokee Nation in all respects as native born Cherokees.   Eli Spears, Pres.

John Lee, Comm.

John L. Adair, Clerk   Andrew Young, Comm.
              (*NOTE: Name spelled both ways.)

Sept. 3, 1884
Case #13

> **REBECCA, PHILIP, EVA, EMMALINE,**
> **CORA, CLEM, & SAMUEL M. SWEETON**
>   (No other information given.)

Sept. 2, 1884
Case #14

> **G.W. WILSON**
> For:
> **HENRY WILSON**
>   (vs)   (Application for Citizenship)
> (Cherokee Nation)

Submitted by Claimant and Solicitor, Sept. 6, 1884.

In the case of Henry Wilson, applicant for citizenship case being referred to the Citizenship Commission by the National Council, November, 1883; and docketed before the Commission on Citizenship, Sept. 4, 1884.

This case coming on for final hearing on this the 6th day of September, 1884. And the affidavit of George Wilson presented to the National Council being read and duly considered by the Commission on Citizenship; It was adjudged by the Commission that said Henry Wilson is a Cherokee Indian by blood and should be and is hereby admitted to the full and complete enjoyment of all rights and privileges as other native Cherokees within the limits of the Cherokee Nation.

Given from under out hands and seal of office, this the 6th day of Sept, 1884.

Eli Spears, President
John Lee
Attest, C.O. Frye   Andrew Young
        Clerk   Comm.

Sept. 2, 1884
Case #15

BITCY(sic) **WILKERSON, POLLY WARD,**
JENNIE WHITE & MARGRATE JONES
            (vs)   (Application for Citizenship)
(Cherokee Nation)

Submitted Sept. 10, 1884, by both parties.

And now on this the 16th day of September, 1884, comes this case for final hearing and all the evidence appertaining thereto having been read and considered by the Commission on Citizenship, It was adjudged by the Commission, the Claimant

(NOTE: Entry incomplete.)

Sept. 2, 1884
Case #16

LOUISA WILSON (Nee: Collins)
& CHILDREN
            (vs)   (Application for Citizenship)
(Cherokee Nation)

Submitted by both parties, Sept. 15, 1884.

And now on this the 16th day of September A.D, 1884, comes this case for final hearing, and all the evidence in relation thereto having been read and considered by the Commission; It was unanimously adjudged that the above applicant, Louisa Wilson, nee Collins, and her children, are Cherokees by blood. She, the applicant, being the daughter of Lydia Joe, a half Cherokee and half Natchez Indian. Being such by blood, the said Louisa Wilson, nee Collins, and her children are entitled to all the rights and benefits of Cherokee citizenship in the Cherokee Nation, and should be and are hereby admitted to

124

Cherokee Citizenship Commission Docket Books
Tahlequah, Cherokee Nation (1880-84, 1887-89)
Volume I

the full and complete enjoyment of the same, in all respects as native born Cherokees.

Eli Spears, Pres.
John Lee

John L. Adair   Andrew Young
      Clerk   Commissioners

Sept. 2, 1884
Case #17   By J.T. Drew, Atty.
      TIP R. BEAN
         (vs)   (Application for Citizenship)
   (Cherokee Nation)

Passed, Sept. 4, 1884;   Submitted by Claimant and Solicitor, Sept. 6, 1884.

And now on this the 6th day of Sept, 1884, this case coming on for final hearing and all the evidence in the case being produced and after being duly read; It was adjudged by the Commission that the said, Tip R. Bean, is a Cherokee Indian by blood and is entitled to all the rights and privileges as other native Cherokees within limits of the Cherokee Nation. And that he should be and is hereby admitted to the full and complete enjoyment of the same within the limits of the Cherokee Nation, as other native Cherokees.

                     Eli Spears, Pres.
                     John Lee
Attest, C.O. Frye   Andrew Young
      Clerk   Comm.

Sept. 2, 1884
Case #18

      NARCISSA BOINGTON*
         vs   Application for Citizenship
   (Cherokee Nation)

Passed, Sept. 4;   Submitted by both parties, Sept. 25, 1884.

And now on this the 25th day of Sept, 1884, This case coming on for final hearing and all the evidence in the case being considered and; It was adjudged by the Commission on Citizenship that the said Narcissa Boingtin* is a Cherokee Indian by blood and that she should be and is hereby admitted to the full and complete enjoyment of all the rights and privileges as other native Cherokees within the limits of the Cherokee Nation.

Eli Spears, Pres.
Attest, C.O. Frye, Clerk   Andrew Young, Comm.
(*NOTE: Name spelled both ways.)

Sept. 3, 1884
Case #19   By Atty. John T. Drew
LAWRENCE S. ALFORD
vs   Application for Citizenship
Cherokee Nation

The affidavits of Mary J. Alford and Thomas I. Harrison were filed by Applicant and are left opened;   Submitted on part of Claimant, Sept. 26, 1884;   Submitted by Solicitor, Sept. 29, 1884.

And now on this the 29th day of Sept. A.D, 1884, this case coming on for final hearing and all the evidence being produced on both sides and both being duly considered; It was adjudged by the Commission on Citizenship that said Lawrence S. Alford had failed to prove the allegation set forth in the application for citizenship stating that he was a Cherokee Indian by blood. The Commission therefore decided that said Lawrence S. Alford is not a Cherokee Indian and should not be allowed to enjoy the rights of citizenship in the Cherokee Nation. The Commission therefore rejects him.

Eli Spears, Pres.
Attest, C.O. Frye, Clerk   Andrew Young,Comm.

Sept. 3, 1884
Case #20   By Atty. T.E. Beavert for Claimant
WM, SHIRLE, & RICHARD MOTTON*
vs   Application for Citizenship
Cherokee Nation

Submitted by both parties Sept. 26, 1884.

And now on this the 26th day of Sept, 1884, this case coming on for final hearing and after all the evidence in the case being introduced and after being read and duly considered; It was adjudged by the Commission on Citizenship that said Wm Moton*, Shirle Motin*, and Richard Moton, are not Cherokees by blood as set forth in the application. And they are hereby duly and legally rejected, this Sept. 26, 1884.

Eli Spears, Pres.
Attest, C.O. Frye, Clerk   Andrew Young, Comm.
(*NOTE: Name spelled three ways.)

Sept. 3, 1884
Case #21   By Atty. T.E. Beavert
HARRIET ELIZABETH HOWEL, et al
vs   Application for Citizenship
Cherokee Nation

Passed till Jan, 1885.

Sept. 3, 1884
Case #22
MARY REBECCA NEAL, EDGAR NEAL,   Atty.
Beavert
ADIE NEAL/Now Adie Lips Neal, CHARLES NEAL,
and **ANNE NEAL/Now Crane**
vs   Application for Citizenship
(Cherokee Nation)

Petition filed Sept. 3, 1884.   (No other information given.)

Sept. 4, 1884
Case #23   E.C. Boudinot, Atty.
GERALDA KENNER
vs   Application for Citizenship
(Cherokee Nation)

Submitted by Claimant, Sept. 24;   Submitted by both parties, Sept. 29,
1884.
And now on this the 29th day of September, 1884, this case coming on for
final hearing and all the evidence on both sides being produced and after being
duly examined by the Commission on Citizenship; It was adjudged by the
Commission that said Geralda Kenner, is not a Cherokee Indian by blood and
not entitled to the rights of citizenship in the Cherokee Nation. The Commission therefore rejects her, this Sept. 29, 1884.
Eli Spears, Pres.

Cherokee Citizenship Commission Docket Books
Tahlequah, Cherokee Nation (1880-84, 1887-89)
Volume I

Attest, C.O. Frye, Clerk   Andrew Young, Comm.

Sept. 4, 1884
Case #24

    MARGERATE J (nee: Miller), **JAMES T,**   E.C. Boudinot, Jr,
    ISAAC C, JOHN W, JULIA A, ADA S,   Atty.
    CALVIN M, ESTHER J, MARY E, &
    ROBERT H. GEORGE
        vs   Application for Citizenship
    (Cherokee Nation)

Withdrawn by Atty until Jan. term, 1884(sic).

Sept. 4, 1884
Case #25   E.C. Boudinot, Jr, Atty.
    J.J. MOURN
        vs   Application for Citizenship
    (Cherokee Nation)

Withdrawn, Sept. 16, 1884.

Sept. 5, 1884
Case #26

    JESSE, Sr, WILLIAM, JOHN, CHRISTOPHER,
    JESSE, Jr, MARY, ALVAH, &
    JEFFERSON JORDEN
        vs   Application for Citizenship
    (Cherokee Nation)

    Case submitted by Claimants, Sept. 10, 1884;   Submitted by Solicitor,
Sept. 18, 1884.
    And now on this the 19th day of September, 1884, comes this case for fi-
nal hearing and all the evidence in relation thereto having been read and considered by the Commission on Citizenship; It was unanimously decided by said
Commission that the above applicants are not Cherokees by blood or otherwise
and are not therefore entitled to any of the rights and privileges of citizenship
in the Cherokee Nation.
                        Eli Spears

John L. Adair, Clerk   Andrew Young, Comm. on Citizenship

Sept. 5, 1884
Case #27   E.C. Boudinot, Jr, Atty.
**AGGIE (Mother), ALBERT, JOHN, FERREL*,
JACKSON, PLEASANT, MARGRET, GURGANNA,
MINNIE, LAURA, AGGIE, WATTIE, MABLE,
& IDA PHARRIS***
            (vs)   (Application for Citizenship)
(Cherokee Nation)

Children of Albert Parris* and grand-children of Aggie Pharris
Submitted by Claimant and Solicitor, Sept. 6, 1884.
And now on this the 6th day of September, 1884, this case coming on for
final hearing and all the evidence in the case being produced and after being
duly considered by the Commission; It was adjudged by the Commission that
said Aggie Pharris, Albert Pharris, John, Farrel*, Jackson, Pleasant, Margret,
and Gunganna Pharris children of Albert Pharris and grand-children to Aggie
Pharris, were Cherokee Indians by blood, and entitled to all the rights and privileges as other native Cherokees. And are hereby admitted to the full and complete enjoyment of the same as other native Cherokees within the limits of the
Cherokee Nation.
Given from under our hands this the day and date above written.
                                    Eli Spears, President
                                    John Lee, Comm.
Attest, C.O. Frye, Clerk   Andrew Young, Comm.
            (*NOTE: Names spelled both ways.)

Sept. 8, 1884
Case #28

        **HANNAH, MARY JANE, LOUISA, CAROLINA,
        JOHN C, VIRGINIA, GULES, TENNESSEE,
        & BILL Z. FLIPPIN**
            vs   Application for Citizenship
        Cherokee Nation

Submitted by both sides this September 25, 1884.
And now on this the 26th day of Sept, 1884, this case coming on for final
hearing and all the evidence in the case being introduced and after being read

and duly considered by the Commission on Citizenship; It was adjudged by the Commission that said Hannah Flippin and children, viz: Mary Jane, Louisa, Carolina, John C, Virginia, Gules, Tennessee, and Bill Z, are Cherokee Indians by blood and are hereby admitted to the full and complete enjoyment of all rights and privileges as other native born Cherokees. Given from under our hands on this the 26th day of Sept, 1884.

Eli Spears, Pres
Attest, C.O. Frye, Clerk   Andrew Young, Comm.
Transcript furnished, Sept. 26, 1884, C.O. Frye, Clk.

Sept. 9, 1884
Case #29

MRS. ANNA FLOURNOY, ELLEN F,   For herself
LILA, ROLLiN, WALTER, and
CLARA FLOURNOY
                vs   (Application for Citizenship)
Cherokee Nation

And now on this the 10th day of September A.D, 1884, this case coming on for final hearing and all the evidence in the case carefully read and considered by the Commission on Citizenship; It was decided that the above named claimants, Mrs. Anna Flournoy and children, Ellen F. Flournoy (ages 12 yrs), Lila Flournoy (aged 10 yrs), Rollin Flournoy (aged 8 yrs), Walter Flournoy (aged 3 yrs), and Clara Flournoy (aged 1 yr). are Cherokees by blood and that they are entitled to all the rights and privileges of citizenship in the Cherokee Nation, and are hereby admitted to the full and complete enjoyment of the same in every particular as other native born Cherokees.

Eli Spears, Pres.
John Lee
John L. Adair   Andrew Young
Clerk   Comm.

Sept. 9, 1884
Case #30   J.M. Bryan & E.C. Boudinot, Attys.
THOMAS JONES, CATHARINE HARGES,
EMILY JONES, ANDY HAMPDEN,
MARY JANE SELLERS, & JOE WHITE
                vs   (Application for Citizenship)
Cherokee Nation

(No other information given.)

Sept. 9, 1883
Case #31

MILLY JANE, CLINTON DAVIS,
ALEXANDER, JAMES IRA, and
IDA LEE MILLER
vs   (Application for Citizenship)
Cherokee Nation

On this the 22nd day of September, 1884, this case coming on (for) final hearing and all the evidence in the case being read and duly considered; It was adjudged by the Commission that said Milly Jane Miller, Clinton, Alexander, James Ira, and Ida Lee Miller, were not Cherokee Indians and not entitled to the rights of citizenship in the Cherokee Nation, as set forth in the petition. And they are hereby rejected by the Commission on Citizenship. This the 22nd day of Sept, 1884.

Eli Spears, Pres.
Attest, C.O. Frye, Clerk   John Lee, Comm.

Sept. 10, 1884
Case #32   E.C. Boudinot, Jr, Atty.
W.C. (Father), **ALMA T, LELIA B,**

& EDDIE C. SHOEMAKE
vs   (Application for Citizenship)
Cherokee Nation

Ready, Sept. 11;   Submitted by Claimants, Sept. 12;   Passed indefinitely;   Referred to Council, Sept. 22, 1884.

Sept. 10, 1884
Case #33   E.C. Boudinot, Jr, Atty.
J.D, JOHN H, HANNAH E, CYRUS R,
& RICHARD E. SHOEMAKE
vs   (Application for Citizenship)
Cherokee Nation

Submitted by Claimants, Sept. 11; Passed indefinitely; Referred to Council.

Sept. 10, 1884
Case #34   C.H. Taylor, Atty.
MARY ANN, HELLEN*, ROBERT LEE,
MARCUS, GRENUP*, JOHN M, &
NEIL BALEY SIGLETON*
            vs   (Application for Citizenship)
(Cherokee Nation)

Passed till Jan, 1885.
                (***NOTE:** Names spelled as given.)

Sept. 11, 1884
Case #35   John O. Drew, Atty.
WILLIAM O. SAYERS
            vs   (Application for Citizenship)
Cherokee Nation

Submitted Sept. 16, 1884, by both parties.

And now on this the 16th day of September, 1884, comes this case for final hearing and all the evidence in relation thereto having been read and considered by the Commission on Citizenship; It was adjudged by the Commission that the above William O. Sayers, is a Cherokee by blood, he being the nephew of Judge J.A. Scales, of the Supreme Court, and son of Jennie Sayers, nee Scales, grand-daughter of Joseph and Jennie Coody; Polly Coody was the sister of Chief John Ross. His descend being such the claimant is entitled to all the rights and privileges of citizenship in the Cherokee Nation and should be and is hereby admitted to the full enjoyment of the same, in all respects as a native born Cherokee.

                                        Eli Spears, Pres.
                                        John Lee
John L. Adair   Andrew Young
       Clerk   Comm.
Transcript furnished, Sept. 17, 1884.

Sept. 11, 1884
Case #36   E.C. Boudinot, Jr, Atty.

Cherokee Citizenship Commission Docket Books
Tahlequah, Cherokee Nation (1880-84, 1887-89)
Volume I

RACHEL M. HAYES, et. al.
vs   (Application for Citizenship)
Cherokee Nation

Passed till Jan, 1885, by Claimant.

Sept. 15, 1884
Case #37   R.L. Owen, Atty.
GEORGE, KATE, ROBT, &
EMILY BLACKENEY*
vs   (Application for Citizenship)
Cherokee Nation

Submitted by both parties, Sept. 15, 1884.

And now on this the 15th day of September, 1884, comes this case for final hearing, and all the evidence in the case having been carefully read and considered by the Commission on Citizenship; It was decided that the above mentioned Claimants to Cherokee citizenship, and as mentioned whom the Roll of Shawnees admitted as citizens of the Cherokee Nation in accordance with the agreement entered into between the Cherokee Nation and the Shawnee Tribe of Indians, on the 7th day of June, 1859, as:

         Shawnee No. 133 - Blackey*, George
         Shawnee No. 134 - Blackey, Kate
         Shawnee No. 135 - Blackey, Robert
         Shawnee No. 136 - Blackey, Emily

are entitled to citizenship in the Cherokee Nation. And are hereby readmitted to the enjoyment of the rights and privileges of the same in all respects as other Shawnee citizens.

                     Eli Spears, Pres.
                     John Lee
John L. Adair   Andrew Young
      Clerk   Comm.
         (***NOTE:** Name spelled both ways.)

Sept. 15, 1884
Case #38   C.H. Taylor, Atty.
       MATTIE & CELIA ASHBY

vs   (Application for Citizenship)
Cherokee Nation

Passed to Jan. term, 1885.

Sept. 15, 1884
Case #39   E.C. Boudinot, Jr, Atty.
LUVINA LONG nee Deshon
& Children
vs   (Application for Citizenship)
Cherokee Nation

Passed till after Mon, Sept. 25, 1884.

Sept. 15, 1884
Case #40
JERRY L. HENRY
vs   (Application for Citizenship)
Cherokee Nation

Submitted by both parties, Sept. 15, 1884.

And now on this the 17th day of September A.D, 1884, comes this case for final hearing and all the evidence in relation thereto having been read and considered by the Commission on Citizenship; It was decided by said Commission that the above Claimant, Jerry L. Henry, is a Cherokee by blood, he being full brother to Miss Annie Benton Henry, who was admitted to Cherokee citizenship by a former Commission on Citizenship, Sept. term, 1883, (See pg. 76, Case #183, Annie Burton(sic) Henry). Being so related, he is entitled to all the rights and privileges of citizenship in the Cherokee Nation, and should be and is hereby admitted to the full enjoyment of the same in all respects as other native born Cherokees.

Eli Spears, Pres.
John Lee
John L. Adair   Andrew Young
Clerk   Comm.

Sept. 16, 1884
Case #41

134

Cherokee Citizenship Commission Docket Books
Tahlequah, Cherokee Nation (1880-84, 1887-89)
Volume I

PETER GRAYBEARD

vs   (Application for Citizenship)

Cherokee Nation

And now on this the 16th day of September, 1884, comes this case for final hearing, and all the evidence in relation thereto, having been read and considered; It was unanimously decided that the above Peter Graybeard is a Cherokee by blood, he being a so-called "North Carolina Cherokee" and a late emigrant from that state, and is entitled to all the rights and privileges of citizenship in the Cherokee Nation, and should be and is hereby admitted to a full and complete enjoyment of the same in all respects, as other native born Cherokees.

Eli Spears, Pres.
John Lee

John L. Adair   Andrew Young

Clerk   Comm.

Sept. 17, 1884

Case #42

MILO HOYT &

His children

vs   (Application for Citizenship)

Cherokee Nation

Submitted by both parties, Sept. 17, 1884.

And now on this the 17th day of September, 1884, comes this case for final hearing and all the evidence in relation thereto having been read and considered by the Commission on Citizenship; It is unanimously decided by them that the above applicant, Milo Hoyt, and his children, Herman L. Hoyt (aged 19 yrs), Emma Hoyt (aged 13 yrs), Milo A. Hoyt, Jr, (aged 16 yrs), and Czarrena Hoyt (aged 11 yrs), are children by blood. The said applicant, Milo Hoyt, being a full brother of Mrs. Nelson Chamberlin, Mrs. Ballentine, Mrs. James Ward and Mrs. Lucy Hays, and son of Lydia, daughter of Old Assistant Chief George Lowry; and they should be and are hereby admitted to the full enjoyment of all the rights and privileges of Cherokee citizenship in the Cherokee Nation as other native born Cherokees.

Eli Spears, Pres
John Lee

John L. Adair   Andrew Young

135

Clerk   Comm.
Transcript furnished, Sept. 18, 1884.

Sept. 19, 1884
Case #43

BENJ. FRANKLIN WILSON
vs   (Application for Citizenship)
Cherokee Nation

Submitted by both parties, Sept. 19, 1884.

And now on this the 19th day of Sept, 1884, comes this case for final hearing, and all the evidence in relation thereto having been read and considered by the Commission on Citizenship; It was unanimously decided by said Commission that the above Benj. Franklin Wilson, is a Cherokee by blood, he being a full brother of Rush Wilson and Dora Wilson, admitted to citizen rights in the Cherokee Nation by a former Commission on Citizenship, Sept term, 1883, (See pg #77, Case #185); and a full cousin of John Wilson, admitted by the present Comm. (See pg #87, Case #1), and being such he is entitled to all the rights and privileges of citizenship in the Cherokee Nation, and should be and he is hereby admitted to the full enjoyment of the same in all respects as other native born Cherokees.

                                        Eli Spears, Pres.
John L. Adair, Clerk   Andrew Young, Comm.
Transcript furnished, Sept. 20, 1884

Sept. 19, 1884
Case #44

ZED CROMWELL
vs   (Application for Citizenship)
Cherokee Nation

Submitted by both parties, Sept. 19, 1884.

And now on this the 19th day of Sept, 1884, comes this case for final hearing and all the evidence in relation thereto having been read and considered by the Commission on Citizenship; It was unanimously decided by said Comm. that the above Zed Cromwell is a Cherokee by blood, he being a son of Margarett Cromwell, nee Whiteallen, a sister to Mrs. Polly Ingram, a N.C. Cherokee, who accepted the invitation of removal to this nation enacted by the National Council, and approved Dec. 3, 1880. Being such, he is entitled and should be and is hereby admitted to all the rights and privileges of citizenship in the Cherokee Nation in all respects as a native born Cherokee.

	Eli Spears, Pres.
John L. Adair	Andrew Young
Clerk	Comm.

Sept. 19, 1884
Case #45   E.C. Boudinott, Atty.
NANCY McGHEE

vs   (Application for Citizenship)
Cherokee Nation

Passed till Jan, 1885.

Sept. 19, 1884
Case #46   L.B. Bell, Atty
**MARY A, MARION C, JOHN R, JAMES W,
HENRY W, MARY J, & LERI T. CROCKET**
vs   (Application for Citizenship)
(Cherokee Nation)

Passed till January, 1885.

Sept. 22, 1884
Case #47

**G,W, G.C, DAVID, JAMES, JOSEPHINE,
JOHN, EDA, WILLIAM, & MAMIE FLOYD**
vs   Application for Citizenship
Cherokee Nation

Passed till Jan, 1885.

Sept. 26, 1884
Case #48   T.E. Beavert,Atty.
**MARTHA, LEE, RANDOLPH,
GINA, & LONNIE SETTLES**
vs   Application for Citizenship

Cherokee Citizenship Commission Docket Books
Tahlequah, Cherokee Nation (1880-84, 1887-89)
Volume I

(Cherokee Nation)

Submitted by Claimants and Solicitor, Sept. 26, 1884.

And now on this the 26th day of September, 1884, this case coming on for final hearing and all the evidence in the case being read and duly considered; It was adjudged by the Commission on Citizenship that said Martha Settles, Lee Settles, Randolph Settles, Gina Settles, and Lonnie Settles are Cherokee Indians by blood. And are entitled to all the rights and privileges as other Cherokees. And that they are hereby admitted to the full and complete enjoyment of the same within the limits of the Cherokee Nation.

Given from under my hand this the 26th day of Sept, 1884.

Eli Spears, Pres.

Attest, C.O.Frye, Clerk

Andrew Young, Comm.

Sept. 29, 1884
Case #49

JOHN, EMILY W, CUSTUS, &
LEEMAR HARNAGE   (Application for Citizenship)

(**NOTE:** The entire entry was marked with an "X".)

APPLICANTS FOR CHEROKEE CITIZENSHIP
vs
Cherokee Nation

Jan. 18, 1887
Docket #1   **KEYS**   A.E. Ivey, Atty.
Roll 1851

Wah-ha-lau

#	NAMES	AGE	SEX
1	W.R.W.C	38	m
~~2~~	~~Mary E. (white)~~	~~30~~	f
3	R.W.M.	4	m
4	M.T.W.	2	m
5	G.A.L.	1	m

Ancestor: Richard Keys

Now on this the 1ˢᵗ day of April, 1887, comes the above case for final hearing. (Applicant having waved(sic) the ninety days notice) and having made application pursuant to the provisions of an act of the National Council of the Cherokee Nation approved, December 8, 1886, and all the evidence being duly considered and found to be sufficient and satisfactory to the commission; It is adjudged and determined by the Commission that W.R.W.C. Keys, R.W.M. Keys, M.T.W. Keys, and G.A.L. Keys, are

Cherokees by blood and are hereby re-admitted to all the rights, privileges and immunities of Cherokee citizens by blood.

And a certificate of said decision of the Commission of re-admission was made and furnished to said parties accordingly.

<table>
<tr><td></td><td>J.T. Adair, Chairman</td></tr>
<tr><td></td><td>John E. Gunter</td></tr>
<tr><td>Henry Eiffert</td><td>D.W. Lipe</td></tr>
<tr><td>Asst. Clerk</td><td>Comm.</td></tr>
</table>

Jan. 18, 1887

Docket #2　　　　　　　**BOOTH**　　　　A.E. Ivey, Atty.

Roll 1851

Chil-　　　　　　　　　　　　　　　　　　　　　　　ders

Sta-

An-

#	NAMES	AGE	SEX
1	Mrs. R.A. Booth	20	f

tion

cestor: Richard Keys

Now on this the 1ˢᵗ day of April, 1887, comes the above case for final hearing (applicant having waved(sic) the ninety days notice) and having made application pursuant to the provisions of an act of the National Council of the Cherokee Nation approved Dec. 8, 1886, and all the evidence being duly considered and found to be sufficient and satisfactory to the Commission; It is adjudged and determined by the Commission that R.A. Booth is Cherokee by blood, and hereby re-admitted to all the rights and privileges and immunities of the(sic) Cherokee by blood.

And a certificate of said decision of the Commission of re-admission was made and furnished to said parties accordingly.

<table>
<tr><td></td><td>J.T. Adair, Chairman</td></tr>
<tr><td></td><td>John E. Gunter</td></tr>
<tr><td>Henry Eiffert</td><td>D.W. Lipe</td></tr>
<tr><td>Asst. Clerk</td><td>Comm.</td></tr>
</table>

Cherokee Citizenship Commission Docket Books
Tahlequah, Cherokee Nation (1880-84, 1887-89)
Volume I

Jan. 21, 1887
Docket #3   **CLELAND**   Wm. Jackson, Atty.
Roll 1835   Marietta, GA

#	NAMES	AGE	SEX
1	George W.	55	m
2	George W, Jr.	25	m
3	Emmet Shaw	22	m
4	Sarah Charlton	19	f
5	James Bancroft	13	m

Ancestor: Geo. M. Waters

Now on this the 13th day of April, 1887, comes the above case for final hearing, the applicant having made application pursuant to the provision of an act of the National Council of the Cherokee Nation, approved Dec. 8, 1886, and all the evidence being duly considered and found to be sufficient and satisfactory to the Commission; It is adjudged and determined by the Commission that George W. Cleland, George W. Cleland, Jr, Emmet Shaw Cleland, Sarah Charlton Cleland, and James Bancroft Cleland, are Cherokees by blood, and are hereby re-admitted to all the rights, privileges, and immunities of a Cherokee citizen by blood.

And a certificate of such decision of the Commission and of re-admission was made and furnished to said parties accordingly.

                                              J.T. Adair, Chairman
Henry Eiffert   D.W. Lipe
      Asst. Clerk   Comm.

Jan. 23, 1887
Docket #4   **MULKEY**   In person
Roll 1835

Park Hill, C.N.

#	NAMES	AGE	SEX
1	William Ross	51	m
2	Eliza Maria	17	f
3	Richard Jonathan	9	m
4	John Ross	6	m

Ancestor: Mariah Ross

Cherokee Citizenship Commission Docket Books
Tahlequah, Cherokee Nation (1880-84, 1887-89)
Volume I

Now this the 30th day of March, 1887, comes the above case for final hearing. (The applicant having waived the ninety days notice) and having made application pursuant to the provision of an act of the National Council of the Cherokee Nation approved Dec. 9, 1886, and all the evidence being duly considered and found to be sufficient and satisfactory to the Commission; It is adjudged and determined by the Commission that William Ross Mulkey, Eliza Maria Mulkey, Richard Jonathan Mulkey, and John Ross Mulkey, are Cherokee by blood, and are hereby re-admitted to all the rights, privileges, and immunities of a Cherokee citizen by blood.

And a certificate of said decision of the Commission and of re-admission was made and furnished to the said parties accordingly.

J.T. Adair, Chairman

Henry Eiffert, Asst. Clerk   D.W. Lipe, Comm.

Jan. 23, 1887
Docket #5   **MULKEY**   William Ross Mulkey, Atty.
Roll 1835

Ballinger, Runnels Co, TX

#	NAMES	AGE	SEX
1	James Daniel Mulkey, Jr.	25	m
2	James E. Mulkey	5m	m

Ancestor: Mariah Ross

Now on this the 30th day of March, 1887, comes the above case for a final hearing. (The applicant having waived the ninety days notice) and having made application pursuant to the provisions of an act of the National Council of the Cherokee Nation approved Dec. 8, 1886, and all the evidence being duly considered and found sufficient and satisfactory to the Commission; It is adjudged and determined by the Commission that James Daniel Mulkey, Jr. and James Elisha Mulkey are Cherokees by blood and are hereby re-admitted to all the rights, privileges and immunities of a Cherokee citizen by blood.

And a certificate of said decisions of the Commission and of re-admission was made and furnished to the said parties accordingly.

J.T. Adair, Chairman Comm.

Henry Eiffert, Asst. Clerk   D.W. Lipe, Comm.

Jan. 23, 1887
Docket #6   **WILLIS**   William Ross Mulkey, Atty.
Roll 1835

Ballinger P.O, Runnels Co, TX

#	NAMES	AGE	SEX
1	Mary Brooks	23	f
2	Fredrick R.	1	m

Ancestor: Mariah Ross

Now on this the 30th day of March, 1887, comes the above case for a final hearing. (The applicant having waived the ninety days notice) and having made application pursuant to the provisions of an act of the National Council of the Cherokee Nation approved Dec. 8, 1886, and all the evidence being duly considered and found to be sufficient and satisfactory to the Commission; It is adjudged and determined by the Commission that Mary Brooks Willis and Fredrick R. Willis are Cherokees by blood and are hereby re-admitted to all the rights, privileges, and immunities of a Cherokee citizen by blood.

And a certificate of said decision of the Commission and of re-admission was made and furnished to the said parties accordingly.

J.T. Adair, Chairman Comm.

Henry Eiffert, Asst. Clerk   D.W. Lipe, Comm.

Jan. 23, 1887
Docket #7   **AMIS**   William Ross Mulkey, Atty.
Roll 1835

Blevins P.O, Bell Co, TX

#	NAMES	AGE	SEX
1	Amanda Avis	20	f
2	William A.	1	m

Ancestor: Mariah Ross

Now on this the 30th day of March, 1887, comes the above case for a final hearing. (Applicant having waived the ninety days notice) and having made application pursuant to the provisions of an act of the National Council of the Cherokee Nation approved Dec. 8, 1886, and all the evidence being duly considered and found to be sufficient and satisfactory to the Commission; It is adjudged and determined by the Commission that Amanda Avis Amis and William A. Amis are Cherokees by blood and are hereby re-admitted to all the rights, privileges, and immunities of a Cherokee by blood.

And a certificate of said decision of the Commission and of re-admission was made and furnished to the said parties accordingly.

J.T. Adair, Chairman Comm.

Henry Eiffert, Asst. Clerk   D.W. Lipe, Comm.

Jan. 24, 1887
Docket #8   **ENGLISH**   C.H. Taylor, Atty.
Roll (Blank)

#	NAMES	AGE	SEX
1	Mary	25	f
2	John	8	m
3	Izade	6	f
4	Stella	2	f

Blue Jacket P.O, C.N.

Ancestor: Lewis Harvey

Now on this date, the 4th day of October, 1888, comes the above case up for final hearing, and all the evidence being duly considered, also the census and pay rolls of Cherokees mentioned in the 7th Sec. of the Act of Dec. 8, 1886, in relation to citizenship. We, the Commission on Citizenship, fail to find the name of Lewis Harvey, from whom the applicant in this case have tried to prove Cherokee descent; neither do we find the names of the applicants themselves, therefore; Mary English, John English, Izade English, and Stella English, cannot under the law be admitted to rights in the Cherokee Nation, but instead, are declared to be intruders upon the public domain of the Cherokee Nation. (See Act of Dec. 8, 1886).

J.T. Adair, Chairman Commission
H.C. Barnes, Commissioner

Jan. 25, 1887
Docket #9   **NEESE**   C.H. Taylor, Atty.
Roll 1848

#	NAMES	AGE	SEX
1	James	58	m

Prairie Grove, AR
Ancestor: (None given.)

Now on this the 12th day of February, 1889, comes the above case, to wit: James Neese, for a final hearing, he having made application pursuant to the provision of an Act of the National Council approved Dec. 8, 1886. An examination of the Rolls of 1835 and other rolls named in the 7th Section of the before mentioned act, fails to show the names of the applicant while the testimony which is composed wholly of affidavits purposing to be taken before Notaries Public in the state of Illinois, does not establish that James Neese was ever a resident of the Cherokee Country; that he had any Cherokee blood in his veins or that he was an Indian or the descendant of an Indian.

It is therefore adjudged and decided by the Commission that James Neese is not a Cherokee and is not entitled to citizenship in the Cherokee Nation.

Will P. Ross
John E. Gunter, Chairman
R. Bunch

Attest, D.S. Williams
Asst. Clerk

Jan. 25, 1887
Docket #10   **WILSON**   C.H. Taylor, Atty.
Roll 1848

Osage Mills, AR

#	NAMES	AGE	SEX
1	Elizabeth (dec.)	38	f
2	Luthena	19	f
3	John B.	17	m
4	Martha	16	f
5	William M.	14	m
6	James E.	12	m
7	Ida Jane	9	f
8	Laura Bell	7	f

Ancestor: Martin B. Many

Now on this the 27th day of Oct, 1887, comes the above case for a final hearing and submitted by agreement between the attorney for Plaintiff and the attorney on part of the Nation on the evidence taken and submitted in the case of Elizabeth Wilson, Luthena Wilson, John B. Wilson, Martha Wilson, William M. Wilson, James E. Wilson, Ida Jane Wilson and Laura Bell Wilson. The Commission on Citizenship after a careful and impartial investigation of the testimony and being also examined the Census Rolls of 1848, failed to find the name of the ancestor Martin B. Many. And the evidence in behalf of applicants not being sufficient, the Commission therefore decides that the above named parties are not Cherokees by blood and not entitled to any of the rights or privileges of Cherokee citizens.

Cherokee Citizenship Commission Docket Books
Tahlequah, Cherokee Nation (1880-84, 1887-89)
Volume I

J.T. Adair, Chairman Comm.
D.W. Lipe, Comm.
John E. Gunter

Jan. 25, 1887
Docket #11   **NEESE**   C.H. Taylor, Atty.
Roll 1835

Prairie Grove, AR

#	NAMES	AGE	SEX
1	Stephen G.	23	m
2	Maggie	4	f
3	Albert	3	m

Ancestor: James Neese

Now on this the 12th day of February, 1889, comes the above case, to wit: Stephen G. Neese, et. al, for a final hearing, they having made application pursuant to the provisions of an Act of the National Council approved Dec. 8, 1886. An examination of the Rolls of 1835 and other rolls named in the 7th Section of the before mentioned Act, fails to show the name of James Neese, Sr, from whom applicant claims. While the testimony which is composed wholly of affidavits purporting to be taken before Notaries Public in the state of Illinois, does not establish the fact that James Neese, Sr, was ever a resident of the Cherokee Country, that he had any Cherokee blood in his veins or that he was an Indian or the descendant of an Indian.

It is therefore adjudged and declared by the Commission that Stephen G. Neese is not a Cherokee and is not entitled to citizenship in the Cherokee Nation.

Will P. Ross, Chairman
John E. Gunter, Comm
Attest, D.S. Williams, Asst. Clerk   R. Bunch

Jan. 25, 1887
Docket #12   **NEESE**   C.H. Taylor, Atty.
Roll 1835

Prairie Grove, AR

#	NAMES	AGE	SEX
1	Oscar L.	26	m
2	Wattie	8	m

3	Muia	6	m
4	Elmer	4	m
5	Gerda Jane	1	f

Ancestor: James Neese

Now on this the 12th day of February, 1889, comes the above case, to wit: Oscar L. Neese, et al, for a final hearing, he having made application pursuant to the provisions of an Act of the National Council approved Dec. 8, 1886. On examination of the Rolls of 1835 and other rolls named in the 9th Section of the before mentioned Act fails to show the name of James Neese from whom applicant claims. While the testimony which is composed wholly of affidavits purporting to be taken before Notaries Public in the state of Illinois, does not establish the fact that James Neese, Sr, was ever a resident of the Cherokee Country, that he had any Cherokee blood in his veins, or that he was an Indian or the descendant of an Indian.

It is therefore adjudged and declared by the Commission that Oscar L. Neese, is not a Cherokee and is not entitled to citizenship in the Cherokee Nation.

Will P. Ross. Chairman
John E. Gunter, Comm.
R. Bunch

Attest, D.S. Williams
Asst. Clerk

Jan. 26, 1887
Docket #13   **PEEBLES**   In person
Siler Roll 1851

Nashville, TN

#	NAMES	AGE	SEX
1	Sarah* E.	52	f
2	James L.	25	m
3	Edginna*	22	f

(Ancestor): Enrolled as Mary E. Nicholson

Now on this the 1st day of April, 1887, comes for final hearing. (Applicant having waived the ninety days notice) and having made application pursuant to the provisions of an Act of the National Council of the Cherokee Nation approved Dec. 8, 1886, and all the evidence being duly considered and found to be sufficient and satisfactory to the Commission; It is adjudged and determined by the Commission that Mary* E. Peebles, James L. Peebles, and Ed-

Cherokee Citizenship Commission Docket Books
Tahlequah, Cherokee Nation (1880-84, 1887-89)
Volume I

garrena* Peebles, are Cherokees by blood and are hereby re-admitted to all the rights, privileges, and immunities of Cherokee citizens by blood. And a certificate of said decision of the Commission was made and furnished to the said parties accordingly.

J.T. Adair, Chairman Comm.
John E. Gunter
D.W. Lipe
Comm.

Henry Eiffert
Asst. Clerk

(***NOTE:** Names given both ways.)

Jan. 26, 1887
Docket #14   **JACKSON**   Mary E. Peebles, Atty.
Siler Roll 1851

Nashville, TN

#	NAMES	AGE	SEX
1	Sarah L.	36	f
2	Chas. C.	2	m

Ancestor: Mary E. Nicholson

Now on this the 1st day of April, 1887, comes for final hearing (applicant having waived the ninety days notice) and having made application pursuant to the provisions of an Act of the National Council of the Cherokee Nation approved Dec. 8, 1886, and all the evidence being duly considered and found to be sufficient and satisfactory to the Commission; It is adjudged and determined by the Commission that Sarah L. Jackson and Charles C. Jackson, are Cherokees by blood, and are hereby re-admitted to all the rights, privileges, and immunities of Cherokee citizens by blood.

And a certificate of said decision of the Commission was made and furnished the said parties.

J.T. Adair, Chairman
John E. Gunter, Comm.
D.W. Lipe, Comm.

Henry Eiffert, Asst. Clerk

Jan. 26, 1887
Docket #15   **WEST**   Mary E. Peebles, Atty.
Siler Roll 1851

Nashville, TN

#	NAMES	AGE	SEX
1	Charlott B.	28	f

Cherokee Citizenship Commission Docket Books
Tahlequah, Cherokee Nation (1880-84, 1887-89)
Volume I

Ancestor: Mary E. Nicholson

Now on this the 1st day of April, 1887, comes the above case for final hearing (applicant having waived the ninety day notice) and having made application pursuant to the provisions of an Act of the National Council of the Cherokee Nation approved Dec. 8, 1886. And all the evidence being duly considered and found to be sufficient and satisfactory to the Commission; It is adjudged and determined by the Commission that Charlott B. West is a Cherokee by blood, and is hereby re-admitted to all the rights and privileges of Cherokee citizens by blood.

And a certificate of said decision of the Commission and of re-admission was made and furnished to said parties accordingly.   J.T. Adair, Chairman Comm.

John E. Gunter, Comm.

Henry Eiffert, Asst. Clerk   D.W. Lipe, Comm.

Jan. 26, 1887
Docket #16   **SPAIN**   Mary E. Peebles, Atty.
Siler Roll 1851

Nashville, TN

#	NAMES	AGE	SEX
1	Bell* K. Spain	32	f
2	George Spain	2	m

Ancestor: Mary E. Nicholson

Now on this the 1st day of April, 1887, comes the above case for final hearing. (Applicant having waived the ninety day notice) and having made application pursuant to the provisions of an Act of the National Council of the Cherokee Nation approved Dec. 8, 1886, and all the evidence being duly considered and found to be sufficient and satisfactory to the Commission; It is adjudged and determined by the Commission that Belle* K. Spain and George Spain are Cherokees by blood and are hereby re-admitted to all the rights, privileges, and immunities of a Cherokee citizen by blood.

And a certificate of said decision of the Commission and of re-admission was made and furnished the parties accordingly.

J.T. Adair, Chairman Comm.

John E. Gunter, Comm.

Henry Eiffert, Asst. Clerk   D.W. Lipe, Comm

(***NOTE:** Name spelled both ways.)

148

Jan. 26, 1887
Docket #17   **MOUDY**   C.H. Taylor, Atty.
Roll 1835

Galena, KS

#	NAMES	AGE	SEX
1	Mahala	40	f
2	Annie M.	15	f
3	John E.	15	m
4	Sallie D.	3	f
5	Hollie E.	3	f

Ancestor: Jack Downing

This case was submitted by Attorneys, April 23, 1889. The applicant alleges that she is a Cherokee by blood and a lineal descendant of Old Jack
Downing, who died in Cherokee County, North Carolina, since the war and
whose name would be found on the Census Rolls of Cherokee taken in 1835.
As no evidence has been presented in support of the application, the Commission on Citizenship adjudges that said applicant, Mahala Moudy, and her children, Annie M. Moudy, John E. Moudy, Sallie D. Moudy, and Hollie E.
Moudy, are not entitled to admission to citizenship in the Cherokee Nation.

                                        Will P. Ross, Chairman
                                        R. Bunch
Attest, D.S. Williams   John E. Gunter
        Clerk   Comm.

(**NOTE:** Cancelled and submitted, April 22, 1889;   Rejected, April 23,
              1889)

Jan. 26, 1887
Docket #18   **POWELL**   C.H. Taylor, Atty.
Rolls 1851 & 52

Carys Ferry, C.N.

#	NAMES	AGE	SEX
1	Arthur	20	m

Ancestor: Francis Powell

Now on this the 23rd day of April, 1889, the Commission on Citizenship
finding that Arthur Powell, the applicant, is a lineal descendant of Francis

Cherokee Citizenship Commission Docket Books
Tahlequah, Cherokee Nation (1880-84, 1887-89)
Volume I

Powell, who was a Cherokee by blood and whose name is found on the census rolls of Cherokees taken and made in 1841(sic) and 1842(sic), is entitled to re-admission to citizenship in the Cherokee Nation.

	Will P. Ross. Chairman
D.S. Williams	John E. Gunter
Clerk	Comm.

(**NOTE:** Cancelled and submitted April 22, 1889.)

Jan. 26, 1887
Docket #19   **BLEDSAW**   C.H. Taylor, Atty.
Roll 1835

Coffeyville, KS

#	NAMES	AGE	SEX
1	Emily	42	f
2	Angie	23	f
3	Samuel	19	m
4	Josie	17	f
5	Susan	15	f
6	Mary	13	f
7	Horace	11	m
8	Christian	9	f
9	Bertia	5	f
10	Cora	10m	f

Ancestor: Soloman Wilkerson

May 2, 1889 - The above case was submitted to the Commission in September, 1888, but was not then decided so far as the records show. It therefore comes up in the course of calling the docket of applications filed for the action of this Commission. The only evidence which accompanies the application filed the 26th day of January, 1887, is the exparte affidavit of our Mary Riley, who makes her mark, taken before P.N. Payton, Notary Public, Lyon County, Kansas, on the 10th day of November, 1884. This affidavit does not establish the identity of the applicant as the daughter of Soloman Bledlaw(sic) or Soloman Wilkerson, nor that such alleged ancestor was of Cherokee descent; although the descent of such person from Aaron Wilkerson or as the half brother of George W. Wilkerson, who is now living, was susceptible of proof.

Cherokee Citizenship Commission Docket Books
Tahlequah, Cherokee Nation (1880-84, 1887-89)
Volume I

The Commission therefore decides that the applicants, Emily Bledsaw, Angie Bledsaw, Samuel Bledsaw, Josie Bledsaw, Susan Bledsaw, Mary Bledsaw, Horace Bledsaw, Christian Bledsaw, Bertie

Bledsaw, and Cora Bledsaw are not of Cherokee blood and therefore are not entitled to citizenship as Cherokees in the Cherokee Nation.

Will P. Ross, Chairman

D.S. Williams, Clk.   John E. Gunter, Comm.

(**NOTE:** Rejected May 2, 1889)

Jan. 27, 1887
Docket #20   **BRUNER**   C.H. Taylor, Atty.
Roll 1848 to 52

Wah-hil-law

#	NAMES	AGE	SEX
1	Polly	62	f
2	L.A.	29	f
3	John	27	m
4	J.N.	24	m
5	George	22	m
6	T.S.	20	m

Ancestor: Polly Keys

The above case is the same as that of Mary Bruner found on page 16, Book B, underlined>admitted</underline>, August 10, 1887, by the former court. This case was filed twice, but the family all show the same names and ages.
This 23rd day of April, 1889.

D.S. Williams
Clerk Comm. on Citizenship

Jan. 29, 1887
Docket #21   **TAYLOR**   C.H. Taylor
Roll 1851 & 52

Chelsea, I.T.

#	NAMES	AGE	SEX
1	Edward	21	m

Ancestor: David Taylor

Cherokee Citizenship Commission Docket Books
Tahlequah, Cherokee Nation (1880-84, 1887-89)
Volume I

On this the 19th day of April, 1887, comes the above named applicant for a final hearing and the applicant having made application in compliance with the provisions of an act of the National Council of the Cherokee Nation approved Dec. 8, 1886, and all the evidence being duly considered and found to be sufficient and satisfactory to the Commission that; It is adjudged and determined by the Commission that Edward E. Taylor, is a Cherokee by blood and he is hereby re-admitted to all the rights, privileges, and immunities of Cherokee citizenship by blood.

And a certificate of said decision of the Commission and of re-admission was made and furnished the parties accordingly.

J.T. Adair, Chairman

Henry Eiffert

Asst. Clerk

D.W. Lipe

Comm.

Jan. 29, 1887
Docket #22   **TAYLOR**   C.H. Taylor, Atty.
Rolls 1851 & 52

Tahlequah, C.N.

#	NAMES	AGE	SEX
1	James E.	31	m
2	Genora	3	f
3	Dora	21	f
4	Samuel	1 mo	m

Ancestor: Thomas J. Taylor

On this the 13th day of April, 1887, comes the above named case for final hearing, and the Applicant having made application in compliance with the provisions of an Act of the National Council of the Cherokee Nation, approved Dec. 8, 1886, and all the evidence being duly considered and found to be sufficient and satisfactory to the Commission; It is adjudged and determined by the Commission, that James E. Taylor, Genora Taylor, Dora Taylor, and Samuel Taylor, are Cherokees by blood, and are hereby re-admitted to all the rights, privileges, and immunities of Cherokee citizens by blood.

And a certificate of said decision of the Commission and of re-admission was made and furnished the parties accordingly.

J.T. Adair, Chairman of Commission

John E. Gunter

Henry Eiffert

D.W. Lipe

Asst. Clerk Commission

Commissioners

152

Cherokee Citizenship Commission Docket Books
Tahlequah, Cherokee Nation (1880-84, 1887-89)
Volume I

Jan. 29, 1887
Docket #23   **GARLIN**   C.H. Taylor, Atty.
Rolls 1851 & 52

Careys Ferry, C.N.

#	NAMES	AGE	SEX
1	Sallie	58	f

Ancestor: Nicy Welch
The above case decided by the former court, decision rendered April 18, 1887. Claimed by the book of admittance but no decision can be found. The applicant was admitted.

D.S. Williams
Clerk Comm.

Jan. 29, 1887
Docket #24   **PARKS**   C.H. Taylor
Roll 1835

Vinora, Ind. Terr.

#	NAMES	AGE	SEX
1	Samuel A.	44	m
2	Alice D.	18	f
3	Nannie O.	16	f
4	Carrie L.	14	f
5	Charles W.	12	m
6	William A.	10	m
7	J. Rex*	5	m
8	G. Ray+	3	m
9	Ora M.	3 mo	f

Ancestor: Samuel Parks, Sr.
Cherokee Nation, I.T.

Tahlequah, May 29, 1889 - The application in the above case was filed on the 29th day of Jan, 1889, and was submitted May 23, 1889, for a final hearing without evidence.

The Commission therefore decides that Samuel A. Parks, whose age is 44 and the following named children: Alice D, Nannie O, Carrie L, Charles W, William A, J. Ray+, and Ora M. Parks, are not of Cherokee blood and are not entitled to citizenship in the Cherokee Nation.
Attest, George O. Bunch(? Difficult to read)
Clerk Comm.

Cherokee Citizenship Commission Docket Books
Tahlequah, Cherokee Nation (1880-84, 1887-89)
Volume I

(***NOTE:** Name omitted from claim.) (**+NOTE:** Name given both ways.)

Feb. 1, 1887
Docket #25   **WALL**   C.H. Taylor, Atty.
Roll 1835

Oaks, I.T.

#	NAMES	AGE	SEX
1	E.A.	38	m
2	Charlie*	15	m

Ancestor: Drew Wall

September 29, 1888

In the matter of the claim of E.A. Wall and family and D.S. Wall and family for Cherokee citizenship in the Cherokee Nation, alleging in their applications that they are the descendants of Drew Wall, whom it is alleges is of Cherokee blood. There is no evidence in these cases at all, and the rolls of Cherokees mentioned in the 7th Sec. of Act of Dec. 8, 1886, in relation to citizenship, fail to contain the name of Drew Wall, therefore; E.A. Wall and his son Charley* Wall, together with D.S. Wall and <u>his</u> four children, viz: Willie, Henry, Mollie and Frank Wall, are not Cherokees by blood and are not entitled to the privileges of citizenship in the Cherokee Nation through virtue of their blood and are intruders upon the public domain of the Cherokee Nation.

J.T. Adair, Chairman
H.C. Burns, Comm.

(***NOTE:** Name spelled both ways.)

Feb. 1, 1887
Docket #26   **CRISMORE***   C.H. Taylor, Atty.
Roll 1835

South West City, MO

#	NAMES	AGE	SEX
1	John	50	m
2	Matilda	30	f
3	Mary Ann	27	f
4	Juda	24	f
5	Nancy	20	f
6	Joseph B.	18	m
7	Thomas J.	16	m
8	Isaac L.	14	m

9	William	10	m
10	Gil	8	m
11	Jennetta	4	f

Ancestor: Wah-lie Crismon*

Sept. 26, 1888

Now on this the 26th day of Sept, 1888, comes the above case up for final hearing and determination. The applicants alleging a Cherokee descent from one Wahlie Crismon.

It rendering an opinion in the case, It is unclear to recount the testimony of applicants, for the names of Wahlie Crismon, or the names even of themselves, do not appear on any of the rolls of Cherokees laid down in the 7th Sec. of Act of Dec. 8, 1886, in relation to citizenship. Therefore, cannot be admitted to citizenship in the Cherokee Nation by this Commission. It is adjudged and determined by the Commission on Citizenship, that John Crismon and his 10 children, viz: Matilda, Mary A, Julia, Nancy, Joseph B, Thomas J, Isaac L, William, Gilbert and Jennetta Crismon, are not Cherokees by blood and are not entitled to any of the rights and privileges of such on account of their blood, and are intruders upon the public domain of the Cherokee Nation.

J.T. Adair, Chairman Comm.

H.C. Barnes, Comm.

(*NOTE: Name spelled both ways.)

Feb. 1, 1887
Docket #27   **WOODSIDE**   C.H. Taylor, Atty.
Roll 1835

Chetopa, KS

#	NAMES	AGE	SEX
1	Thomas	38	m
2	William	7	m
3	Thomas A.	5	m
4	George R.	1	m
5	Andrew J.	3	m

Ancestor: Malinda Watts

This case embraces the application of Thomas Woodside,* et.al, Dillard Woodsides,* Margaret Shirly, Charles M. Shirly, and Nancy* N. Day, all claiming a Cherokee descent from Malinda Watts, Nancy Pathkiller, and Margaret Shirly; all descend as per application, set forth from Nancy Pathkiller -

who it is alleged will appear on the census rolls of Cherokees of the year 1835. Supposing such to be the case, the testimony in this case, or cases, fail to establish a lineal descent from the above named ancestors, and the Commission on Citizenship, after a thorough examination of the testimony, find that the evidence is insufficient to establish the rights of the applicant to Cherokee citizenship (see Act of Dec. 8, 1886); and Thomas Woodsides,* William Woodsides, Thomas A. Woodsides, Andrew J. Woodsides, George Woodsides, Dillard Woodsides, Margaret Shirly, Charles M. Shirly, and Mary* N. Day, the applicants in this cause, are not Cherokees by blood and are not entitled to the rights and privileges of such on account of their blood. And the Commission so declares.

J.T. Adair, Chairman Commission
D.W. Lipe
H.C. Barnes
Commissioners

Feb. 1, 1887
Docket #28   **WALL**   C.H. Taylor, Atty.
Roll 1835

Oak P.O, I.T.

#	NAMES	AGE	SEX
1	D.W. Wall	31	m
2	Wallie	12	m
3	Henry	10	m
4	Mollie	8	f
5	Frank	6	m

Ancestor: Drew Wall
(**NOTE:** No other information given.)

Feb. 3, 1887
Docket #29   **McDANIEL**   C.H.   Taylor,
Atty.
Roll 1835

Cherryvale, KS

#	NAMES	AGE	SEX
1	Richard	45	m
2	Gurney D.	17	m
3	Addie	15	f

| 4 | Edgar P. | 13 | m |
| 5 | Beatruce | 4 | f |

Ancestor: Matilda* Underdoo

Oct. 4, 1888

Now on this the above written dates, comes this case up for final hearing. And all the evidence being duly considered, as well as the rolls of Cherokees laid down in the 7th Section of the Act of Dec. 8, 1886, in relation to citizenship, and the failure of the name of Malinda* Underdoo, the alleged Cherokee ancestor of the parties in the above case, or their own names; to appear thereon; It is adjudged and determined by the Commission on Citizenship, that Richard McDaniel and his four children, viz: Gurney D, Addie, Edgar P. and Beatrice McDaniel, are not Cherokees by blood and are not entitled to the rights and privileges of the citizens of the Cherokee Nation on account of their blood, and showed they be within the confines of the Cherokee Nation as intruders upon the public domain of said Nation.

J.T. Adair, Chairman Commission
H.C. Barnes, Commissioner

Feb. 8, 1887
Docket #30   **PEAKE**   B.N. Stone, Atty.
Rolls 1848 to 1852

Tahlequah, C.N.

#	NAMES	AGE	SEX
1	R.T.	56	m
2	James R.	31	m
3	Eli C.	26	m
4	Arab	21	m
5	Harry	19	m
6	John	10	m

Ancestor: James Peek*

Now on this the 6th day of June, 1887, comes the above case for final hearing; and having made application pursuant to the provisions of an Act of the National Council approved Dec. 8, 1886. And all the evidence being duly considered and examined and after an impartial investigation of all testimony admitted and from the evidence given by applicant's witnesses; It is clearly proven that the ancestor James Peak* and his descendant are not Cherokees by blood. Therefore the Commission unanimously agrees and determines that the applicant R.T. Peak, James R. Peak, Eli C. Peak, Arab Peak, Harry Peak, and John Peak are not Cherokees by blood and are therefore not entitled to any rights and privileges of Cherokee citizens by blood.

J.T. Adair, Chairman Commission
John E. Gunter
D.W. Lipe
Commissioners

Henry Eiffert
Asst. Clerk Comm.

(***NOTE:** Name spelled both ways.)

Feb. 8, 1887
Docket #31   **THOMAS**   (No Atty. given)
Rolls 1848 to 1852

Flint P.O.

#	NAMES	AGE	SEX
1	Manerva T.	43	f
2	James M.	17	m
3	Caldoney E.	14	f
4	Nancy C.	12	f
5	Luces* F.	8	m
6	Mordecia A.	5	f
7	George E.	10	m

Ancestor: John Tucker

Now on this the 2nd day of April, 1887, comes the above named case for final hearing (Applicant having waived the 90 days notice) and having made application in pursuant to an act of the National Council of the Cherokee Nation approved Dec. 8, 1886, and all the evidence being duly considered and found to be sufficient and satisfactory to the Commission; It is adjudged and determined by the Commission that Manerva J. Thomas, James M. Thomas, Caldoney E. Thomas, Nancy C. Thomas, Lucy* F. Thomas, and Mordecia A. Thomas, are Cherokees by blood, and are hereby re-admitted to all the rights, privileges, and immunities of Cherokee citizens by blood.

And a certificate of said decision of the Commission and of re-admission was made and furnished the parties accordingly. (**NOTE:** On the 5th day of June, 1887, the certificate of admission to citizenship was returned to the court by Mrs. Thomas for correction and the name of George E. Thomas was inserted, having been left off by mistake.)

J.T. Adair, Chairman Commission

Cherokee Citizenship Commission Docket Books
Tahlequah, Cherokee Nation (1880-84, 1887-89)
Volume I

Henry Eiffert
Asst. Clerk Comm.

John E. Gunter
D.W. Lipe
Comm.

(*NOTE: Both names given.)

Feb. 8, 1887
Docket #32   **CALLAHAN**   (No Atty. given.)
Rolls 1848 to 1852

Flint P.O.

#	NAMES	AGE	SEX
1	Martha E.	19	f
2	Drury Q.	6 mo	*(blank)*

Ancestor: John Tucker

Now on this the 2nd day of April, 1887, comes the above case for final hearing (Applicant having waived the ninety days notice) and having made application in pursuant to the provisions of an act of the National Council of the Cherokee Nation approved Dec. 8, 1886, and all the evidence in the case being duly considered and found to be sufficient and satisfactory to the Commission; It is adjudged and determined by the Commission that Martha E. Callahan and Drury Q. Callahan, are Cherokees by blood, and are hereby re-admitted to all the rights, privileges, and immunities of Cherokee citizens by blood.

And a certificate of said decision of the Commission and of re-admission was made and furnished the parties accordingly.

J.T. Adair, Chairman Comm.
John E. Gunter
D.W. Lipe
Comm.

Henry Eiffert
Asst. Clerk Comm.

Feb. 8, 1887
Docket #33   **TUCKER**   In person.
Rolls 1848 to 1852

Flint P.O. C.N.

#	NAMES	AGE	SEX
1	Sutiza M.	37	f

Ancestor: John Tucker

Tahlequah, Aug. 16, 1889

The application in the above case in presented by Minerva T. Thomas in behalf of Sutiza M. Tucker, as her best friend and sister, because she is "non compos mentis" (Not legally competent) and is an inmate of the Cherokee National Home for the Blind and Insane. The evidence is conflicting as the legitimacy of Sutiza M. Tucker. Her father, John Tucker, at one time denying her as his child and refusing to show per capita for her when drawing for the other members of his family. At one payment, it does not appear that he refused to receive her allowance of per capita and the evidence shows that she was born in wedlock and raised in the house with the recognized children of John Tucker, from whom they derive their Cherokee blood.

The Commission therefore decides in favor of Applicant as of Cherokee blood and entitled to citizenship in the Cherokee Nation.   (**NOTE**) Readmitted Aug. 16, 1889.

(No other names given)

Attest, D.S. Williams
      Asst. Clerk Comm.

Feb. 8, 1887
Docket #34   **WILSON**   In person.
Roll 1852

Tahlequah, C.N.

#	NAMES	AGE	SEX
1	Mary E.	28	f
2	Sarah Jane	11	f
3	Liddie Matilda	7	f
4	Manda Letitia*	4	f
5	James Marcum	1	m

Ancestor: Caleb S. Thompson

On this the 4th day of April, 1887, comes the above case for final hearing. (Applicant having waived the ninety days notice) and having made application in pursuant to the provisions of an act of the National Council of the Cherokee Nation, approved Dec. 8, 1886, and all the evidence in the case being duly considered and found to be satisfactory to the commission; It is adjudged and determined by the Commission that, Mary E. Wilson, Sarah Jane Wilson, Liddie Matilda Wilson, Manda Luticia* Wilson, and James Marcum Wilson, are Cherokees by blood and are hereby re-admitted to all the rights, privileges, and immunities of Cherokee citizens by blood.

And a certificate of said decision and of re-admission was made and furnished to said parties accordingly.   J.T. Adair, Chairman of Commission

John E. Gunter
Henry Eiffert
Asst. Clerk Comm.

D.W. Lipe
Comm.

(*NOTE: Name spelled both ways.)

Feb. 8, 1887
Docket #35   **THOMPSON**   Self.
Roll 1852

Tahlequah, C.N.

#	NAMES	AGE	SEX
1	William D.	37	m
2	Ruben* C.	17	m
3	John M.	15	m
4	Lydia S.	13	f
5	Hiram A.	11	m
6	Martha J.	9	f
7	Mary L.	7	f
8	William J.	5	m
9	Lucy A.	2	f

Ancestor: Caleb S. Thompson

On this the 4th day of April, 1887, comes the above case for final hearing. (Applicant having waived the ninety days notice) and having made application in compliance to the provisions of an act of the National Council, approved Dec. 8, 1886, and all the evidence being duly considered and found sufficient and satisfactory to the Commission; It is adjudged and determined by the Commission that, Willia D. Thompson, Reubin* C. Thompson, John M. Thompson, Lydia S. Thompson, Hiram A. Thompson, Martha J. Thompson, Mary L. Thompson, William J. Thompson, and Lucy A. Thompson, are Cherokees by blood, and are hereby re-admitted to all the rights, privileges, and immunities of Cherokee citizens by blood.

And a certificate of said decision of the Commission and of re-admission was made and furnished to said parties accordingly.

J.T. Adair, Chairman of Comm.
John E. Gunter
Henry Eiffert   D.W. Lipe
Asst. Clerk Comm.   Commissioners

Cherokee Citizenship Commission Docket Books
Tahlequah, Cherokee Nation (1880-84, 1887-89)
Volume I

(***NOTE:** Name spelled both ways.)

Feb. 10, 1887
Docket #36   **BOROUGHS**   Self.
Roll 1835

Tahlequah, C.N.

#	NAMES	AGE	SEX
1	Mary A.	33	f
2	Pony F	4	m

Ancestor: Alex West

Now on this the 16th day of April, 1887, comes the above case for final hearing. The applicant having filed her application in compliance with the provisions of an act of the National Council of the Cherokee Nation, approved Dec. 8, 1886. And all the evidence being submitted; We the Commission on Citizenship after a careful and impartial investigation of the testimony, and having also examined the census rolls of 1835, 1848, 1851, and 1852, in the case of Mary A. Boroughs and Pony F. Boroughs, find that there is not sufficient testimony in behalf of the applicants to justify them to any rights of Cherokee citizens.

J.T. Adair, Chairman Comm

Henry Eiffert   D.W. Lipe
   Asst. Clerk   Comm.

Feb. 11, 1887
Docket #37   **DAWSON**   C.H. Taylor, Atty.
Roll 1835

Nevada, MO

#	NAMES	AGE	SEX
1	Andrew J.	44	m
2	E.E.	16	m
3	Olive M.	14	f
4	William N.	11	m
5	Jessie K.	9	m
6	Glennie D.	8	f

Ancestor: (No name given.)

Cherokee Citizenship Commission Docket Books
Tahlequah, Cherokee Nation (1880-84, 1887-89)
Volume I

The decision in this case is that of P.R. Dawson, rendered April 26, 1889.
Rejected.

D.S. Williams
    Clerk Comm.

Feb. 11, 1887
Docket #38   **DUNN**   S.N Benge
Roll 1835

Fort Gibson, C.N.

#	NAMES	AGE	SEX
1	Alice	34	f
2	Mariah	16	f
3	Eliza	13	f
4	James J.	11	m
5	Davis N.	8	m
6	Martin J.	4	m
7	Andrew T.	18 mo	m

Ancestor: James Griffin

Oct. 3, 1888

In the matter of the claim of Alice Dunn and family to Cherokee citizenship before the Commission, and who having filed her application pursuant to the provisions of an act of the National Council approved Dec. 8, 1886, and claiming as her ancestor James Griffin, from where she claims Cherokee descent.

The Commission after a careful examination of all the evidence offered in the case, and a careful examination of all the rolls mentioned in the 7th Section of the law creating this Commission, fail to find the name of ancestor as claimed in the application, and hereby declare Alice Dunn and family, to wit: Mariah Dunn, Eliza Dunn, James J. Dunn, Davis N. Dunn, Martin J. Dunn, and Andrew T. Dunn, not to be Cherokees by blood, and are not entitled to any of the rights, privileges, and immunities of other Cherokees; and are hereby declared to be intruders on the public domain.

                             J.T. Adair, Chairman Comm.
Attest, C.C. Lipe   H.C. Barnes
    Clerk Comm.   Commissioner

Feb. 12, 1887
Docket #39   **MILLIGAN**   Isaac Milligan, Atty.

Roll 1852

Webber Falls, C.N.

#	NAMES	AGE	SEX
1	Susan J.	34	f
2	Annie	13	f
3	Cabel	10	m
4	Grace	5	f

Ancestor: Polly Mayfield

Now on this the 31st day of March, 1887, comes the above case for final hearing. (Applicant having waived the ninety days notice) and having made application pursuant to the provisions of an act of the National Council of the Cherokee Nation approved Dec. 8, 1886, and all the evidence being duly considered and found to be sufficient and satisfactory to the Commission; It is adjudged and determined by the Commission that Susan Jane Milligan, Annie Milligan, Cabel Milligan, and Grace Milligan are Cherokees by blood, and are hereby re-admitted to all the rights, privileges and immunities of a Cherokee citizen by blood.

And a certificate of said decision of the Commission and of re-admission was made and furnished to said parties accordingly.

> J.T. Adair, Chairman Comm.
> John E. Gunter
>
> Henry Eiffert   D.W. Lipe
> Asst. Clerk Comm.   Comm.

Feb. 14, 1887
Docket #40   **ALSTON**   Wm. Jackson, Atty.
Rolls 1851 & 1852

Marietta, GA

#	NAMES	AGE	SEX
1	Williamina	31	f
2	Mary Christian	1	f

Ancestor: Geo. W. Cleland

Now on this the 31st day of August, 1887, comes the above case for final hearing and the above named parties having made application pursuant to the provisions of an act of the National Council approved Dec. 8, 1886, and all the evidence being duly considered and found to be sufficient and satisfactory to

Cherokee Citizenship Commission Docket Books
Tahlequah, Cherokee Nation (1880-84, 1887-89)
Volume I

the Commission; It is adjudged and determined by the Commission that Williamina Alston and Mary Christian Alston are Cherokees by blood and are hereby re-admitted to all the rights, privileges, and immunities of Cherokee citizens by blood.

And a certificate of said decision of the Commission and of re-admission was made and furnished to said parties accordingly.

J.T. Adair, Chairman, Commission

Henry Eiffert   John E. Gunter

Clerk Comm.   Comm.

Feb. 14, 1887

Docket #41   **BARNELL***   Wm. Jackson, Atty.

Rolls 1851 & 1852

Marietta, GA

#	NAMES	AGE	SEX
1	Elizabeth S.	29	f
2	Stephen	6	m
3	Middleton	3	m
4	Dudley	7 mo	m

Ancestor: Geo. W. Cleland

Tahlequah, May 8, 1889

Now on this day comes the above named case for the final hearing. The evidence shows that the applicant for re-admission to citizenship is the daughter of George W. Cleland, a citizen of Cooweescoowee District, Cherokee Nation and the grand-daughter of George M. Waters, whose names are found on the Silar Roll of 1851 and the Chapman Roll of 1852, of Cherokees by blood and the Commission therefore, decides that Elizabeth S. Barnwell* is of Cherokee blood and is hereby re-admitted to citizenship in the Cherokee Nation, and her children, to wit: Stephen Barnwell, Middleton Barnwell, Dudley Barnwell, and Carlton Barnwell, aged 7 months, (born after date of application).

Will P. Ross, Chairman

Attest, D.S. Williams   John E. Gunter

Clerk Comm.   Comm.

(***NOTE:** Name spelled both ways.)

Feb. 14, 1887

Docket #42   <u>**SPRIGGS**</u>   (No Atty. given)
Rolls 1851 & 1852

Cleveland, TN

#	NAMES	AGE	SEX
1	Polly Ann	55	f
2	Mary Adda	21	f
3	Lillie Ann	16	f

Ancestor: George W. Cleland

Now on this the 26th day of April, 1887, comes this case for final hearing, and having made application pursuant to the provisions of an act of the National Council, approved Dec. 8, 1886, and all the evidence being duly considered and found to be sufficient and satisfactory to the Commission; It is adjudged and determined by the Commission, that Polly Ann Spriggs, Mary Adda Spriggs, and Lillie Ann Spriggs, are Cherokees by blood and they are hereby re-admitted to all the rights, privileges and immunities of Cherokee citizenship by blood.

And a certificate of said decision of the Commission and of re-admission was made and furnished said parties accordingly.

J.T. Adair, Chairman Comm.
John E. Gunter, Comm.
Henry Eiffert, Asst. Clerk Comm.   D.W. Lipe, Comm.

Feb. 14, 1887
Docket #43   <u>**McDONALD**</u>   (No Atty. given.)
Roll 1851

Gibson Station

#	NAMES	AGE	SEX
1	Charles C.	18	m
2	Cherokee Isabella	15	f

Ancestor: Martha Blythe

Now on this the 26th day of April, 1887, comes the above case for final hearing and having made application pursuant to the provisions of an act of the National Council approved Dec. 8, 1886, and all the evidence being duly considered and found to be sufficient and satisfactory to the Commission; It is adjudged and determined by the Commission that Charles C. McDonald and Cherokee Isabella McDonald are Cherokees by blood and they are hereby re-admitted to all the rights, privileges, and immunities of Cherokee citizenship by blood.

And a certificate of said decision of the Commission and of re-admission was made and furnished said parties accordingly.

J.T. Adair, Chairman Comm.

John E. Gunter

Henry Eiffert   D.W. Lipe

Asst. Clerk Comm.   Commissioners

Feb. 16, 1887

Docket #44   **HEATH**   (No Atty. given.)

Rolls 1851 & 52

Muscogee, I.T.

#	NAMES	AGE	SEX
1	Charles	19	m

Ancestor: Jane Biggs

The motion in this case is that of William H. Rush, <u>by</u> default, in this book on page (125, See Docket #47), rendered April 24, 1889.

D.S. Williams

Clerk Comm.

Feb. 17, 1887

Docket #45   **RUSH**   (No Atty. given.)

Roll 1835

#	NAMES	AGE	SEX
1	J. P.	39	m
2	Willis M.	7	m
3	Purnia D.	5	f
4	Dora E.	3	f
5	Arthur T.	6 mo	m

Prairie City, I.T.

Ancestor: Rachel Bryant

The applicant in the above case asked to withdraw his application for Cherokee citizenship, upon the grounds that he had been misinformed as to his

Cherokee Citizenship Commission Docket Books
Tahlequah, Cherokee Nation (1880-84, 1887-89)
Volume I

Cherokee blood relationship, and that he had no further claims as such. The applicant not owning or pretending to own any improvement in the Nation, the Attorney for the Nation consented to the withdrawal of said application, therefore the case is dismissed from the docket. This April 6, 1887.

J.T. Adair, Chairman Commission
John E. Gunter
Henry Eiffert   D.W. Lipe
   Asst. Clerk Comm.   Commissioners

Feb. 16, 1887
Docket #46   **DUNCAN**   (No Atty. given.)
Rolls 1851 & 52

Uniontown, AR

#	NAMES	AGE	SEX
1	Charles	37	m
2	Charles, Jr.	14	m
3	Sarah	12	f
4	Juda	8	f
5	Eddie	5	m
6	Hannah	2	f

Ancestor: Charles R. Duncan

The motion in this case is that of William H. Rush, by default, in this book on this page, (Docket #47); rendered April 24, 1889.

George O. Butler
   Clerk Comm. Pro tem.

Feb. 17, 1887
Docket #47   **RUSH**   (No Atty. given)
Roll 1835

Whitt, Parker Co, TX

#	NAMES	AGE	SEX
1	William H.	40	m
2	T.E.	19	m
3	W.E.	11	m
4	John G.	6	m

Cherokee Citizenship Commission Docket Books
Tahlequah, Cherokee Nation (1880-84, 1887-89)
Volume I

Ancestor: Rachael Bryant

Before the Commission on Citizenship   Hon. W.P. Ross, Chairman   Hon. John E. Gunter, Presiding
Now comes Richard M. Wolfe, Atty. for Cherokee Nation and moves that judgment be entered against the above entitled cases, together with children for the following reasons; 1st - the cases were all filed in 1887 by the applicants as appears from their papers, respectfully; therefore they knew that their personal attention was necessary. 2nd - They have had ample notice, the Commission having given 30 days notice of the time fixed for its siting in all of the newspapers in the country and the further notice of one month of the time when the call of the docket would begin also given in the newspapers of the country. Not withstanding the parties failed to answer either in person or by atty. to the call of their respective cases and thereby have disregarded and ignored (the) Commission on Citizenship.

Respectfully,
Richard M. Wolfe,
Atty. Cherokee Nation, C.C.

Notice sustained by the Commission and judgment entered against the applicant together with children. This April 24, 1889.

Will P. Ross, Chairman
John E. Gunter, Commissioner

Feb. 18, 1887
Docket #48   **SUMTER**   (No Atty. given.)
Roll 1835

Evansville, AR

#	NAMES	AGE	SEX
1	Hester	25	f
2	Lafeyette	6	m
3	Mt. Edney	5	f
4	Birdie	3	f
5	Minnie	2	f

Ancestor: Buck Hargus
The motion in this case is that of William H. Rush, by default - rendered April 24, 1889, in this book page 125 (Docket #47).

D.S. Williams
    Clerk Commission

Feb. 21, 1887
Docket #49   **LUSK**   A.E. Ivey, Atty
Roll 1851

Wah-hil-law, I.T.

#	NAMES	AGE	SEX
1	Huldah	34	f
2	L.J.	6	m
3	James	4	m

Ancestor: James M. Keys

Now on this the 1st day of April, 1887, comes the above named case for final hearing. (Applicant having waived the ninety days notice) and having made application pursuant to the provisions of an act of the National Council of the Cherokee Nation approved Dec. 8, 1886. And all the evidence in the case being duly considered and found to be sufficient and satisfactory to the Commission; It is adjudged and determined by the Commission that Huldah Lusk, L.J. Lusk, and James Lusk are Cherokees by blood and are hereby re-admitted to all the rights, privileges, and immunities of a Cherokee citizen by blood.

And a certificate of said decision of the Commission and of re-admittance was made and furnished the said parties accordingly.

                     J.T. Adair, Chairman Comm.
                     John E. Gunter, Comm
Henry Eiffert. Asst. Clerk   D.W. Lipe, Comm.

Feb. 21, 1887
Docket #50   **KEYS**   A.E. Ivey, Atty.
Roll 1851

Wah-hil-law, I.T.

#	NAMES	AGE	SEX
1	D.C.	22	m
2	M.G.	20	m
3	V.C.	24	f
4	M.O.	16	f
5	Martha	14	f

| 6 | Ophelia | 10 | f |

Ancestor: James M. Keys

Now on this the 1st day of April, 1887, comes the above case for final hearing. (Applicant having waived the ninety days notice) and having made application pursuant to the provisions of the National Council of the Cherokee Nation, approved Dec. 8, 1886, and all the evidence in the case being duly considered and found sufficient and satisfactory to the Commission; It is adjudged and determined by the Commission that; D.C. Keys, M.G. Keys, V.C. Keys, M.O. Keys, Martha Keys, and Ophelia Keys, are Cherokees by blood and are hereby re-admitted to all the rights, privileges, and immunities of Cherokee citizens by blood.

And a certificate of said decision and of re-admission was made and furnished to the parties.

J.T. Adair, Chairman of Comm.

John E. Gunter

Henry Eiffert　　　　　　　　　D.W. Lipe
　　Asst. Clerk　　　　　　　　　Commissioners

Feb. 23, 1887
Docket #51　　　　　　　**MARTIN**　　　　　　Self
Roll 1835

Sanders, Ind. Ter.

#	NAMES	AGE	SEX
1	A.J.	44	m
2	Mattie	20	f
3	Victoria	16	f

Ancestor: Samuel Martin

Now on this the 5th day of October, 1888, comes the above case for a final hearing, and the parties having made application in compliance with the provisions of an act of the National Council, approved Dec. 8, 1886, and all the evidence having been duly considered and found to be sufficient and satisfactory to the Commission; It is adjudged and determined by the Commission that A.J. Martin and his two children; to wit: Mattie Martin and Victoria Martin are Cherokees by blood and is hereby re-admitted to all the rights, privileges, and immunities of other Cherokees by blood.

Cherokee Citizenship Commission Docket Books
Tahlequah, Cherokee Nation (1880-84, 1887-89)
Volume I

And a certificate of said decision of the Commission and of re-admission was made out and furnished said parties accordingly.

J.T. Adair, Chairman Comm.

Attest, C.C. Lipe
Clerk Comm.

H.C. Barnes
Commissioner

Feb. 23, 1887
Docket #52   **WHITTINGTON**   Self
Roll 1835

Cincinnati, AR

#	NAMES	AGE	SEX
1	Cynthia	61	f

Ancestor: Enrolled as Sally Langley

On this the 15th day of April, 1887, comes the above case for final hearing, and application having been made in compliance with the provisions of an act of the National Council of the Cherokee Nation, approved Dec. 8, 1886, and all the evidence being duly considered and found to be sufficient and satisfactory to the Commission; It is adjudged and determined by the Commission that Cynthia Whittington is a Cherokee by blood, and is hereby re-admitted to all the rights, privileges, and immunities of a Cherokee by blood.

And a certificate of said decision and of re-admission was made and furnished the said party accordingly.

J.T. Adair, Chairman of Commission
John E. Gunter
D.W. Lipe
Commissioners

Henry Eiffert
Asst. Clerk

Feb. 23, 1887
Docket #53   **WHITTINGTON***   C.H. Taylor, Atty.
Roll 1851

Sexton, AR

#	NAMES	AGE	SEX
1	Cornelius	28	m
2	Jana	7 mo	f

Ancestor: John Langley

On this the 15th day of April, 1887, comes the above case for final hearing and having made application pursuant to the provisions of an act of the National Council of the Cherokee Nation approved Dec. 8, 1886, and all the evidence in the case being duly considered and found to be sufficient and satisfactory to the Commission; It is adjudged and determined by the Commission that Cornelius Whitington* and Jana Whitington are Cherokees by blood, and are hereby re-admitted to all the rights, privileges and immunities of Cherokees by blood.

And a certificate of said decision and of re-admission was made and furnished to said parties.

J.T. Adair, Chairman of Commission
John E. Gunter

Henry Eiffert
Asst. Clerk

D.W. Lipe
Commissioners

Feb. 24, 1887
Docket #54   **HULSEY**   (No Atty. given.)
Rolls 1835

Echo, Ind. Terr.

#	NAMES	AGE	SEX
1	Josephine Hulsey	28	f

Ancestor: Betsy Kell

Now on this the 12th day of Oct, 1887, comes the above case for a final hearing and the parties having made application pursuant to the provisions of an act of the National Council approved Dec. 8, 1886. And all the evidence being duly examined and found to be sufficient and satisfactory to the Commission and the names of the ancestor, Betsy Kell, appearing on the rolls of 1835; It is adjudged and determined by the Commission that Josephine Hulsey is a Cherokee by blood, and is hereby re-admitted to all the rights, privileges, and immunities of Cherokees by blood.

And a certificate of said decision of the Commission and re-admission was made and furnished accordingly.

D.W. Lipe, Acting Chairman
John E. Gunter, Commissioner

Feb. 23, 1887
Docket #55   **RALSTON***   James M. Bell, Atty.
Roll 1835

Vinita, Ind. Ter.

#	NAMES	AGE	SEX

| 1 | Zachariah T. | 38 | m |

Ancestor: Betsy Kell

Now on this the 12th day of Oct, 1887, comes the above case for a final hearing and the parties having made application pursuant to the provisions of an act of the National Council, approved Dec. 8, 1886. And all the evidence being duly examined and found to be sufficient and satisfactory to the Commission and the name of the ancestor, Betsy Kell, appearing on the rolls of 1835; It is adjudged and determined by the Commission that Zachariah T. Raulston* is a Cherokee by blood and is hereby re-admitted to all the rights, privileges, and immunities of Cherokees by blood.

And a certificate of said decision of the Commission and re-admission are made and furnished to said parties accordingly.

D.W. Lipe, Act. Chairman
John E. Gunter, Comm.

(***NOTE:** Name spelled both ways.)

Feb. 23, 1887
Docket #56   **RALSTON***   James M. Bell, Atty.
Roll 1835

Echo, Ind. Terr.

#	NAMES	AGE	SEX
1	James D.	30	m

Ancestor: (Betsy) Kell

Now on this the 12th day of Oct, 1887, comes the above case for a final hearing. And the parties having made application pursuant to the provisions of an act of the National Council, approved Dec. 8, 1886. And all the evidence being duly examined and found to be sufficient and satisfactory to the Commission. And the name of the ancestor, Betsy Kell, appearing on the roll of 1835; It is determined and adjudged by the Commission that James D. Raulston*, is a Cherokee by blood, and is hereby re-admitted to all the rights, privileges, and immunities of Cherokees by blood.

And a certificate of said decision of the Commission and re-admission was made and furnished accordingly.

D.W. Lipe, Acting Chairman

Cherokee Citizenship Commission Docket Books
Tahlequah, Cherokee Nation (1880-84, 1887-89)
Volume I

John E. Gunter, Commissioner

(*NOTE: Name spelled both ways)

Feb. 25, 1887
Docket #57   **HAIL**   C.H. Taylor, Atty.
Roll 1835

Tahlequah, C.N.

#	NAMES	AGE	SEX
1	James M.	35	m
2	Margarett	11	f
3	Ida T.	9	f
4	John G.	6	m
5	Lillie B.	4	f
6	Elizabeth F.	8 mo.	f

Ancestor: Geo. W. Hail

Now on this the 23 day of May, 1887, comes the above case for final hearing and after having made application pursuant to the provisions of an act of the National Council approved Dec. 8, 1886. And all the evidence having been duly considered and found to be sufficient and satisfactory to the Commission; It is adjudged and determined by the Commission that James M. Hail, Margarett Hail, Ida T. Hail, John G. Hail, Lillie B. Hail, and Elizabeth F. Hail, are Cherokees by blood and they are hereby re-admitted to all the rights, privileges, and immunities of Cherokee citizens by blood.

And a certificate of said decision of the Commission and of re-admission was made and furnished said parties accordingly.

J.T. Adair, Chairman Commission
Henry Eiffert   John E. Gunter
          Asst. Clerk   Commissioner

Feb. 25, 1887
Docket #58   **BOWERS**   C.H. Taylor, Atty.
Roll 1835

Paris, AR

#	NAMES	AGE	SEX
1	M.H.	33	m
2	Martha E.	9	f
3	Lillie J.	7	f

4	Ellen E. (Twin)	4	f
5	Dollie (Twin)	4	f
66	Charles D.	1	m

Ancestor: Ned Christy*

In the matter of the claim of M.J. Bowers and family, applicants for Cherokee citizenship; on this 3rd day of Oct, 1888, who having made application in compliance with an act of the National Council, approved Dec. 8, 1886, and claiming as their ancestor Ned Christie* from whom they claim their Cherokee descend. The Commission after a careful and impartial examination of all the evidence in the case and a careful examination of all the rolls mentioned in the law creating this Commission; fail to find said ancestor as claimed in the application. Therefore, we the Commission declare that M.J. Bowers and family; Martha E. Bowers, Lillie Bowers, Ellen E. Bowers, Dollie Bowers, and Charles Bowers, are not Cherokees by blood and are not entitled to any of the rights and privileges of other Cherokee citizens of this Nation.

J.T. Adair, Chairman Comm.

H.C. Barnes, Commissioner

Attest, C.C. Lipe
Clerk Comm.
(**NOTE:** Name spelled both ways.)

Feb. 25, 1887
Docket #59   **TIPTON**   C.H.   Taylor,
Atty.
Roll 1835

Coffeyville, KS

#	NAMES	AGE	SEX
1	Mary E.	50	f
2	Susie H.	19	f
3	Jessie L.	17	f
4	Samuel	15	m
5	Eddie	11	m
6	Eliza S.	9	f
7	Jane H.	7	f
8	Howard	5	m

Ancestor: Lander* Carter

Cherokee Citizenship Commission Docket Books
Tahlequah, Cherokee Nation (1880-84, 1887-89)
Volume I

In the matter of the above claimant and her children for Cherokee citizenship, it appears she claims her Cherokee blood from her father Landen* Carter, who was the son of Alford Carter, and that her mother was a mulatto woman owned by her alleged grand-father. We have examined all the rolls taken by the Government East of the Mississippi River, and find that there were a lot of Carters living in that section of country, or rather in the state of North Carolina, but fail to find either the name of Alford or Landen Carter. The Carters we find enrolled by Mr. Siler proved not to be of Cherokee blood, but under the head of <u>Remarks</u> find them to be Catawba Indians. If the applicant had proven that she was a descendant from any of the Carters enrolled, that would not entitle her and her children to any rights in the Cherokee Nation, for the reason they were Catawba and not Cherokees. Under the law creating this Commission, passed Dec. 8, 1886, it plainly states that applicants must prove a descent from an ancestor (Cherokee) on some(sic) one of these rolls mentioned in law.

After carefully summing up the evidence in this case, the Commission adjudges the applicant not to be of Cherokee blood. Therefore, Mary E. Tipton and her seven children, viz: Susie H, Jessie L, Samuel, Eddie, Eliza S, Jane H, and Howard Tipton, are intruders upon the public domain of the Cherokee Nation and not entitled to any of the rights and privileges of the Cherokee Nation.

> J.T. Adair, Chairman Commission
> D.W. Lipe, Commissioner
> H.C. Barnes, Commissioner

Tahlequah, I.T, Sept. 24, 1888
(***NOTE:** Name spelled both ways.)

Feb. 25, 1887
Docket #60　　　　　　　　**LETT**　　　　C.H. Taylor, Atty.
Roll 1835

Prairie City, I.T.

#	NAMES	AGE	SEX
1	Moses	63	m
2	Aquilla	21	m
3	Lander	18	m
4	Benj.	17	m
5	Amanda	12	f
6	Nelson	8	m

Ancestor: Betsey Caliman

Tahlequah, Sept. 29, 1888

Cherokee Citizenship Commission Docket Books
Tahlequah, Cherokee Nation (1880-84, 1887-89)
Volume I

In the matter of the above case for citizenship in the Cherokee Nation, filed on the 25th day of February, 1887. Mr. C.H. Taylor, Atty. We the Commission on Citizenship, find that there is no evidence submitted whatever in support of the allegation set forth in the application of the applicants. That Betsey Caliman is not Cherokee or that they are descended from her. It is the opinion of the Commission, therefore, that Moses Lett and his five children, viz: Aquilla, Lander, Benjamin, Amanda, and Nelson Lett are not Cherokees by blood and not entitled to any of the rights of citizenship in the Cherokee Nation and are intruders thereof.

J.T. Adair, Chairman Comm.

H.C. Barnes, Commissioner

Feb. 26, 1887
Docket #61   **COMEIFORD***   C.H. Taylor, Atty.
Roll 1835

South West City, MO

#	NAMES	AGE	SEX
1	Pleasant	31	m
2	Rose May	9	f
3	R.S.	7	f
4	H.S.	5	f

Ancestor: Mary Sutton or Fisher

Now on this the 28th day of January, 1888, comes the above case for a final hearing and the parties having made application pursuant to the provisions of an act of the National Council approved Dec. 8, 1886, and all the evidence having been duly examined and found to be sufficient and satisfactory to the Commission and the name of the ancestor being on the Roll. It is adjudged and determined by the Commission that; Pleasant Cumiford*, Rose May Cumiford, R.S. Cumiford, and H.S. Cumiford, are Cherokees and are hereby re-admitted to all the rights and privileges of Cherokee citizens by blood.

And a certificate of said decision of the Commission and of re-admission was made and furnished said parties accordingly.

J.T. Adair, Chairman Commission

John E. Gunter, Commissioner

D.W. Lipe, Commissioner

Attest, C.C. Lipe, Clerk

(***NOTE:** Name spelled both ways.)

Feb. 26, 1887

Docket #62   <u>**WILLIS**</u>   C.H. Taylor, Atty.
Rolls 1851 & 52

Cincinnati, AR

#	NAMES	AGE	SEX
1	Hester	39	f
2	Thomas J.	18	m
3	J.W.	13	m
4	Carrie R.	11	f
5	J.R.	8	m
6	G.G.	6	m
7	C.C.	4	m
8	Lula	2	f

Ancestor: John Langley

On this the 15th day of April, 1887, comes the above case for final hearing and application having been made in pursuant to the provisions of an act of the National Council of the Cherokee Nation, approved Dec. 8, 1886. And all the evidence being duly considered and found sufficient and satisfactory to the Commission; It is adjudged and determined by the Commission that Hester Willis, Thomas J. Willis, J.W. Willis, Carrie R. Willis, J.R. Willis, G.G. Willis, C.C. Willis, and Lula Willis, are Cherokees by blood and are hereby re-admitted to all the rights, privileges, and immunities of Cherokee citizens by blood.

And a certificate of said decision and of re-admission was made and furnished the parties accordingly.

                J.T. Adair, Chairman of Comm.
                John E. Gunter, Comm.
Henry Eiffert, Asst. Clerk   D.W. Lipe, Comm.

Feb. 28, 1887
Docket #63   <u>**CORBITT**</u>   C.H. Taylor, Atty.
Roll 1835

Echo, Ind. Terr.

#	NAMES	AGE	SEX
1	Jane	60	f

Ancestor: Jack Downing

The foregoing case having been submitted by attorneys without evidence, the Commission decides that Jane Corbitt is not a Cherokee by blood as alleged in her application and not entitled to citizenship in the Cherokee Nation. This 23rd day of April, 1889.

Will P. Ross, Chairman
R. Bunch, Comm.

Attest, D.S. Williams, Clerk

John E. Gunter, Comm.

March 3, 1887
Docket #64   **DEMPSEY**   Geo. O. Butler, Atty.
Roll 1835

Buffalo Gap, Dak.

#	NAMES	AGE	SEX
1	Melvin	(blank)	(blank)

Ancestor: Melvin Dempsey

In the matter of the claim of Melvin Dempsey, applicant for Cherokee citizenship, before the Commission, filed on the 3rd day of March, 1887, and alleging as his ancestor, one Melvin Dempsey, from whom he claims his Cherokee descent. We the Commission on Citizenship after a careful examination of all the evidence offered in the case, agree that the said Melvin Dempsey is not a Cherokee by blood. His ancestor not appearing on any of the census rolls of Cherokees mentioned in the 7th Section of the act of the National (Council) approved Dec. 8, 1886, in relation to Cherokee citizenship. Therefore, we the Commission declare said Melvin Dempsey not entitled to any of the rights, privileges, and immunities of Cherokee citizenship and is hereby declared to be an intruder upon this public domain of the Cherokee Nation. This Oct. 21, 1888.

J.T. Adair, Chairman Commission
H.C. Barnes, Commissioner

March 4, 1887
Docket #65   **PEAK**   C.H. Taylor, Atty.
Roll 1835

Rogers, AR

#	NAMES	AGE	SEX
1	Lafayette	40	m
2	Norris*	19	m
3	Ollie	12	f
4	Mary Isabella	7	f

| 5 | Rena* | 7 mo | f |

Ancestor: Absolum Peak

Tahlequah, June 12, 1889

Now on this day the Commission adjudges that the applicant in the above case Lafayette Peak, aged 40 yrs; and his son Norus* Peak, aged 19 yrs; and daughters, Ollie Peak, aged 13 yrs; Mary Isabella Peak, aged 7 yrs; and Renni-ah* Peak, aged 7 months; at the filing of this application on the 4th day of March, 1887, are not of Cherokee blood because the evidence shows that Absolum Peak was not an Indian and because his name does not appear on the census roll of Cherokees by blood taken in 1835. See case of Wm. A. Peak, Docket #120, P.O. Rogers, AR. Rejected June 12, 1889.

J.E. Gunter, Comm.

Attest, D.S. Williams, Asst. Clerk   R. Bunch, Comm.

(***NOTE:** Names spelled both ways.)

March 9, 1887
Docket #66   **GREGORY**   (No Atty. given.)
Roll (None given)

Chetope, KS

#	NAMES	AGE	SEX
1	George W.	25	m

Ancestor: H.C. Gregory

The motion in this case is that of William H. Rush, by default, in this book on page 125 (Docket #47). Rendered April 24, 1889.

D.W. Williams,
Clerk Comm.

March 9, 1887
Docket #67   **GREGORY**   (No Atty. given.)
Roll (None given)

Chetopa, KS

#	NAMES	AGE	SEX
1	William	33	m

Ancestor: H.C. Gregory

The motion in this case is that of William H. Rush, by default, in the book on page 125, (Docket #47). Rendered, April 24, 1889.

D.W. Williams
Clerk Comm.

March 14, 1887
Docket #68   **NIGHT**   (No Atty. given.)
Rolls 1835 to 1852

Webbers Falls, C.N.

#	NAMES	AGE	SEX
1	Miles	21	m
2	Nancy	3	f
3	Everett	2	m
4	Frank	1 mo	m

Ancestor: Bashabea Russell

Now this day comes for the final hearing, the above named case. No evidence accompanies the application and the applicant having been called there several times at an interval of one hour apart; the Commission decides that Miles Night, who filed his application March 11, 1887, and his family Nancy Night, Everett Night, and Frank Night, are not of Cherokee blood and not entitled to re-admission to citizenship in the Cherokee Nation and so decree. This April 26, 1889.

Will P. Ross, Chairman
D.S. Williams, Clerk   John E. Gunter, Comm.

March 11, 1887
Docket #69   **GADAS**   B.H. Stone, Atty.
Rolls 1835 to 1852

Tahlequah, C.N.

#	NAMES	AGE	SEX
1	Jemima E.	42	f

Ancestor: John Eavans

Now on this day comes the above named case for the final hearing. Jemima E. Gadas filed her application for re-admission to citizenship in the Cherokee Nation on the 11th day of March, 1887, alleging that she is the niece of one John Eavens. The testimony fails to show that she is of Cherokee blood as to identify her in any way with the Cherokee people. The Commission therefore adjudges that Jemima E. Gadas is not of Cherokee blood and is not entitled to citizenship in the Cherokee Nation. Post office address, Tahlequah, I.T. This April 26, 1889.

	Will P. Ross, Chairman
D.W. Williams, Clerk	John E. Gunter, Comm.

March 11, 1887
Docket #70   **RUSSELL**   (No Atty. given.)
Rolls 1835 to 1852

Webber Falls, C.N.

#	NAMES	AGE	SEX
1	William	60	m
2	Callie	38	f
3	Payton	40	m
4	Arzelia	36	f
5	Perry G.	35	m
6	Henry	32	m
7	Joseph	25	m
8	Ficelia	21	m
9	Jasper	19	m
10	Texa	17	f
11	Robert	11	m
12	Minnie	6	f
13	Andrew	4	m
14	Hescue	2	m
15	Cister	16	f

Ancestor: Bashabea Russell

Now on this the 31st day of May, 1887, comes the above case for final hearing and after having made application pursuant to the provisions of an act of the National Council approved Dec. 8, 1886, and after a careful and impartial investigation of all the testimony submitted in the case find that they are not Cherokees by blood, but find from the testimony of Thomas Taylor, that they are Catawba Indians, which is corroborated by the decision of William Siler on the Rolls taken in the year 1851.

Therefore, we the Commission on Citizenship unanimously agree and decide that the said William Russell, Callie Russell, Payton Russell, Arzelia

Cherokee Citizenship Commission Docket Books
Tahlequah, Cherokee Nation (1880-84, 1887-89)
Volume I

Russell, Perry G. Russell, Henry Russell, Joseph Russell, Ficelia Russell, Jasper Russell, Texa Russell, Robert Russell, Minnie Russell, Andrew Russell, Hescue Russell, and Cister Russell, are not entitled to any rights and privileges of Cherokee citizens by blood.

J.F. Adair, Chairman Comm.
John E. Gunter

Henry Eiffert
Clerk

D.W. Lipe
Commissioners

March 12, 1887
Docket #71   **SINGLETON**   C.H. Taylor, Atty.
Roll 1835

Coffeyville, KS

#	NAMES	AGE	SEX
1	Mary A.	47	f
2	Robt. L.	18	m
3	Marcus S.	16	m
4	Greenip A.	14	m
5	John M.	12	m
6	William Stul.	8	m

Ancestor: Phillip* Daffron

Tahlequah, Sept. 29, 1888

In the matter of the Mrs. Singleton's claim for citizenship in the Cherokee Nation, We the Commission on Citizenship find that the name of Philip* Daffron, or that of the applicants themselves, fail to appear on the rolls of Cherokees as laid down in the 7th Sec. of Act of Dec. 8, 1886, in relation to citizenship, consequently, under the law, this Commission cannot grant the applicant citizenship in the Cherokee Nation, and it now becomes our duty to declare, that Mary A. Singleton and her five children; viz: Robert L. Singleton, Marcus S. Singleton, Greenip A Singleton, John M. Singleton, and William S. Singleton, are not Cherokees by blood and are not entitled to any of the rights and privileges of such, on account of their blood, and should they be in the Cherokee Nation are intruders upon the public domain thereof.

J.T. Adair, Chairman Comm.
H.C. Barnes, Com.

(***NOTE:** Name spelled both ways.)

March 12, 1887

Docket #72   **WEST**   C.H.   Taylor,
Atty.
Roll 1835

Echo, Ind. Terr.

#	NAMES	AGE	SEX
1	Perry	45	m
2	Kerchin Y.	21	m
3	R.B.	17	m
4	William W.	14	m
5	Celia	13	f
6	John A.	12	m
7	Ida G.	10	f
8	Melvina	5	f
9	Charlotte	5	f
10	Ruba B.	3	f
11	Isham L.	21	m

Ancestor: William Y. West

The above case was filed in the office of the Commission on Citizenship on the 8th day of March, 1887, and upon the 4th day of Oct, 1886, it was taken up and duly disposed of under the law. Mr. Perry West claims as his Cherokee ancestor, his father, William Y. West, whom it is alleged appears on the census rolls of Cherokees taken in the year 1835, in the states of Tennessee, Alabama, North Carolina, and Georgia, and that William Y. West was usually called and known as "Honi-fly" West. And that the testimony shows him in the state of Tennessee in the year 1835. The testimony in this case would have us at once believe that the applicant was of Cherokee Indian descent, but the failure of the name of their ancestor or that of themselves to appear on some of the rolls laid down in the 7th Sec. of the Act of Dec. 8, 1886, in relation to citizenship works against them, and under the law this Commission has no option whatever, only to declare Perry West, Kerchin Y. West, R.B. West, William W. West, Celia West, Jr, John A. West, Ida G. West, Melvina West, Charlotte West, Ruba B. West, and Isham West not Cherokee citizens by blood, and are intruders upon the public domain of the Cherokee Nation. Oct. 4, 1886.

         J.T. Adair Chairman Comm.
         H.C. Barnes, Commissioner

March 18, 1887

Docket #73　　　　　**CANNON**　　　　A.E. Ivey, Atty.
Rolls 1851 & 52

Baptist, C.N.

#	NAMES	AGE	SEX
1	Edward B.	32	m
2	Cornelia	12	f
3	Charley*	10	m
4	Ira	8	m
5	Dubbin	6	f
6	Claude*	4	m
7	Maud	2	f

Ancestor: Elizabeth Cannon

Now on this the 13th day of August, 1887, comes the above case for final hearing, and having made application pursuant to the provisions of an act of the National Council approved Dec. 8, 1886. And all the evidence having been duly considered and found to be sufficient and satisfactory to the Commission, and upon an examination the name of ancestor, Elizabeth Cannon appears upon the Rolls of 1851 & 52; It is adjudged and determined by the Commission that Edward B. Cannon, Cornelia Cannon, Charlie* Cannon, Ira Cannon, Dubbin Cannon, Claud* Cannon, and Maud Cannon, are Cherokees by blood and are hereby re-admitted to all the rights, privileges, and immunities of Cherokee citizens by blood.

And a certificate of said decision of the Commission and of re-admission was made and furnished to said parties accordingly.

　　　　　　　　　　　　　　J.T. Adaid, Chairman Comm.
Henry Eiffert　　　　　　　　　　　D.W. Lipe
　　　　Clerk　　　　　　　　　　　Commissioner

(***NOTE:** Names spelled both ways.)

March 18, 1887
Docket #74　　　　　**PALMOUR**　　　　A.E. Ivey, Atty.
Rolls 1835, 1851 & 52

Baptist, Ind. Terr.

#	NAMES	AGE	SEX
1	J.A.	36	m

Ancestor: J.D. Palmour

Cherokee Citizenship Commission Docket Books
Tahlequah, Cherokee Nation (1880-84, 1887-89)
Volume I

Now on this the 11th day of August, 1887, comes the above case for final hearing, and having made application pursuant to the provisions of an act of the National Council approved Dec. 8, 1886, and all the evidence having been duly considered and found to be sufficient and satisfactory to the Commission; It is adjudged and determined by the Commission that J.A. Palmour, is a Cherokee by blood and he is hereby re-admitted to all the rights, privileges and immunities of a Cherokee by blood.

And a certificate of said decision of the Commission and of re-admission was made and furnished him accordingly.

	J.T. Adair, Chairman Comm.
Henry Eiffert, Clerk	D.W. Lipe, Comm.

March 29, 1887
Docket #75   **DAVIS**   A.E. Ivey, Atty.
Roll 1838(sic)

Atlanta, GA

#	NAMES	AGE	SEX
1	Delilah* J.	39	f
2	Mary	12	f
3	Susan	9	f

Ancestor: Lorenzo D. Davis

Now on this the 7th day of June, 1887, comes the above case for final hearing and having made application pursuant to the provisions of an act of the National Council approved Dec. 8, 1886, and all the evidence having been duly considered and found to be sufficient and satisfactory to the Commission; It is adjudged and determined by the Commission that Delila* J. Davis, Mary Davis, and Susan Davis, are Cherokees by blood and they are hereby re-admitted to all the rights, privileges, and immunities of Cherokee citizens by blood.

And a certificate of said decision of the Commission was made and furnished said parties accordingly.

	J.T. Adair, Chairman Comm.
Henry Eiffert, Asst. Clerk	John E. Gunter, Commissioner

(***NOTE:** Name spelled both ways.)

March 22, 1887
Docket #76   **PACE**   J.L. McCoy, Atty.
Roll 1835

Allawa, I.T.

#	NAMES	AGE	SEX
1	Elizabeth E.	48	f
2	Thomas	18	m
3	Mary	15	f
4	Edward	12	m

Ancestor: Nancy Lynch

Tahlequah, Oct. 23, 1888

We, the Commission on Citizenship after carefully examining all the evidence in the above case, and also the sworn statement of the applicant, who claims she is the grand-daughter if Nancy McWhorter, formerly Nancy Lynch, find that the testimony of James Wofford, which goes to show that Nancy McWhorter, the widow of Gater Lynch, did have one child by said McWhorter, but he did not know what became of it, nor did he know its name. He also states that Nancy McWhorter was a Cherokee, and there is no doubt of this.

The testimony of John T. Adair, who was formerly acquainted with the Lynch family and who was a near neighbor to them, and knows all the Lynch family, even every name, is very plain; he states that Gater Lynch's widow did marry McWhorter about the same time, and this was the only child she, Nancy, ever had by McWhorter.

The evidence of Johnson Thompson, who is a grand-son of Nancy McWhorter, knows nothing of the applicant, not even acquainted with her. From what he was told by the family, his grand-mother had one child by McWhorter, but don't(sic) remember whether it was a girl or boy; but was told that his grand-mother died in giving birth to the child, and that the mother and child both died about the same time.

Now after carefully summing up the whole of the testimony in this case, we are unable to find any proof whatsoever that the applicant is of Cherokee blood. Therefore, we the Commission unanimously agree and decide that Elizabeth E. Pace and her three children, Thomas, Mary, and Edward Pace, are not Cherokees by blood and not entitled to any rights and privileges of the Cherokee Nation, and are declared to be intruders upon the public domain of the same.

J.T. Adair, Chairman Comm.
D.W. Lipe, Comm.
H.C. Barnes, Comm.

March 22, 1887
Docket #77   **PACE**   J.L. McCoy, Atty.

188

Cherokee Citizenship Commission Docket Books
Tahlequah, Cherokee Nation (1880-84, 1887-89)
Volume I

Roll 1835

Allawa, I.T.

#	NAMES	AGE	SEX
1	Samuel E.	54	m

Ancestor: James Pace

Now comes this case for the final hearing. The application is accompanied by no evidence whatsoever and the name of the applicant and his attorney having been called three several times at an interval of one hour apart. The Commission adjudges that Samuel E. Pace is not a Cherokee by blood and is not entitled to citizenship in the Cherokee Nation. Rejected April 26, 1889.

Will P. Ross, Chairman
R. Bunch, Comm.

D.S. Williams, Clerk　　　　　　　John E. Gunter, Comm.

March 23, 1887
Docket #78　　　　　　**FURGUSON***　　　　C.H. Taylor, Atty.
Roll 1835

New Burnside, IL

#	NAMES	AGE	SEX
1	Minnie L.	20	f

Ancestor: Thomas F. Waters

On this the 5th day of April, 1889, the application of Minnie L. Ferguson* for re-admission to citizenship in the Cherokee Nation was submitted by her attorney, C.H. Taylor, to the Commission for decision. The applicant alleges that she is of Cherokee blood, being the daughter of Thomas F. Waters, who was the son of Wallace Waters, whose name can be found as she believes, on the census roll of 1835. There being no evidence whatever to support the application and the name of neither Thomas F. nor Wallace Waters being found on the roll of either 1835 or 1852, the Commission decides that Minnie L. Ferguson is not of Cherokee blood and therefore decree that she is not entitled to citizenship in the Cherokee Nation. Post Office address, New Burnside, IL. Rejected April 5, 1889

Will P. Ross, Chairman

D.S. Williams, Clerk　　　　　　John E. Gunter, Comm.

(***NOTE:** Name spelled both ways.)

March 23, 1887
Docket #79   <u>COX</u>   C.H. Taylor, Atty.
Roll 1835

New Burnside, IL

#	NAMES	AGE	SEX
1	Olive L.	18	f

Ancestor: Thomas F. Waters

The application of Olive L. Cox for re-admission to citizenship in the Cherokee Nation was filed the 23rd day of March, 1887, and submitted by Attorneys, April 24, 1889. There being no evidence whatever to identify claimant or establish her allegations in this premise; it is alleged by the Commission that Olive L. Cox, aged 18 yrs, is not entitled to citizenship in the Cherokee Nation by virtue of her Cherokee blood alleged to be the grand-daughter of one Wallace Waters, whose name may be found on the census rolls of Cherokees by blood taken in the year 1835. Post office New Burnside, IL. <u>Rejected</u> April 25, 1889.

Will P. Ross, Chairman
D.W. Williams, Clerk   John E. Gunter, Comm.

March 23, 1887
Docket #80   <u>WATERS</u>   C.H. Taylor, Atty.
Roll 1835

Falls River, KS

#	NAMES	AGE	SEX
1	Thomas F.	42	m
2	Thomas B.	13	m
3	Ernest H.	11	m
4	Charles F.	3	m
5	Mabel C.	2	f

Ancestor: Wallace Waters

The application of Thomas F. Waters for re-admission to citizenship on the grounds that he is a Cherokee by blood and that the name of his ancestor, Wallace Waters, may be found on the census rolls of Cherokees taken in the year 1835, was submitted to the Commission on the 24th day of April, 1889. This application was filed (the) 23rd day of March, 1887, but is submitted without evidence. The Commission therefore decrees that Thomas F. Waters, Thomas B. Waters, Ernest H. Waters, Charles F. Waters and Mable C. Waters, are not Cherokees by blood. P.O. address, Falls River, KS. Rejected April 25, 1889.

	Will P. Ross, Chairman
D.S. Williams, Clerk	John E. Gunter, Comm.

March 23, 1887

Docket #81	**GRANT**	(No Atty. given.)
Roll 1835		

Chouteau, I.T.

#	NAMES	AGE	SEX
1	Martha A.	40	f
2	William E.	13	m
3	James Oskar*	11	m
4	Henry Virgil	8	m

Ancestor: James G. Adams

This application filed the 23rd day of March, 1887, alleges that Martha A. Grant derives her Cherokee blood from her father, James G. Adams, whose name may be found on the census rolls of Cherokees by blood taken and made in the year 1835. The evidence in support of this application is found in the affidavit of Wiley Adams of Polk Co, Mx(sic), who states that Martha A. Grant is his niece and is the grand-daughter of James G. Adams, who moved west in the detachment of emigrating Cherokees conducted by Mr. Bushyhead, but stopped in Missouri (because of) impaired health and died there. The affidavit is inadmissible under the rule of the Commission because it is ex parte and the credibility of the affiant is not certified by the clerk of the county before whom it was made. Besides this, the name of James G. Adams is not found on the census rolls of 1835. The Commission therefore adjudges Martha A. Grant and her children, William E. Grant, James Oscar* Grant, and Henry Virgil Grant, are not of Cherokee blood and not entitled to citizenship in the Cherokee Nation and so decree. This 25th day of April, 1889.

	Will P. Ross, Chairman
George O. Butler, Clerk, Pro Tem.	John E. Gunter, Comm.

(***NOTE:** Name spelled both ways.)

March 24, 1887

Docket #82   **SHIVELY**   C.H. Taylor, Atty.
Roll 1835

Coffeyville, KS

#	NAMES	AGE	SEX
1	Margarett	47	f

Ancestor: Nancy Pathkiller

See decision in this case in the Thomas Woodsides case in this book on page 115, (Docket #27). Sept. 18, 1888.

Cornell Rogers, Clerk   John E. Gunter, Commissioner

March 24, 1887
Docket #83   **SHIVELY**   C.H.
Taylor, Atty.
Roll 1835

Coffeyville, KS

#	NAMES	AGE	SEX
1	Charles M.	20	m

Ancestor: Margarett Shively
See decision in the above case in the Thomas Woodsides case on page 115 of this book (Docket #27). Adverse. Sept. 18, 1888
Cornell Rogers, Clerk

March 24, 1887
Docket #84   **DAY**   C.H. Taylor, Atty.
Roll 1835

Coffeyville, KS

#	NAMES	AGE	SEX
1	Mary N.	22	f

Ancestor: Margarett Shively

See decision in this case on page 115 of this book (Docket #27) in the Thomas Woodsides case. Adverse. Sept. 18, 1888

March 24, 1887
Docket #85   **WOODSIDES**   C.H. Taylor, Atty.
Roll 1835

Coffeyville, KS
192

Cherokee Citizenship Commission Docket Books
Tahlequah, Cherokee Nation (1880-84, 1887-89)
Volume I

#	NAMES	AGE	SEX
1	Dillard	34	m

Ancestor: Nancy Pathkiller

See decision in this case on page 115, (Docket #27) of this book, in the case of Thomas Woodsides. Adverse. Sept. 18, 1888

Cornell Rogers, Clerk

March 25, 1887
Docket #86   **ROGERS**   A.E. Ivey, Atty.
Roll 1835
Dalton, GA

#	NAMES	AGE	SEX
1	Jackson	70	m
2	Sarah Blackburn	67	f
3	Ridge W.	27	m
4	Sarah F.	23	f
5	Ella Wofford	12	f
6	Laura Wofford	10	f

Ancestor: John Rogers

Now on this the 18th day of Oct, 1887, comes the above case for a final hearing, and the parties having made application pursuant to the provisions of an act of the National Council approved Dec. 8, 1886. And all the evidence being duly examined and found to be sufficient and satisfactory to the Commission and the name of the ancestor John Rogers, appearing on the rolls of 1835; It is adjudged and determined by the Commission that Jackson Rogers, Sarah B. Rogers, Ridge W. Rogers, Sarah F. Rogers, Ella Wofford, and Laura Wofford, are Cherokees by blood and are hereby re-admitted to all the rights, privileges, and immunities of Cherokees by blood.

And a certificate of said decision of this Commission and re-admission was made and furnished to said parties accordingly.

D.W. Lipe, Acting Chairman
John E. Gunter, Commissioner

March 25, 1887
Docket #87   **BARD**   (No Atty. given.)
Roll 1835

Cherokee Citizenship Commission Docket Books
Tahlequah, Cherokee Nation (1880-84, 1887-89)
Volume I

Dalton, GA

#	NAMES	AGE	SEX
1	Laura M.	42	f
2	Lizzie H.*	18	f
3	Sallie B.	16	f
4	Laura May	14	f
5	James R.*	12	m
6	Thomas D.	9	m
7	Lovely	7	f
8	Robert B.	1 mo	m

Ancestor: Jackson Rogers

Now on this the 13th day of Oct, 1887, comes the above case for a final hearing and the parties having made application pursuant to the provisions of an act of the National Council approved Dec. 8, 1886. And all the evidence being duly examined and found to be sufficient and satisfactory to the Commission, and the name of the ancestor Jackson Rogers, appearing on the roll of 1835; It is adjudged and determined by the Commission that Laura M. Bard, Lizzie B.* Bard, Sallie B. Bard, Laura May Bard, James M.* Bard, Thomas D. Bard, Lovely Bard, and Robert B. Bard, are Cherokees by blood and are hereby re-admitted to all the rights, privileges, and immunities of Cherokees by blood.

And a certificate of said decision of the Commission and re-admission was made and furnished to said parties accordingly.

J.T. Adair, Chairman Comm.

John E. Gunter, Commissioner

(*NOTE: Both initials given.)

March 25, 1887

Docket 88 **ROGERS** C.H. Taylor

Roll 1835

Dalton, GA

#	NAMES	AGE	SEX
1	Henry C.	62	m
2	Mary K.	61?	f
3	Louisa P.	27	f
4	E.O.	25	f

194

5	W.W.	23	m
6	Stonewall	21	m

Ancestor: John Rogers

Now on this the 14th day of Oct, 1887, comes the above case for a final hearing and the parties having made application pursuant to the provisions of an act of the National Council approved Dec. 8, 1886. And all evidence being duly examined and satisfactory to the Commission and the name of the ancestor, John Rogers, appearing on the roll of 1835; It is adjudged and determined by the Commission that Henry C. Rogers, Mary K. Rogers, Louisa P. Rogers, E.O. Rogers, W.W. Rogers, and Stonewall Rogers, are Cherokees by blood, and are hereby re-admitted to all the rights and privileges of Cherokees by blood.

And a certificate of said decision of the Commission and re-admission was made and furnished to said parties accordingly.

D.W. Lipe, Acting Chairman
John E. Gunter, Commissioner

March 25, 1887
Docket #89　　　　　　　　**STRICKLIN**　　　　　　(No Atty. given.)
Roll 1835

Duluth, GA

#	NAMES	AGE	SEX
1	Sarah C.	30	f
2	Kate Clare	7	f
3	Elizabeth Louisa	4	f

Ancestor: Henry C. Rogers

Now on this the 18th day of Oct. 18, 1887, comes the above case for a final hearing, and the parties having made application pursuant to the provisions of an act of the National Council approved Dec. 8, 1886. And all the evidence being duly examined and found to be sufficient and satisfactory to the Commission and the name of the ancestor, Henry C. Rogers, appearing on the rolls of 1835; It is adjudged and determined by the Commission that Sarah C. Stricklin, Kate Clare Stricklin, and Elizabeth Louisa Stricklin, are Cherokees by blood and are hereby re-admitted to all the rights and privileges and immunities of Cherokees by blood.

And a certificate of said decision of the Commission and re-admission was made and (furnished) to said parties accordingly.

195

D.W. Lipe, Act. Chairman
John E. Gunter, Commissioner

March 25, 1887
Docket #90   **SCUDDER**   (No Atty. given)
Roll 1835

Dalton, GA

#	NAMES	AGE	SEX
1	Louis Blackburn	48	m
2	Jacob McCarty	16	m
3	Narcissa G.	14	f
4	Cherokee G.	7	f
5	Alphred B.	3	m
6	Louis B.	5	m

Ancestor: Elizabeth Blackburn

Now on this the 18th day of Oct, 1887, comes the above case for a final hearing and the parties having made application pursuant to the provisions of an act of the National Council approved Dec, 1886, and all the evidence being duly examined and found to be sufficient and satisfactory to the Commission and the name of the ancestor, Elizabeth Blackburn, appearing on the roll of 1835; It is adjudged and determined by the Commission that Louisa B. Scudder, Jacob McC. Scudder, Narcissa G. Scudder, Cherokee G. Scudder, Alphred B. Scudder, and Louis B. Scudder, are Cherokees by blood and are hereby re-admitted to all the rights, privileges, and immunities of Cherokees by blood.

And a certificate of said decision of the Commission and re-admission are made and furnished to said parties accordingly.

D.W. Lipe, Acting Chairman
John E. Gunter, Commissioner

March 28, 1887
Docket #91   **DANIEL***   B.H. Stone, Atty.
Roll 1835

Silomo(sic) Spgs, AR

#	NAMES	AGE	SEX
1	William H.	33	m

Ancestor: Ned Daniels*

Cherokee Citizenship Commission Docket Books
Tahlequah, Cherokee Nation (1880-84, 1887-89)
Volume I

Now came on this day for the final hearing of the above entitled case the Commission after investigating the papers in said case find that the applicant produces no evidence whatever to sustain his allegation, relying entirely on his application. Therefore, the Commission renders a decision adversely to claimant, William H. Daniels. <u>Rejected</u> April 26, 1889.

Will P. Ross, Chairman

D.S. Williams, Clerk

John E. Gunter, Commissioner

(***NOTE:** Both names given.)

March 28, 1887
Docket #92   **<u>CLEVELAND</u>**   C.H. Taylor, Atty.
Roll 1835

Jacksbouro(sic), TX

#	NAMES	AGE	SEX
1	Maggie	45	f
2	Rosa	17	f
3	Lillie	14	f
4	Thomas	8	m

Ancestor: Thomas Burnette*

Tahlequah, Ind. Ter. Sept. 25, 1888
    Maggie Cleveland, et.al.
    P.T. Gooing, et.al.
    John B. Leach, et.al.
    In examining the applications and indexes in the above cases, we find they claim their Cherokee blood from Thomas Burnett, who moved from South Carolina to the state of Alabamma(sic) in the year 1820. There lived until the year 1857, and died. Now if Thos. Barnett* was of Cherokee blood, his name should appear on the census rolls of 1835, and if he lived until 1857, his name should appear on
the census and pay roll of 1851 & 52 of Cherokees residing east of the Mississippi River at that time. We have carefully examined the rolls of 1835 -51 & 52, and fail to find the name of Thomas Barnett, the alleged ancestor. This Commission is govered(sic) in making up these decisions, by the 7th Sec. of the act creating this court, passed and approved, Dec. 8, 1888(sic), in which it requires all applicants to name their ancestor on some one of the several rolls. In this case, the applicants have failed to do, and thereby have not established their Cherokee blood. Therefore, we the Commission do hereby declare that,

Cherokee Citizenship Commission Docket Books
Tahlequah, Cherokee Nation (1880-84, 1887-89)
Volume I

Maggie Cleveland and her three children, Rosa, Lilly and Thomas Cleveland, in application #24; R.T. Gooing and Desser Gooing, in application #26; John B. Leach and Jesse L. Leach, in application #27; are not Cherokees by blood, and not entitled to any rights and privileges of the Nation. And if on the public domain of this nation are hereby declared to be intruders.

J.T. Adair, Chairman of Commission
D.W. Lipe, Commissioner
H.C. Barnes

(***NOTE:** Name spelled both ways.)

April 2, 1887
Docket #93   **HUBBARD**   E.C. Boudinot, Jr, Atty.
Rolls 1835, 1852 & 52

Tahlequah, C.N.

#	NAMES	AGE	SEX
1	Wilkerson [or Wick]	65	m

Ancestor: (No name given.)

In the matter of the claim of Wilkerson Hubbard for Cherokee citizenship, filed before this Commission on the 2nd day of April, 1887, alleging that his own name would appear on the rolls of Cherokees of the years 1851-1852 and 1835. This case is one that for a long time born(sic) before the court of the Cherokee Nation praying for citizenship. It was determined adversely to Mr. Hubbard, as the records show, on the 23rd day of June, 1879, by what is known as the "Cherokee Court".

The testimony before us is both for and against Mr. Hubbard as a Cherokee Indian, but the preponderance of it is in his favor, outside of the fact that the rolls of Cherokees contain his name. Mr. Siler says in his remarks on this family, "The wives of Benjamin Bracket, Lock Langley and Migs Bracket, claim they are sisters and daughters of Mr. Hubbard whose wife was a Wilkerson and a native of the Cherokee Nation. This is corroborated by persons of high standing who have long been well acquainted with Cherokee affairs. I find, however, their claim has been disputed by some persons, but from the best information I can get, they have enjoyed the benefits of the treaty" marked "allowed". The Mr. Hubbard spoken of in the remarks of Mr. Siler just quoted, is Urich Hubbard who married Nelly Wilkison, who were the parent of Wilkerson Hubbard, the applicant. Wilkerson Hubbard's name appears in the Pay rolls of Emigrant Cherokees of the year 1852, where he received money as such and receipted for the same.

We the Commission on Citizenship do hereby re-admit Wilkerson Hubbard to all the rights and privileges of a citizen of the Cherokee Nation. Nov. 1, 1888.

J.T. Adair, Chairman Comm.
H.C. Barnes, Commissioner
D.W. Lipe, Commissioner

April 2, 1887
Docket #94   **HUBBARD**   E.C. Boudinot, Jr, Atty.
Rolls, 1851 & 51, & 1835

Tahlequah, C.N.

#	NAMES	AGE	SEX
1	Thomas	33	m

Ancestor: Wilkerson Hubbard

Now on this the 24th day of April, 1889, comes for final hearing, the application of Thomas Hubbard for re-admission to citizenship in the Cherokee Nation as a Cherokee by blood. The evidence shows that Thomas Hubbard is the son of Wilkerson Hubbard, whose name appears on the roll of Cherokees made in 1852, and whose right to citizenship was decreed by the Commission on Citizenship Nov. 1, 1888, [See page 147, Docket #93].

The Commission therefore decrees that Thomas Hubbard is of Cherokee blood and is entitled as such to the rights and privileges of citizenship in the Cherokee Nation. April 24, 1889.

Will P. Ross, Chairman
P. Bunch, Commissioner
D.S. Williams, Clerk   John E. Gunter, Commissioner

April 2, 1887
Docket #95   **RICHIE**   E.C. Boudinot, Jr, Atty.
Rolls 1851 & 52 & 1835

Tahlequah, I.T.

#	NAMES	AGE	SEX
1	Mary Jane Richie	29	f
2	Andrew	6	m

Wilkerson Hubbard

Cherokee Citizenship Commission Docket Books
Tahlequah, Cherokee Nation (1880-84, 1887-89)
Volume I

The application of Mary Jane Richie for admission of herself and son, Anderson Richie, who was 6 yrs old at the date of filing of the same, April 2, 1887. Case of final hearing this 24th of April, 1889. The evidence shows that Mary Jane Richie is the daughter of Wilkerson Hubbard who was admitted to citizenship by the Commission, Nov. 1, 1888, [See page 147, Docket #93]. She and her son are therefore admitted to citizenship as of Cherokee blood. Rendered April 24, 1889.

Will P. Ross, Chairman
R. Bunch, Commissioner
Attest, D.S. Williams, Clerk   John E. Gunter, Commissioner

April 2, 1887
Docket #96   **BRACKETT**   A.E. Ivey, Atty.
Roll 1851

Wauhilla*, I.T.

#	NAMES	AGE	SEX
1	Benjamin	38	m
2	(Daniel R.)+	(17)	(m)
3	Caldonia S.	15	f
4	William T.	10	m
5	Louisa E.	7	f
5	Martha J.	4	f
6	(Arnelia E.)+	(6 mo)	(?)

Ancestor: (No name given.)

Now on this the 24th day of April, 1889, comes this case for final hearing and satisfactory showing having been made that the name of applicant, Benjamin Brackett, appears on the Siler roll of Cherokees by blood, taken and made in the year 1851. It is adjudged by the Commission that Benjamin Brackett is a Cherokee by blood and as such is entitled to citizenship in the Cherokee Nation. This decision includes the children of the said Benjamin Brackett, to wit: Daniel R. Brackett+, aged 17 yrs, Caldonia S. Brackett, William T. Brackett, Louisa E. Brackett, and Martha J. Brackett, and Arnelia E. Brackett+, aged 6 months. P.O. address, Wauhillau*, C.N. April 24, 1889.

Will P. Ross, Chairman
D.S. Williams, Clerk   John E. Gunter, Comm.

(***NOTE:** Place spelled both ways.) (**+NOTE:** Names added to chart.)

April 2, 1887
Docket #97   **BRACKETT**   A.E. Ivey
Roll 1851
Tahlequah, I.T.

#	NAMES	AGE	SEX
1	R.L.	22	m

Ancestor: Francis Brackett

Rejected April 23, 1889.

Now on this the 23rd day of April, 1889, comes the above case for final hearing. The only evidence supporting the application of R.L. Brackett is that of Benjamin Brackett, who is an applicant for admission to citizenship and testifies that he is the first cousin of Francis Brackett, whose name appears on the Chapman roll of Cherokees by blood, taken in the year 1852, and who was never married, but is the mother of two children, viz: R.L. Brackett and a daughter named Jane, who is now 26 or 26 years old.

The Commission regards the testimony as sufficient to establish the right as a Cherokee by blood of R.L. Brackett to citizenship in the Cherokee Nation and so decree. **Reconsidered and Admitted** - April 23, 1889.

                                        Will P. Ross, Chairman
D.S. Williams, Clerk   John E. Gunter, Comm.

Oct. 22, 1889

The above case was called for a final hearing and rejected on the 23rd day of April, 1889, upon the grounds of not being properly identified and now comes E.C. Boudinott, Atty for applicant and makes and files a motion asking for a Reconsideration of said case. Said case had been neglected by former Atty. for Applicant in getting of the necessary testimony. Now on this 22nd day of Oct, 1889, the Commission grants the above motion and proceeds to reconsider the above case and after the examination of the testimony of Benjamin Brackett, a cousin of applicant and Mrs. Anna Leach, a citizen of this Nation, and offers a careful investigation of the census rolls taken and made in the year 1852, find the name of Francis Brackett, the mother of applicant does appear now in view of this. . . (The entry stops here. No other information given.

April 6, 1887
Docket #98   **ORME**   A.E. Ivey, Atty.
Rolls 1835, 1848, 1851 & 52
                            Van Buren, AR

#	NAMES	AGE	SEX
1	S.F.	62	f

Ancestor: Mima Edwards

Now on this the 9th day of January, 1888, comes the above case for a final hearing. And the parties having made application pursuant to the provisions of an act of the National Council approved Dec. 8, 1886. And all the evidence being duly examined and found not to be sufficient and satisfactory to the Commission, and the name of the ancestor not appearing on the rolls as claimed in the application.

It is adjudged and determined by the Commission that S.F. Orme is not a Cherokee by blood and is hereby <u>rejected</u> and declared (an) intruder.

J.T. Adair, Chairman Commission
John E. Gunter, Commissioner

Attest, C.C. Lipe, Clerk   D.W. Lipe, Commissioner

April 6, 1887
Docket #99   **COUCH**   A.E. Ivey & J.M. Bell, Attys.
Roll 1835, 1848, 1851 & 52

Van Buren, AR

#	NAMES	AGE	SEX
1	Mary A.	64	f

Ancestors: Mary M. Couch, Mima Edwards

Now on this the 9th day of Jan, 1888, comes the above case for a final hearing. And the parties having made application pursuant to the provisions of an act of the National Council approved Dec. 8, 1886. And all the testimony being duly examined, and found not to be sufficient and satisfactory to the Commission. And the name of the ancestor, not appearing on the rolls as claimed in the application.

It is adjudged and determined by the Commission that Mary A. Couch is not a Cherokee by blood and is hereby <u>rejected</u> and declared (an) intruder.

J.T. Adair, Chairman
John E. Gunter, Comm.

Attest, C.C. Lipe, Clerk   D.W. Lipe, Comm.

Testimony in the above case will be found on Journal page 277 & 78. (Is below)

Tahlequah, I.T, Jan. 9, 1888

Cherokee Citizenship Commission Docket Books
Tahlequah, Cherokee Nation (1880-84, 1887-89)
Volume I

In the matter of the following named persons for citizenship, will be found in application [#1] of Mary A. Couch, all the testimony that relates to the parties named in applications #2 to 36, inclusive. They claiming the same ancestor, Mima Edwards, and the Attorney for Defendant and also the Attorney for the Nation mutually agreed that the case of Mary A. Couch should govern all as they claim their Cherokee blood through Mima Edwards, their ancestor who is also the ancestor of Mary A. Couch.

Therefore we, the Court, after carefully investigating the case, and examining the evidence, and see the census and pay rolls find that [Mary A. Couch in application #1; William Couch in application #2; Mo. J. Orme and daughter S.F, in application #3; Samuel N, John, Sarah E, Malissie, Emily, Silas, Laura Ann, Polly Ann and James Calvin Baker, in application #4; W.H, John A, Ada, William C, Peter A, George, Jr, and Jacob C. Beller in application #5; Henry M. Couch, and [those children not named] in application #6; Andrew, A.L, Maggie, Mamy, William H, Joseph, James, Sarah, Laradia, and Lizzie Couch in application #7; Louisa N, Mary E, Peter G, Soloman E, Julia A, James W, and Disia L. Wagner in application #8; Mary Ann, Samuel and Mary Magazino Smith in application #9; Sarah E, Mary F, William A, M.J, Henry P, and A.M. Huston in application #10; Andrew M, J.W, P.S, E.W, A.M, M.F, Ex(sic), H.M, and James Couch in application #11; James H, George W, William B, Andrew J, Lucrecia, James, Gorrer(sic) E, and Arthur L. Edwards in application #12; Mary E, Walter, Wallace, Eugene, Cathie, Sidney and Charlie Stewart in application #13; T.C, Daisy Bell, and Delilah May Stewart in application #14; Tempie, John, James, William, Ollie, Etta, Columbus, Tempie Jr, and Emma Whitam in application #15; James H. Wm C, James M, Mary L, Irena, George O, Nancy A, and Alabama Edwards in application #16; G.W, Anna L, James W, Mary M, Lucy A, and Pery W. Edwards in application #17; L.A, D.L, William, Wallace, Callie, Lizzie, and Eula Orme in application #18; P.C, Mary J, Lula, William, May and Lilly Orme in application #19; Malissa and Edna Burton in application #20; W..L.H, W.A.M, T.D.M, John C, Minnie E. and R.J. Couch in application #21; William Couch and four sons and daughters not named in application #22; Benjamin Franklin, Hiram H, Mary Paul, and Henry B. Edwards in application #23; Arizona and Tracy F. Bearden in application #24; E.M. Maney in application #25; B.C, G.W, and H.M. Orme in application #26; John Ann Couch and four children [minors] not named in application #27; William, C.P, George Washington, Anna Lee, Elizabeth, Silas and James Daniel Edwards in application #28; Mary Kirby and four children not named ages from 2 to 10 years in application #29; Mary Manerva, Rosa Mabell and Adell Brooks in application #30; Sarah M. and P.A. Long in

Cherokee Citizenship Commission Docket Books
Tahlequah, Cherokee Nation (1880-84, 1887-89)
Volume I

application #31; Silas P. Edwards in application #32; Ollie Edwards in application #33; Mary Thompson in application #34; F.J. and Melissa Orme in application #35; Dirinda, Rosa and May Huston in application #36; are not entitled to any rights and privileges of Cherokee citizens by blood.

J.T. Adair, Chairman Commission
John E. Gunter, Comm.
D.W. Lipe, Comm.

The names of Andrew Wagoner, James H, George A, Mallissa C, and Emory W. Wagoner in application #37; Henry M. Wagoner in application #38; And John C. Wagoner in application #39; were omitted on the other side, and the decision stands against them the same as in all the other cases where Mima Edwards appears as the ancestor.

John T. Adair, Chairman
John E. Gunter, Comm.
D.W. Lipe, Comm.

The names Adalia Creekmore in application #40; Emma Claunt and Allice(sic) Claunt in application #41; were also omitted and the decision stands against them as Minnie Franklin is a direct descendant of Mima Edwards.

D.W. Lipe, Commissioner
John E. Gunter, Commissioner

The names John M. Beller, Ada Lee, Arthur Eli, and Luler May Beller in application #772; W.R. Stone, J.A, Robt. A, Lellia M, and Bean Stone in application #488; James C. Stone in application #489; John Speld, William D, Pat, Robt B, and Columbus Speld in application #1896; Samuel A. Stone in application #490; Sarah E. Johnson in application #495; William Couch, wife & four children in application #856; Andrew Jackson Howell, Robt E. Lee, George Washington, William Oscar, William Hulbert, Joseph Matthew, William Edward; Ednor Olly; Deby Perline; and Maggie Howell in application #1472; Mary Catherine Moss, James R, George N, Mary E, Rebecca M; Alice and John T. Moss in application #1381; Mary T. Neal and Ollie Neal in application #1981; Rebecca Spears and her infant son 2 weeks old in application #1890; John G. Pennington, Jos W, Mary E, George R, and Gertrude Pennington in application #1309; Mary F. Smith, Sidnia Henrietta, Mary J, Jesse B, Sarah A, Augusta W, and Nelly M. Smith in application #1611; Harriette L Whittington, Sarah E, William T, Mary E, Stella M, and Fanny A. Whittington in application #1816; Elizabeth Speld, Henry T, and Delilah E. Speld in application #1617.

J.T. Adair, Chairman Commission
D.W. Lipe, Commissioner

April 6, 1887
Docket #100   **KIRBY**   C.H. Taylor, Atty.
Roll 1835

Harris Ferry, TX

#	NAMES	AGE	SEX
1	James D.	40	m
2	Asa R.	17	m
3	John H.	15	m
4	Goobah B.	13	m
5	Richard P.*	10	m
6	Jiler J.	8	m
7	James D.	6	m
8	Sophia L.	4	f
9	Sudie A.	2	f
10	Boy Baby not named	2 days	m

Ancestor: Richard Kirby

Tahlequah, Aug. 2, 1888

    The above case being submitted by Plaintiff's Atty. Mr. C.H. Taylor, on the above written date. The Commission on Citizenship after a careful and complete examination of the evidence, together with the rolls mentioned in the 7th Sec. of the law of Dec. 8, 1886, in relation to citizenship and known as the Rolls of 1835, 1848, 1852, and 1852, of Eastern Cherokees, find: that the name of Richard Kirby, the alleged Cherokee ancestor of the applicant, James D. Kirby, does not appear on any of these records of Cherokees; and in the matter of the testimony, it is useless for us to enter into a detailed summary of the same in the absence of the fact that the name of the person, or themselves, the applicants in this case, from whom they have tried to prove a Cherokee descent, fail to appear on any of the before mentioned rolls of Cherokees. The law says in substance is, that a person, an applicant, must be a person or the lineal descendant of a person whose name appears on some of these rolls, before this Commission can re-admit them to Cherokee citizenship. It is therefore adjudged and determined that James D. Kirby and his nine children, now residing in Texas, viz: Asa R. John H. Goobah B. Rachel P*, Jiler J, James D. Jr, Sophia L, Susie A. Kirby, and boy not named just down as 2 days old, are not Cherokees by blood, and are not entitled to the rights and privileges of such, and do hereby so declare.

J.R. Adair, Chairman Commission
H.C. Barnes, Commissioner

(***NOTE:** Both names given.)

April 6, 1887
Docket #101　　　　　**HOHIMER**　　　　C.H. Taylor, Atty.
Roll (None given)

Fall River, KS

#	NAMES	AGE	SEX
1	William E.	40	m
2	Nancy M.	17	f
3	Laura J.	13	f
4	James O.	9	m

Ancestor: Elizabeth Sidebottom

This application was filed the 6th day of April, 1887, and submitted by attorneys to the Commission April 24, 1889. The applicant alleges he derives his Cherokee blood from his grand-mother, Elizabeth Hohimer, nee Elizabeth Sidebottom whose name he believes may be found on the census rolls of Cherokees by blood taken and made in the year 1852. The evidence in this case consists of their exparte affidavits taken in Kansas and Missouri and which go to establish the fact the Wm E. Hohimer is the son of John Hohimer, the son of Elizabeth Hohimer whose maiden name was Elizabeth Sidebottom, but it does not show that he was a Cherokee or that he descended from a Cherokee and the name of his alleged ancestor not being found on the census rolls of 1835 is adjudged by the Commission and so declared that Wm E. Hohimer is not Cherokee by blood and as such not entitled to citizenship in the Cherokee Nation. This decision includes his children Nancy M. Hohimer, Laura J. Hohimer, and James O. Hohimer. Post Office Fall River, Kansas. This 25th of April, 1889.

Will P. Ross, Chairman Comm.
R. Bunch
Geo. O. Butler　　　　　　John E. Gunter
　　Clerk Pro. Tem.　　　　Commissioners

April 6, 1887
Docket #102　　　　　**SMITH**　　　E.C. Boudinot, Atty.

Rolls 1835, 1852, 1852

Vinita, Ind. Terr.

#	NAMES	AGE	SEX
1	Kansas	28	f
2	John Essey	3	f

Ancestor: Young Davis

Tahlequah, May 17, 1889

This day the above case coming on for final hearing and after examining the papers which was filed (the) 6th of April, 1887, we fail to find any evidence accompanying the application in support of claimant's Cherokee blood and in view of this fact, the Commission decides that applicants, Kansas Smith and his(sic) daughter John Essey Smith are not Cherokees by blood and are not entitled to Cherokee citizenship. P.O. Vinita, I.T.

J.E. Gunter, Comm.

Attest. D.S. Williams, Asst Clk.   R. Bunch, Comm.

April 7, 1887
Docket #103   **DAVIS**   (No Atty. given.)
Roll 1851

Cassandra, GA

#	NAMES	AGE	SEX
1	John, Jr.	40	m
2	Julia M.	18	f
3	Susan E.	14	f
4	Rachael	12	f
5	Mary	10	f
6	Burlvell M.	6	m

Ancestor: Martin Davis

On this the 7th day of April, 1887, comes the above case for final hearing, and having made application pursuant to the provisions of an act of the National Council of the Cherokee Nation approved Dec. 8, 1886. And all the evidence being duly considered and found to be sufficient and satisfactory to the Commission; It is adjudged and determined by the Commission that John Davis Jr, Julia M. Davis, Susan E. Davis, Rachael Davis, Mary Davis, and Burlvell M. Davis, are Cherokees by blood, and are hereby re-admitted to all the rights, privileges, and immunities of Cherokee citizens by blood.

And a certificate of said decision of the Commission and of re-admission was made and furnished the said parties accordingly.

J.T. Adair, Chairman of Commission
John E. Gunter, Commissioner
Henry Eiffert, Asst. Clerk   D.W. Lipe, Commissioner

April 7, 1887
Docket #104   **RIDGE**   E.C. Boudinot, Atty.
Roll 1835

Grass Valley, CA

#	NAMES	AGE	SEX
1	Andrew J.	52	m
2	Darsie B.*	25	m
3	Frank B.	14	m

Ancestor: John Ridge

Now on this the 7th day of April, 1887, comes the above named case for final hearing. And having made application pursuant to the provisions of an act of the National Council of the Cherokee Nation, approved Dec. 8, 1886. And all the evidence being duly considered and to be sufficient and satisfactory to the Commission; It is adjudged and determined by the Commission that Andrew J. Ridge, Darsie R.* Ridge, and Frank B. Ridge are Cherokees by blood and are hereby re-admitted to all the rights, privileges, and immunities of Cherokees by blood.

And a certificate of said decision of the Commission and re-admission was made and furnished to said parties accordingly.

J.T. Adair, Chairman of Comm.
John E. Gunter, Commissioner
Henry Eiffert, Asst. Clerk   D.W. Lipe, Commissioner

April 7, 1887
Docket #105   **BEATTY**   E.C. Boudinott, Atty.
Roll 1835

Nevada City, CA

#	NAMES	AGE	SEX
1	Alice* B.	39	f

Ancestor: John Ridge

Now on this the 7th day of April, 1887, comes the above case for final hearing and having made application in compliance with the provisions of an act of the National Council of the Cherokee Nation, approved Dec. 8, 1886. And all the evidence having been duly considered and found to be sufficient and satisfactory to the Commission; It is adjudged and determined by the Commission that Allis* B. Beatty is a Cherokee by blood, and is hereby re-admitted to all the rights, privileges, and immunities of a Cherokee by blood.

And a certificate of said decision of the Commission and of re-admission was made and furnished said parties.

J.T. Adair, Chairman
John E. Gunter, Comm.
Henry Eiffert, Asst Clerk   D.W. Lipe, Comm.

(*NOTE: Name spelled both ways.)

April 7, 1887
Docket #106   **RIDGE**   E.C. Boudinot, Atty.
Roll 1835

San Francisco, CA

#	NAMES	AGE	SEX
1	John R.	30	m
2	Noble John	2	m
3	George McLean	2 mo	m

Ancestor: John Ridge

Now on this the 7th day of April, 1887, comes the above case for final hearing. And the applicant having applied pursuant to the provisions of an act of the National Council dated Dec. 8, 1886. And all the evidence in the case being duly considered and found to be sufficient and satisfactory to the Commission; It is adjudged and determined by the Commission that John R. Ridge, Noble John Ridge, and George McLean Ridge are Cherokees by blood, and are hereby re-admitted to all the rights, privileges, and immunities of Cherokees by blood.

And a certificate of said decision of the Commission and of re-admission was made and furnished the parties accordingly.

J.T. Adair, Chairman Comm.
John E. Gunter, Comm.
Henry Eiffert, Asst. Clerk   D.W. Lipe, Comm.

April 7, 1887
Docket #107   **FRICK**   E.C. Boudinot, Atty.
Roll 1835

Nevada City, CA

#	NAMES	AGE	SEX
1	Nannie N. Frick	28	f

Ancestor: John Ridge

Now on this the 7th day of April, 1887, comes the above case for final
hearing and the applicant having made application in compliance with the provisions of an act of the National Council dated Dec. 8, 1886. And all the evidence in the case being duly considered and found to be satisfactory to the
Commission; It is adjudged and determined by the Commission that Nannie N.
Frick is a Cherokee by blood and is hereby re-admitted to all the rights, privileges, and immunities of a Cherokee citizen by blood.

And a certificate of such decision of the Commission and of re-admission
was furnished to said party accordingly.

John T. Adair, Chairman
John E. Gunter, Comm.
Henry Eiffert, Asst. Clerk   D.W. Lipe, Comm.

April 7, 1887
Docket #108   **NIVENS**   E.C. Boudinott
Roll 1835

Nevada City, CA

#	NAMES	AGE	SEX
1	Jessie B.	23	f

Ancestor: John Ridge

On this the 7th day of April, 1887, comes the above case for final hearing.
And the party having made application pursuant to the provisions of an act of
the National Council of the Cherokee Nation, approved Dec. 8, 1886. And all
the evidence in the case having been duly considered and found to be sufficient
and satisfactory in the case; It is adjudged and determined by the Commission
that Jessie B. Nivens is a Cherokee by blood and is hereby re-admitted to all
the rights, privileges, and immunities of a Cherokee by blood.

And a certificate of such re-admission by the Commission was furnished
the parties accordingly.

Cherokee Citizenship Commission Docket Books
Tahlequah, Cherokee Nation (1880-84, 1887-89)
Volume I

J.T. Adair, Chairman
John E. Gunter, Comm.

Henry Eiffert, Asst. Clerk   D.W. Lipe, Comm.

April 8, 1887
Docket #109   **RIGGLE**   E.C. Boudinot, Atty.
Roll 1835

Chouteau, I.T.

#	NAMES	AGE	SEX
1	Abe F.	40	m
2	Nannie Lee	17	f
3	Montie	15	f
4	Lula	1	f

Ancestor: Letha West

Now on this the 7th day of March, 1888, comes the above case for final hearing, and having made application pursuant to the provisions of an act of the National Council approved Dec. 8, 1886, and all the evidence being duly considered and found to be insufficient and unsatisfactory to the Commission; It is adjudged and determined by the Commission that Abe F. Riggle, Nannie Lee Riggle, Montie Riggle, and Lula Riggle, are not Cherokees by blood, and are therefore not entitled to any rights and privileges of Cherokee citizens by blood and are hereby rejected and declared intruders.

J.T. Adair, Chairman
Cornell Rogers, Clerk   John E. Gunter, Comm.

April 13, 1887
Docket #110   **WAKEFIELD**   C.H. Taylor
Rolls 1851 & 1852

Chouteau, Ind. Terr.

#	NAMES	AGE	SEX
1	Escobedo	20	m

Ancestor: Lydia Wakefield

Now on this the 22nd day of April, 1887. comes the above case for final hearing and having made application pursuant to the provisions of an act of the National Council approved Dec. 8, 1886. And all the evidence being duly considered and found to be sufficient and satisfactory to the Commission; It is adjudged and determined by the Commission that Escobedo Wakefield is a Cherokee by blood and he is hereby re-admitted to all the rights, privileges, and immunities of Cherokee citizens by blood.

And a certificate of said decision of the Commission and of re-admission was made and furnished said parties accordingly.

J.T. Adair, Chairman
John E. Gunter, Comm.

C.C. Lipe, Clerk   D.W. Lipe, Comm.

April 16, 1887
Docket #111   **SMITH**   J.H. Aiken, Atty.
Rolls 1835 & 1851

Chouteau, I.T.

#	NAMES	AGE	SEX
1	Emeline T.	40	f
2	James A.	20	m
3	Dedril T.	18	m
4	John E.	13	m
5	Landan C.	11	m
6	Captola	9	f
7	William G.	6	m
8	Arthur J.	3	m

Ancestor: Mahala Jones

On this the 11th day of Oct, 1888, comes the above case up for final hearing; it having been regularly submitted on the 8th inst. Mrs. Emaline T. Smith, the applicant in the above case claiming a Cherokee descend from, nee Mahaly Jones, whom they align was the daughter of William Jones, a Cherokee. The testimony in this case would lead one to suppose that Mahaly Jones was the daughter of William Jones, but the "Old Settler" roll of Cherokees made in this Nation in the year 1851, shows that

William Jones lived in Delaware Dist, Cherokee Nation, and was a Cherokee Indian, and that he had at that time, children in his family named as follows: Mary Jones, Lucinda Jones, Drew Jones, and Julian Jones, but no Mahaly Jones appears thereon as the daughter of William Jones, or otherwise, hence; It is useless for the Commission on Citizenship to recount the testimony of Mrs. Smith, for in the absence of the fact that the rolls laid down in the 7th Sec. of the act of Dec. 8, 1886, and the amendment thereto of Feb. 7, 1888, do not contain the name of Mahaly Jones, who married a Mayes or the applicant herself, in the absence of which, we say; This Commission cannot grant citizenship in the Cherokee Nation. Therefore, We, the Commission on Citizenship, after fully considering the testimony submitted, as well as the rolls of Cherokees mentioned in the laws before named, are of the opinion and do hereby declare, that Emaline T. Smith and her seven children, viz: James A, Dedril T, John E, Landan C, Captola, William G, and Arthur J. Smith are not Cherokees by blood, and are not entitled to any of the rights and privileges of citizens of the Cherokee Nation by blood, and are intruders upon the public domain of the Cherokee Nation. Oct. 11, 1888.

J.T. Adair, Chairman
H.C. Barnes, Comm.

April 16, 1887
Docket #112   **SWIFT**   A.E. Ivey, Atty.
Roll 1835

Girara, KS

#	NAMES	AGE	SEX
1	Martha	39	f
2	Frank T.	20	m
3	Ben W.	19	m
4	James F.	17	m

Ancestor: Polly Sanders

Now on this the 19th day of April comes the above named case for final hearing and having made application pursuant to the provisions of an act of the National Council approved Dec. 8, 1886. And all the evidence being duly considered and found to be sufficient and satisfactory to the Commission; It is adjudged and determined by the Commission that Martha Swift, Frank T. Swift, Benj. W. Swift, and James F. Swift are Cherokees by blood and they are hereby re-admitted to all the rights, privileges, and immunities of Cherokee citizens by blood.

And a certificate of said decision of the Commission and of re-admission was made and furnished said parties accordingly.

J.T. Adair, Chairman
John E. Gunter, Commissioner

C.C. Lipe, Clerk   D.W. Lipe, Commissioner

April 18, 1887
Docket #113   **MONTGOMERY**   B.H. Stone, Atty.
Roll 1835

Maysville, AR

#	NAMES	AGE	SEX
1	John M.	48	m
2	James K.	15	m
3	Isaac L.	13	m

Ancestor: Thomas Gobbare

Now on this the 15th day of September, 1887, comes the above case for final hearing. And having made application pursuant to the provisions of an act of the National Council approved Dec. 8, 1886. And all the evidence being duly considered and found not to be sufficient and satisfactory to the Commission; It is adjudged and determined by the Commission that John M. Montgomery, James K. Montgomery, and Isaac L. Montgomery, are not Cherokees by blood and they are hereby rejected and declared intruders by said Commission, and are not entitled to any rights of Cherokee citizenship.

J.T. Adair, Chairman

C.C. Lipe, Clerk　　　　　　　　　　　John E. Gunter, Commissioner

April 20, 1887

Docket #114　　　　　　　**HARRISS**　　　　　E.C. Boudinot, Atty.

Rolls 1835, 1848, 1852 & 1852

Vinita, Ind. Terr.

#	NAMES	AGE	SEX
1	Mary J.	37	f
2	J.G. Cass	18	m
3	Cora B. Cass	17	f
4	Lewis P. Cass	14	m

Ancestors: Wm P. Keys, Susan Holt

The applicant in this case claims to be the daughter of Susan Holt and William Pleasant Keys and claims that Susan Holt was a half-sister of Wm Holt, and also that she was born in the Cherokee Nation near Maysville, AR, and was taken from the Nation when about six months old by her parents and settled in Sereio(sic) County, AR. The applicant claims that her father, William P. Keys, was also a Cherokee Indian.

Polly Parris states that the applicant's father was Geo. Keys, and that she only knew from hearsay that Susan Holt was a half-sister of Wm. Holt, and the first time she even saw the applicant was in the fall of 1886, and that she does not remember of ever seeing the applicant's mother; said she did not remember

214

any Keys by the name of Ples - all she knows of the case is from what the applicant and Geo. Parris told her.

Mary J. Harris, the applicant's sworn statement shows that her father was named William Pleasant Keys. Levi Keys, a citizen of Tahlequah Dist. states in connection with this case that he was born in Alabama in the year 1828, and gives the name of all the Keys that he remembers of ever marrying among the Cherokees, but makes no mention of Pleasant Keys. The testimony of John L. McCoy is altogether of a hearsay nature. He seems to know nothing whatever of himself (this sentence stated as is on original); only from what he had been told and most of this by the applicant herself.

The affidavit of Winnie Ratcliff is conflicting. She said she was born in Alabama, and been here all her life, came here in 1828. Claims she is acquainted with M.J. Harris, the applicant, and that she know her when a child about six years old and that she was then living with Bill Holt, her brother, in Flint.

The applicant, Mary J. Harris, claims she left the Nation, near Maysville, AR, when she was about six months old and went to AR to live, if such was the case it was impossible for Winnie Ratcliff to have known anything about the applicant at the time of which she speaks. She also claims that the applicant lived in Flint Dist, about 12 years. Taking the statement of Winnie Ratcliff as a whole, there cannot be much importance attached to it. None of the census or pay rolls of "Old Settler" Cherokees show either the name of Susan B. Holt or William Pleasant Keys, the parents of the applicant, as set up. If the parents of Mary J. Harris were Cherokee Indians, why leave the home of their folks and go into the state of AR, as is clearly set up, taking the statement of the applicant herself. And then too, if Cherokees, why do the rolls of Cherokees mentioned in the 7th Section of Act of Dec. 8, 1886, and the amendment thereto of Feb. 7, 1888, in relation to citizenship, fail to contain their names?

It is the opinion of the Commission on Citizenship in the absence of the fact that the mentioned rolls, do not contain the name or names, of the ancestors of Mary J. Harris, the applicant, that she is not of Cherokee blood, and do therefore declare that she, Mary J. Harris, and her three children, namely: J.G. Cass, Cora B. Cass and Lewis P. Cass, are not Cherokees by blood and are not entitled to any of the rights and privileges of citizens of the Cherokee Nation on account of their blood, and are intruders upon the public domain of the same.

J.T. Adair, Chairman
H.C. Barnes, Comm.

Cherokee Citizenship Commission Docket Books
Tahlequah, Cherokee Nation (1880-84, 1887-89)
Volume I

D.W. Lipe, Comm.

April 21, 1887
Docket #115   **DAVIS**   B.H. Stone, Atty.
Roll 1835

Bartlesville, Ind. Terr.

#	NAMES	AGE	SEX
1	J. Newton	42	m

Ancestor: Nancy Davis

Now on this the 21st day of April, 1887, comes the above named case for final hearing, and having made application pursuant to the provisions of an act of the National Council approved Dec. 8, 1886, and all the evidence being duly considered and found to be sufficient and satisfactory to the Commission; It is adjudged and determined by the Commission that J. Newton Davis is a Cherokee by blood and he is hereby re-admitted to all the rights, privileges, and immunities of a Cherokee citizen by blood.

And a certificate of said decision of the Commission and of re-admission was made and furnished said parties accordingly.

J.T. Adair, Chairman
John E. Gunter, Comm.
C.C. Lipe, Clerk   D.W. Lipe, Comm.

April 22, 1887
Docket #116   **ALFRED**   A.E. Ivey, Taay.
Rolls 1835, 1848, 1851 & 1852

Adair, I.T.

#	NAMES	AGE	SEX
1	James I.	15	m
2	William L.	13	m
3	Walter H.	7	m
4	Ollie R.	5	f
5	C.L.	2	m
6	L.S.	41	m

Ancestor: Polly Alford

Tahlequah, May 9, 1889

The application in this case was filed the 21st day of April, 1887. It is sustained by no evidence and having been called three several times at inter-

216

vals of not less than one hour apart, the Commission decides that said Lawrence Alfred and his children, James J. Alfred, Wm L. Alfred, Walter H. Alfred, Ollie R. Alfred, and C.L. Alfred, are not Cherokees by blood and not entitled to citizenship in the Cherokee Nation. Post office Adair, Ind. Ter.

Will P. Ross, Chairman

E.G. Ross, Clerk John E. Gunter, Comm.

April 22, 1887
Docket #117 **MONTGOMERY** C.H. Taylor, Atty.
Roll 1835

Slatten*, AR

#	NAMES	AGE	SEX
1	Druciler* C.	28	f
2	Lee	11	m
3	David* N.	9	m
4	Martha C. [Twin]	5	f
5	Amanda O. [Twin]	5	f
6	John C.	3	m
7	Rosey E.	2	f

Ancestor: Martha E. Black

Tahlequah, I.T, Aug. 2, 1888

The above case being submitted by Descendants Atty. Mr. C.H. Taylor, on the above written date. We, the Commission on Citizenship, after a careful and complete examination of the evidence together with the rolls mentioned in the 7th Sec. of the law of Dec. 8, 1886, which are of the years 1835, 1848, 1851, and 1852, of Eastern Cherokees, find that the name of Martha E. Black, or that of the applicant, Drucilla* C. Montgomery, are not enrolled thereon, and in the matter of the testimony in this case it is useless for us to enter into a detailed summary of the same in the absence of the fact that the name of the person or themselves, the applicant in this case, from whom they have tried to prove a Cherokee descent fail to appear on any of the before mentioned rolls of Cherokees.

The law says, or in substance is, that a person, an applicant, must be a person or the lineal descendant of a person whose name appears on some of the before mentioned rolls before this Commission can re-admit them to Cherokee citizenship.

It is therefore determined and adjudged that Drucilla C. Montgomery and her six children, viz: Lee, Davey* H, Martha C. Amanda O, John C, and

Rosey E. Montgomery of Slattler, AR, are not Cherokees by blood, and are not entitled to the rights and privileges of such, and do hereby so declare.

J.T. Adair, Chairman Commission

H.C. Barnes, Commissioner

(***NOTE:** Names spelled both ways.)

April 22, 1887
Docket #118   **PARKER**   C.H. Taylor, Atty.
Roll 1835

Vinita, I.T.

#	NAMES	AGE	SEX
1	Geo.* W.	46	m
2	John	21	m
3	Josephine	17	f
4	Edward	14	m
5	Thomas	10	m

Ancestor: Henry Parker

Sept. 25, 1888

George* W. Parker, et.al.   John A. Parker & son
Joseph P. Parker   E.A. Parker, et.al
Joseph A. Parker   Wm. A. Parker
Millie E. Christopher & daughter   Joseph P. Parker, et.al.

In the matter of the above claimants to Cherokee citizenship, will say that we have examined the various affidavits in the several cases, and we fail to find any positive proof that they are Cherokees, all the affidavits in the matter seem to only state what the parties told themselves, the applicant may be of Cherokee blood, but they have failed to convince the Commission that they are of Cherokee Indian blood. It is more than probable they are of Catawba Indian blood, as the evidence shows their ancestors were from South Carolina, once the abode of the Catawba. Render the 7th Section of the act creating this Commission, and formed by the National Council Dec. 8, 1886. It technically states that all persons, applicants before the Commission, must name some ancestor whose name appears on some one of the several rolls taken by the government from 1835 up to 1852. We have carefully examined all the said rolls and failed to find any of the alleged ancestors of the within applicants.

Now we the Commission after summing up all the testimony in these cases, find that there is not sufficient proof to justify a decision in the favor,

Cherokee Citizenship Commission Docket Books
Tahlequah, Cherokee Nation (1880-84, 1887-89)
Volume I

therefore we are of the opinion they are not Cherokees by blood, and so decide, and are not entitled to any rights and privileges of the Cherokee Nation. Therefore, John W.* Parker and his four children, John, Josephine, Edward and Thomas in application #17; Millie E. Christopher and daughter, Gertrude in application #18; William A. Parker in application #19; Joseph A. Parker in application #20; E.A. Parker and his two children, Earnest and Clandy(sic) in application #21; Joseph P. Parker in application #22; John A. Parker and son, William E. in application #23; Joseph P. Parker and his five children, Frank, Willie A, Fannie L, Lucy M, and James G. Parker; are intruders upon the public domain of the Cherokee Nation.

> J.T. Adair, Chairman of the Commission
> D.W. Lipe, Comm.
> H.C. Barnes, Comm.

(***NOTE:** Both names given.)

April 26, 1887
Docket #119   **SPRIGGS**   E.C. Boudinot, Atty.
Rolls 1835, 1851, 1852

(No Post Office given)

#	NAMES	AGE	SEX
1	Alexander A.	28	m
2	John Benjamin	2	m

Ancestor: Polly Ann Spriggs

Now on this the 26th day of April, 1887, comes the above case for a final hearing. And having made application pursuant to the provisions of an act of the National Council approved Dec. 8, 1886, and all of the evidence having been duly considered, and found to be sufficient and satisfactory to the Commission; It is adjudged and determined by the Commission that Alexander A. Spriggs and John Benjamin Spriggs are Cherokees by blood and are hereby re-admitted to all the rights, privileges, and immunities of Cherokees by blood.

And a certificate of said decision of the Commission and of re-admission was made and furnished to said parties accordingly.

> J.T. Adair, Chairman Commission
> John E. Gunter, Commissioner

Henry Eiffert, Asst. Clerk   D.W. Lipe, Commissioner

April 26, 1887

Docket #120   **PEAK**   C.H. Taylor, Atty.
Roll 1835

Rogers, AR

#	NAMES	AGE	SEX
1	William A.	52	m
2	Charles O.	32	m
3	Daniel L.	28	m

Ancestor: Absolum Peak

Tahlequah, June 12, 1889

The application in this case alleges that he is descended from one Absolum Peak, whose name he believes will be found on the census rolls of Cherokees by blood taken and made in the year 1835. The evidence shows that Absolum Peak was a white man and not an Indian by blood or intermarriage. Further his name does not appear on the census roll of 1835. The Commission decides that William A. Peak, and his sons, Charles A. Peak and David S. Peak, are not of Cherokee blood and not entitled to admission to citizenship in the Cherokee Nation. P.O. Rogers, AR.

J.E. Gunter, Comm.

Attest, D.S. Williams, Asst. Clerk Comm.   R. Bunch, Comm.

April 27, 1887
Docket #121   **RICH**   B.H. Stone, Atty.
Rolls 1835 & 1852

Fort Gibson, I.T.

#	NAMES	AGE	SEX
1	Albert Rich	31	m

Ancestor: Ellie Rich

Now comes on this day for the final hearing of the above entitled case. The Commission after investigating the papers in said case find that the applicant produces no evidence whatever to sustain the allegations set forth in his application relying entirely on his application. Therefore the Commission renders a decision adversely to Albert Rich. Rejected, this April 26, 1889.

Will P. Ross, Chairman
R. Bunch, Comm.

D.S. Williams, Clerk   John E. Gunter, Comm.

April 28, 1887

Docket #122   **HICKS**   (No Atty. given.)
Roll 1835

Mountain City, NE

#	NAMES	AGE	SEX
1	Senora*	64	m
2	Jane	12	f
3	Hannah	10	f
4	Polly	8	f
5	Charles	6	m
6	Edward	3	m
7	Jessie*	2 mo	m

Ancestor: Elija Hicks

Now on this the 13th day of January, 1888, comes the above case for a final hearing and the parties having made application pursuant to the provisions of an act of the National Council approved Dec. 8, 1886, and all the evidence being duly examined and found to be sufficient and satisfactory to the Commission, and the name of the ancestor appearing on the roll of 1835. It is adjudged and determined by the Commission, that Sonora* Hicks, and his six children, Jane Hicks, Hannah Hicks, Polly Hicks, Charles Hicks, Edward Hicks, and Jesse* Hicks, are Cherokees by blood, and are hereby re-admitted to all the rights, privileges, and immunities of Cherokees by blood.

And a certificate of said decision of the Commission and re-admission was made and furnished to said parties accordingly.

J.T. Adair, Chairman
John E. Gunter, Comm.

Attest, C.C. Lipe, Clerk   D.W. Lipe, Comm.

(***NOTE:** Names spelled both ways.)

May 10, 1887
Docket #123   **MORRIS**   E.C. Boudinot, Atty.
Rolls 1851, 1852, 1835

Paw Paw, I.T.

#	NAMES	AGE	SEX
1	William A.	27	m
2	Sallie A.	23	f
3	Emma L.	19	f
4	Mattie C.	17	f

5	James J.	13	m
6	Madge L.	11	f
7	John Y.	6	m
8	Answell F.	51	m

Ancestor: Letitia Little

Now on this the 16th day of June, 1887, comes the above case for final hearing. The applicants having filed this application on compliance with an act of the National Council approved Dec. 8, 1886, and all the evidence having been submitted and examined and having also made a careful examination of the rolls of 1848, 1835, 1851 & 2, fail to find any of the names of applicants or their ancestor upon said rolls. Therefore, we the Commission declare the above applicants, William A. Morris, Sallie A. Morris, Emma L. Morris, Walter C. Morris, James J. Morris, Madge L. Morris, John Y Morris and Answell F. Morris, not entitled to any rights or privileges of Cherokee citizens by blood.

J.T. Adair, Chairman

Attest, Henry Eiffert, Clerk   John E. Gunter, Comm.

May 11, 1887
Docket #124   **SCOTT**   A.E. Ivey, Atty.
Rolls 1835, 1848, 1851

Maysville, AR

#	NAMES	AGE	SEX
1	M.C.	56	m
2	Matilda	25	d
3	Julia	23	f
4	Sarah E. (Lester)	6	f

Ancestor: Abraham Scott

Tahlequah, May 9, 1889

The application in this case was filed the 11th day of May, 1887. It is supported by no evidence. And the parties having been called three several times at intervals of not less than one hour apart. The Commission decided that M.C. Scott and his daughters, Matilda Scott, Julia Ann Scott, and his grand-daughter, Sarah E. Lester, are not of Cherokee blood and not entitled to citizenship in the Cherokee Nation.

Will P. Ross, Chairman

Attest, D.S. Williams, Clk.   John E. Gunter, Comm.

April 28, 1887
Docket #125   **WELCH**   C.H. Taylor, Atty.
Roll 1851
Flint, I.T.

#	NAMES	AGE	SEX
1	Rebecca	21	f

Ancestor: John E. Welch

Now on this the 28th day of April, 1887, comes the above case for final hearing and having made application pursuant to the provisions of an act of the National Council approved Dec. 8, 1886, and all the evidence being duly considered and found to be sufficient and satisfactory to the Commission; It is adjudged and determined by the Commission that Rebecca Welch is a Cherokee by blood and she is hereby re-admitted to all the rights, privileges, and immunities of a Cherokee citizen by blood.

And a certificate of said decision of the Commission and of re-admission was made and furnished said parties accordingly.

J.T. Adair, Chairman
John E. Gunter, Comm.
Henry Eiffert, Asst. Clerk   D.W. Lipe, Comm.

May 16, 1887
Docket #126   **ROGERS**   L.B. Bell, Atty.
Roll 1835
Sheltonville, GA

#	NAMES	AGE	SEX
1	Robert N.	49	m
2	Mary L.	20	f
3	Joseph R.	16	m
4	Julia E. McNair	14	f
5	Raymona C.	12	m
6	Sarah L.	9	f
7	Cleo A.	6	f
8	Ernest H.	1	m

Ancestors: Wm. Rogers and Mary V. McNair

Now on this the 18th day of October, comes the above case for a final hearing and the parties having made application pursuant to the provisions of an act of the National Council approved Dec. 8, 1886. And the evidence being duly examined and found to be sufficient and satisfactory to the Commission and the name of the ancestors, Wm Rogers and Mary V. McNair, appearing on the rolls of 1835. It is adjudged and determined by the Commission that Robert N. Rogers, Mary L. Rogers, Joseph R. Rogers, Julia E. McNair, Raymona C. Rogers, Sarah L. Rogers, Cleo A. Rogers, and Ernest H. Rogers, are Cherokees by blood and are hereby re-admitted (to) the rights, privileges, and immunities of Cherokees by blood.

And a certificate of said decision of the Commission and re-admission were made and furnished to said parties accordingly.

D.W. Lipe, Act. Chairman
John E. Gunter, Comm.

May 16, 1887
Docket #127   **ROGERS**   L.B. Bell, Atty.
Roll 1835

Sheltonville, GA

#	NAMES	AGE	SEX
1	Augustus L.	35	m
2	Mary E.	13	f
3	Julia E.	10	f
4	May (or Mary) M.	6	f
5	John W.	4	m
6	Louisa E.	1	f

William Rogers

Now on this the 13th day of Oct, 1887, comes the above case for a final hearing. And the parties having made application pursuant to the provisions of an act of the National Council approved Dec. 8, 1886. And the evidence being duly examined and found to be sufficient and satisfactory to the Commission and the name of the ancestor, Wm Rogers, appearing on the rolls of 1835. It is adjudged and determined by the Commission that Augustus L. Rogers, Mary E. Rogers, Julia E. Rogers, Mary M. Rogers, John W. Rogers, and Louisa E. Rogers, are Cherokees by blood and are hereby re-admitted to all the rights, privileges, and immunities of Cherokees by blood.

And a certificate of said decision of the Commission and re-admission was made and furnished to said parties accordingly.

D.W. Lipe, Chairman
John E. Gunter, Commissioner

May 16, 1887

Docket #128   **BELL**   L.B. Bell, Atty.
Roll 1835

Sheltonville, GA

#	NAMES	AGE	SEX
1	Albina M.	56	f
2	Raphael L.	18	m
3	William P.	15	m
4	Allyus G.	11	m

Ancestors: Wm Rogers & Mary V. McNair

Now on this the 13th day of Oct, 1887, comes the above case for a final hearing. And the parties having made application pursuant to the provisions of an act of the National Council approved Dec. 8, 1886. And all the evidence being duly examined and found to be sufficient and satisfactory to the Commission, and the names of the ancestors Wm Rogers and Mary V. McNair, appearing on the rolls of 1835. It is adjudged and determined by the Commission that Albina M. Bell, Raphael L. Bell, William P. Bell, Allyus G. Bell, are Cherokees by blood and are hereby re-admitted to all the rights, privileges, and immunities of Cherokees by blood.

And a certificate of said decision of the Commission and re-admission was made and furnished to said parties accordingly.

J.T. Adair, Chairman
John E. Gunter, Comm.

May 16, 1887
Docket #129   **BELL**   (No Atty. given.)
Rolls 1851 & 52

Milledgeville, GA

#	NAMES	AGE	SEX
1	Edward E.	31	m

Ancestor: Josephine Scudder

Now on this the 13th day of October, 1887, comes the above case for a final hearing and the parties having made application pursuant to the provisions of an act of the National Council approved Dec. 8, 1886. And all (the) evidence being duly examined and found to be satisfactory and sufficient to the Commission and the name of the ancestor, Josephine Scudder, appearing on the rolls of 1851 and 1852. It is adjudged and determined by the Commission that Edward E. Bell is a Cherokee by blood and is hereby re-admitted to all the rights, privileges, and immunities of Cherokees by blood.

Cherokee Citizenship Commission Docket Books
Tahlequah, Cherokee Nation (1880-84, 1887-89)
Volume I

And a certificate of said decision of the Commission and re-admission was made and furnished to said parties accordingly.

J.T. Adair, Chairman
John E. Gunter, Commissioner

May 16, 1887
Docket #130   **BELL**   L.B. Bell, Atty.
Roll 1835

Sheltonville, GA

#	NAMES	AGE	SEX
1	Albert M.	31	m
2	Walter L.	28	m
3	Mary J.	22	f

Ancestor: W. Rogers

Now on this the 13th day of Oct, 1887, comes the above case for a final hearing. And the parties having made application pursuant to the provisions of an act of the National Council, approved Dec. 8, 1886. And all the evidence being duly examined and found to be sufficient and satisfactory to the Commission, and the name of the ancestor, Wm. Rogers, appearing on the roll 1835. It is adjudged and determined by the Commission that, Albert M. Bell, Walter L. Bell, and Mary J. Bell, are Cherokees by blood. And are hereby re-admitted to all the rights, privileges, and immunities of Cherokees by blood.

And a certificate of said decision by the Commission and re-admission was made and furnished to said parties accordingly.

J.T. Adair, Chairman
John E. Gunter, Comm.

May 16, 1887
Docket #131   **COUCH**   A.E. Ivey
Rolls 1835 to 1852

Van Buren, AR

#	NAMES	AGE	SEX
1	W.L.H.	31	m
2	W.A.M.	11	m
3	John C.	9	m
4	Minnie E.	4	f
5	R.J.	3	m

Cherokee Citizenship Commission Docket Books
Tahlequah, Cherokee Nation (1880-84, 1887-89)
Volume I

Ancestor: Mima Edwards

Now on this the 9th day of January, 1888, comes the above case for a final hearing and the parties having made application pursuant to the provisions of an act of the National Council, approved Dec. 8, 1886. And all the evidence being duly examined and found not to be sufficient and satisfactory to the Commission. And the name of the ancestor not appearing on the rolls as claimed in the application.

It is adjudged and determined by the Commission, that W.L.H. Couch, W.A.M. Couch, John C. Couch, Minnie E. Couch, and R.J. Couch, are not Cherokees by blood and are hereby <u>rejected</u> and declared intruders.

J.T. Adair, Chairman
John E. Gunter, Comm.

Attest, C.C. Lipe, Clerk   D.W. Lipe, Comm.

May 16, 1887
Docket #132   **COUCH**   A.E. Ivey, Atty.
Rolls 1835 to 1852

Van Buren, AR

#	NAMES	AGE	SEX
1	Andrew M.	44	m
2	J.W.	23	m
3	P.S.	19	m
4	E.W.	16	m
5	A.M.	9	m
6	F.M.	7	f
7	Ex	6	m
8	H.M.	3	m
9	James	1	m

Ancestor: Mima Edwards

Now on this the 9th day of January, 1888, comes the above case for a final hearing. And the parties having made application pursuant to the provisions of an act of the National Council, approved Dec. 8, 1886. And all the evidence having been duly examined and found not to be sufficient and satisfactory to the Commission, and the name of the ancestor, not appearing on the rolls as claimed in the application.

It is adjudged and determined by the Commission, that Andrew M. Couch, J.W. Couch, P.S. Couch, E.W. Couch, A.M. Couch, F.M. Couch, Ex

Couch, M.H. Couch, and James Couch, are not Cherokees by blood, and is hereby rejected and declared intruders.

	J.T. Adair, Claimant
	John E. Gunter, Comm.
Attest, C.C. Lipe, Clerk	D.W. Lipe, Comm.

May 16, 1887
Docket #133   **ORME**   A.E. Ivey, Atty.
Rolls 1835 to 1852

Van Buren, AR

#	NAMES	AGE	SEX
1	P.C.	34	m
2	Mary J.	14	f
3	Lula	12	f
4	William	8	m
5	May	6	f
6	Lillie*	4	f

Ancestor: Mima Edwards

Now on this the 9th day of January, 1888, comes the above case for a final hearing, and the parties having made application pursuant to the provisions of an act of the National Council, approved Dec. 8, 1886. And all the evidence being duly examined and found not to be sufficient and satisfactory to the Commission, and the names of the ancestor, not appearing on the rolls, as claimed in the application.

It is adjudged and determined by the Commission that P.C. Orme, Mary J. Orme, Lula Orme, William Orme, May Orme, and Lilly* Orme, are not Cherokees by blood and are hereby rejected and declared intruders.

	J.T. Adair, Chairman
	John E. Gunter, Comm.
Attest, C.C. Lipe, Clk.	D.W. Lipe, Comm.

(***NOTE:** Name spelled both ways.)

May 16, 1887
Docket #134   **ORME**   A.E. Ivey, Atty.
Rolls 1835 to 1852

Van Buren, AR

Cherokee Citizenship Commission Docket Books
Tahlequah, Cherokee Nation (1880-84, 1887-89)
Volume I

#	NAMES	AGE	SEX
1	L.A.	35	m
2	D.C.	16	f
3	William	14	m
4	Wallace	12	m
5	Callie	10	f
6	Lizzie	8	f
7	Eula	6	f

Ancestor: Mima Edwards

Now on this the 9th day of January, 1888, comes the above case for a final hearing, and the parties having made application pursuant to the provisions of an act of the National Council, approved Dec. 8, 1886. And all the evidence being duly examined and found to not be sufficient and satisfactory to the Commission. And the name of (the) ancestor not appearing on the rolls, as claimed in the application.

It is adjudged and determined by the Commission, that L.A. Orme, D.L. Orme, William Orme, Wallace Orme, Callie Orme, Lizzie Orme, and Eula Orme, are not Cherokees by blood and are hereby rejected, and declared to be intruders.

	J.T. Adair, Chairman
	John E. Gunter
Attest, C.C. Lipe	D.W. Lipe
Clerk	Commissioners

May 16, 1887
Docket #135   **ORME**   A.E. Ivey, Atty.
Rolls 1835 to 1852

Van Buren, AR

#	NAMES	AGE	SEX
1	B.C.	26	m
2	G.W.	4	m
3	H.M.	1	m

Ancestor: Mima Edwards

Now on this the 9th day of Jan, 1888, comes the above case for a final hearing. And the parties having made application pursuant to the provisions of an act of the National Council, approved Dec. 8, 1886. And all the evidence being duly examined and found not to be sufficient and satisfactory to the Commission.

It is adjudged and determined by the Commission, that B.C. Orme, G.W. Orme, and H.M. Orme, are not Cherokees by blood, and are hereby rejected and declared intruders.

J.T. Adair, Chairman
John E. Gunter, Comm.
Attest, C.C. Lipe, Clerk   D.W. Lipe, Comm.

May 16, 1887
Docket #136   **ORME**   A.E. Ivey, Atty.
Roll 1835 to 1852

Van Buren, AR

#	NAMES	AGE	SEX
1	F.J.	16	m
2	Melissa	14	f

Ancestor: Mima Edwards

Now on this the 9th day of Jan, 1888, comes the above case for a final hearing. And the parties having made application pursuant to the provisions of an act of the National Council approved Dec. 8, 1886. And all the evidence being duly examined and found not to be sufficient and satisfactory to the Commission. And the name of the ancestor not appearing on the rolls, as claimed in the application.

It is adjudged and determined by the Commission that F.J. Orme and Melissa Orme, are not Cherokees by blood, and are hereby rejected and declared intruders.

J.T. Adair, Chairman
John E. Gunter, Comm.
Attest, C. C. Lipe, Clerk   D.W. Lipe, Comm.

May 16, 1887
Docket #137   **HOUSTON**   A.E. Ivey, Atty.
Rolls 1835 to 1852

Van Buren, AR

#	NAMES	AGE	SEX
1	Sarah E.	45	f
2	Mary J.	21	f
3	William A.	16	m

4	M.J.	13	f
5	Henry P.	9	m
6	A.M.	5	f

Ancestor: Mima Edwards

Now on this the 9th day of January, 1888, comes the above case for a final hearing and the parties having made application pursuant to the provisions of an act of the National Council, approved Dec. 8, 1886. And all the evidence being duly examined and found not to be sufficient and satisfactory to the Commission, and the name of the ancestor not appearing on the rolls as claimed in the application.

It is adjudged and determined by the Commission that Sarah E. Houston, Mary F. Houston, Wm A. Houston, M.J. Houston, Henry P. Houston and A.M. Houston, are not Cherokees by blood and are hereby rejected and declared intruders.

J.T. Adair, Chairman
John E. Gunter, Comm.

Attest, C.C. Lipe, Clerk   D.W. Lipe, Comm.

May 17, 1887
Docket #138   **BURTON**   A.E. Ivey, Atty.
Rolls 1835 to 1852

Van Buren, AR

#	NAMES	AGE	SEX
1	Melissa*	32	f
2	Edna	8	f

Ancestor: Mima Edwards

Now on this the 9th day of Jan, 1888, comes the above case for a final hearing, and the parties having made application pursuant to the provisions of an act of the National Council, approved Dec. 8, 1886. And all the evidence being duly examined and found not to be sufficient and satisfactory to the Commission, and the name of the ancestor not appearing on the rolls as claimed in the application.

It is adjudged and determined by the Commission that Malissa* Burton and Edna Burton are not Cherokees by blood, and are hereby declared intruders.

J.T. Adair, Chairman
John E. Gunter, Comm.

Attest, C.C. Lipe, Clerk   D.W. Lipe, Comm.

(*NOTE: Name spelled both ways.)

May 17, 1887
Docket #139   **BEARDEN**   A.E. Ivey, Atty.
Rolls 1835 to 1852

Van Buren, AR

#	NAMES	AGE	SEX
1	Arizona	28	f
2	Tray F.	1	m

Ancestor: Mima Edwards

Now on this the 9th day of Jan, 1888, comes the above case for a final hearing, and the parties having made application pursuant to the provisions of an act of the National Council, approved Dec. 8, 1886. And all the evidence having been duly examined and found not to be sufficient and satisfactory to the Commission, and the (name) of the ancestor not appearing on the rolls, as claimed in the application.

It is adjudged and determined by the Commission that Arizona Bearden and Tray F. Bearden are not Cherokees by blood and are hereby <u>rejected</u> and declared intruders.

                                        J.T. Adair, Chairman
                                        John E. Gunter, Comm.
Attest, C.C. Lipe, Clerk   D.W. Lipe, Comm.

May 17, 1887
Docket #140   **MONEY**   A.E. Ivey, Atty.
Rolls 1835 to 1852

Van Buren, AR

#	NAMES	AGE	SEX
1	M.E.	26	f

Ancestor: Mima Edwards

Now on this the 9th day of Jan, 1888, comes the above case for a final hearing, and the parties having made application pursuant to the provisions of an act of the National Council, approved Dec. 8, 1886. And all the evidence being duly examined and found not to be sufficient and satisfactory to the commission. And the name of the ancestor not appearing on the rolls as claimed in the application.

It is adjudged and determined by the Commission that M.E. Money is not a Cherokee by blood and is hereby rejected and declared to be (an) intruder.

> J.T. Adair, Chairman
> John E. Gunter, Comm.

Attest, C.C. Lipe, Clerk   D.W. Lipe, Comm.

May 17, 1887
Docket #141   **STEWART**   A.E. Ivey, Atty.
Rolls 1835 to 1852

Van Buren, AR

#	NAMES	AGE	SEX
1	Mary E.	40	f
2	Walter	16	m
3	Wallace	14	m
4	Eugenia	12	f
5	Cathie	10	f
6	Sidney	8	m
7	Charles	6	m

Ancestor: Mima Edwards

Now on this the 9th day of Jan, 1888, comes the above case for a final hearing, and the parties having made application pursuant to the provisions of an act of the National Council, approved Dec. 8, 1886. And all the evidence being duly examined and found not to be sufficient and satisfactory to the commission. And the name of the ancestor not appearing on the rolls as claimed in the application.

It is adjudged and determined by the Commission that Mary E. Stewart, Walter Stewart, Wallace Stewart, Eugenia Stewart, Cathie Stewart, Sidney Stewart, and Charles Stewart are not Cherokees by blood and are hereby rejected and declared intruders.

> J.T. Adair, Chairman
> John E. Gunter, Comm.

Attest, C.C. Lipe, Clerk   D.W. Lipe, Comm.

May 17, 1887
Docket #142   **LONG**   A.E. Ivey, Atty.
Rolls 1835 to 1852

Van Buren, AR

#	NAMES	AGE	SEX

1	Sarah M.	25	f
2	P.A.	2	m

Ancestor: Mima Edwards

Now on this the 9th day of Jan, 1888, comes the above case for a final hearing, and the parties having made application pursuant to the provisions of an act of the National Council, approved Dec. 8, 1886. And all the evidence being duly examined and found not to be sufficient and satisfactory to the commission. And the name of the ancestor not appearing on the rolls as claimed in the application.

It is adjudged and determined by the Commission that Sarah M. Long and P.A. Long are not Cherokees by blood and are hereby rejected and declared intruders.

J.T. Adair, Chairman
John E. Gunter, Comm.
Attest, C.C. Lipe, Clerk   D.W. Lipe, Comm.

May 17, 1887
Docket #143   **HOUSTON**   A.E. Ivey, Atty.
Rolls 1835 to 1852

Van Buren, AR

#	NAMES	AGE	SEX
1	Derinda	7	m
2	Rose May	4	f

Ancestor: Mima Edwards

Now on this the 9th day of Jan, 1888, comes the above case for a final hearing, and the parties having made application pursuant to the provisions of an act of the National Council, approved Dec. 8, 1886. And all the evidence being duly examined and found not to be sufficient and satisfactory to the commission. And the name of the ancestor not appearing on the rolls as claimed in the application.

It is adjudged and determined by the Commission that Derinda Houston and Rose May Houston are not Cherokees by blood and are hereby rejected and declared intruders.

J.T. Adair, Chairman
John E. Gunter, Comm.
Attest, C.C. Lipe, Clerk   D.W. Lipe, Comm.

234

May 17, 1887
Docket #144   **BANKHEAD**   A.E. Ivey, Atty.
Rolls 1835 to 1852
Van Buren, AR & Morgan, TX

#	NAMES	AGE	SEX
1	Geo. W.	34	m
2	Trader	7	m
3	Mary	6	f
4	John	4	m
5	Charles	2	m

Ancestors: Richard and Polly Blevins

Tahlequah, I.T, Oct. 30, 1888
 Geo. W. Bankhead, et.al.
 John T. Bankhead, et.al.
 E.J. Thompson

The above entitled case this day came up for final hearing. The applicants claiming for their ancestors Polly and Richard Blevins, who were their
grand-parents, and Elizabeth Jane Bankhead, nee Blevins, as their mother. After examining all the testimony in this case carefully, the Commission is of the
opinion that the applicants are Cherokees by blood. It is proven by the several
affidavits that the parties are what is termed "Old Settler" Cherokees, and were
living in the state of Texas at the time of the Old Settler payment in the year
1851. After carefully examining the Old Settler pay rolls, under the head of
"New Resident" we fail to find the name of Elizabeth Jane Blevins, but we find
that of Mahala Jane Blevins, we are of the opinion it was a mistake in the copy-
ing of the names, as we have discovered that mistake of the kind appears in
several families, and we were informed by one of the delegation, that the original rolls in the department were so mutilated that some of the names could not
be made out.
 Now, we the Commission on Citizenship after carefully deliberating on
the above cases for several weeks, unanimously agree, that George W. Bankhead, Trader, Mary, John, and Charles Bankhead, in application #1; John T.
Bankhead, Frank G, Elizabeth J, Eunice A. Bankhead, in application #2; and
E.J. Thompson, James P, William Carrol, George Taylor, Ora Lee, Stella S,
and Rhoda F. Thompson in application #3, are Cherokees by blood and under
the law creating the Commission, approved Dec. 8, 1886, and the amendment

thereto, are hereby re-admitted to all the rights and privileges of Cherokee citizens by blood.

J.T. Adair, Chairman of the Commission
D.W. Lipe, Commissioner
H.C. Barnes, Commissioner

May 17, 1887
Docket #145   **BANKHEAD**   A.E. Ivey, Atty.
Rolls 1835 to 1852

Morgan, TX

#	NAMES	AGE	SEX
1	John T.	32	m
2	Frank G.	9	m
3	Elizabeth J.	6	f
4	Eunice A.	2	f

Ancestors: Richard and Polly Blevins
See decision in this case in that of Geo W. Bankhead in this book, page 174 (Docket #144).
Admitted.

May 17, 1887
Docket #146   **ELLIOTT**   A.E. Ivey, Atty.
Rolls 1835 to 1852

Prairie City, I.T.

#	NAMES	AGE	SEX
1	Rebecca	61	f
2	George	26	m
3	Arminta	20	f
4	Nancy	18	f
5	Lydia	16	f
6	William	14	m

Ancestor: James Shook
Tahlequah, Sept. 29, 1888
In the matter of the application of Rebecca Elliott and her children for Cherokee citizenship, filed 16th day of May, 1887. We the Commission on Citizenship after a thorough search on the rolls of Cherokees mentioned in the 7th Sec. of the Act of Dec. 8, 1886, in relation to citizenship find that the name of Jane Shook from whom the applicants claim a Cherokee descent fail to appear

thereon. It is useless to recount the evidence in this case or any other in the absence of the only evidence that can be sufficient to re-admit parties to citizenship in the Cherokee Nation; i.e. to prove a descent from some one on the rolls mentioned above, (see Act of Dec. 8, 1886). Therefore, Rebecca Elliott and her five children, viz: George, Arminta, Nancy, Lydia and William Elliott, are not Cherokees by blood, and not entitled to the rights and privileges of such on account of their blood, and are declared to be intruders upon the public domain of the Cherokee Nation.

J.T. Adair, Chairman
H.C. Barnes, Commissioner

May 18, 1887
Docket #147   **DAVIS**   (No Atty. given.)
Rolls 1835

Cassandra, GA

#	NAMES	AGE	SEX
1	John	74	m
2	Jane	18	f
3	Robert	16	m

Ancestors: Daniel & Rachel Davis

Now on this the 18th day of May, 1888, comes the above case for a final hearing, and the parties having made application pursuant to the provisions of an act of the National Council, approved Dec. 8, 1886. And all the evidence being duly examined and found to be sufficient and satisfactory to the commission. It is adjudged and determined by the Commission that John Davis, Jane Davis, and Robert Davis are Cherokees by blood and are hereby re-admitted to all the rights, privileges, and immunities of Cherokees by blood.

And a certificate of said decision of the Commission and of re-admission was made and furnished to said parties accordingly.

J.T. Adair, Chairman
John E. Gunter, Comm.

Attest, Henry Eiffert, Clerk

May 18, 1887
Docket #148   **DAVIS**   (No Atty. given.)
Rolls 1851 & 52

Dahlonega, GA

#	NAMES	AGE	SEX

| 1 | Berilla | 27 | f |
| 2 | Daniel | 8 | m |

Ancestor: L.D. Davis

Now on this the 18th day of May, 1888, comes the above case for a final hearing, and having made application pursuant to the provisions of an act of the National Council, approved Dec. 8, 1886. And all the evidence being duly examined and found to be sufficient and satisfactory to the commission. It is adjudged and determined by the Commission that Berilla Davis and Daniel Davis are Cherokees by blood and they are hereby re-admitted to all the rights, privileges, and immunities of Cherokee citizens by blood.

And a certificate of said decision of the Commission and of re-admission was made and furnished to said parties accordingly.   J.T. Adair, Chairman

John E. Gunter, Comm.

Attest, Henry Eiffert, Clerk

May 18, 1887
Docket #149   **HARNAGE**   (No Atty. given.)
Roll 1835

Kilgore, TX

#	NAMES	AGE	SEX
1	Emily W.	55	f
2	Lena	17	f
3	John G.	70	m

Ancestor: Jessie Mayfield

Now on this the 21st day of May, 1887, comes the above case for a final hearing, and having made application pursuant to the provisions of an act of the National Council, approved Dec. 8, 1886. And all the evidence being duly considered and found to be sufficient and satisfactory to the Commission. It is adjudged and determined by the Commission that Emily W. Harnage and Lena Harnage are Cherokees by blood and they are hereby re-admitted to all the rights, privileges, and immunities of Cherokees by blood.

And a certificate of said decision of the Commission and of re-admission was made and furnished to said parties accordingly.

J.T. Adair, Chairman
John E. Gunter, Comm.
Attest, Henry Eiffert, Clerk   D.W. Lipe, Comm.

238

Cherokee Citizenship Commission Docket Books
Tahlequah, Cherokee Nation (1880-84, 1887-89)
Volume I

We the Commission on Citizenship after examining the evidence also the Old Settler Pay rolls of 1851, find that the applicant, John G. Harnage, is a Cherokee by blood and is hereby re-admitted to all the rights and privileges of a Cherokee citizen by blood, which is in compliance with an amendment of an act of the National Council dated Feb. 7, 1888, creating this Commission.

J.T. Adair, Chairman
D.W. Lipe, Commissioner

May 19, 1887
Docket #150   **HENDRICKS**   (No Atty. given.)
Roll 1852

Oklahoma, I.T.

#	NAMES	AGE	SEX
1	Carolina D.	14	f
2	Harriett	12	f
3	Milo A.	10	m
4	Theodosha	8	f

Ancestor: Lydia Holt

Tahlequah, I.T, Sept. 1, 1887

We the Commission on Citizenship after a careful examination of the evidence in the case of Carolina Hendricks and her three children, Harriett Hendricks, Milo A. Hendricks, and Theodosha Hendricks, find they are Cherokees by blood and are entitled to all the rights and privileges of Cherokee citizens by blood.

J.T. Adair, Chairman
D.W. Lipe, Commissioner

May 19, 1887
Docket #151   **BARNES**   (No Atty. given.)
Roll 1851

Briar Town, C.N.

#	NAMES	AGE	SEX
1	Alexander	28	m
2	Hiram	26	m
3	John	22	m

Ancestor: Elizabeth Brown

Cherokee Citizenship Commission Docket Books
Tahlequah, Cherokee Nation (1880-84, 1887-89)
Volume I

This application filed May 18, 1887, claims admission as Cherokees by blood for applicant and for his brothers, Hiram Barnes and John Barnes, as the grand-sons of one Elizabeth Brown, whose name is enrolled on the census rolls of Cherokees by blood taken and made in the year 1851. The application is supported by no evidence and the applicant having been called three several times at intervals of one hour apart each and not having answered in person or by attorney, the Commission declares judgment against the said Alexander Barnes, Hiram Barnes and John Barnes and direct them to report to the Principal Chief as intruders in the Cherokee Nation. Post Office, Briartown, C.N. This 25th of April, 1889.

| | Will P. Ross, Chairman |
| George Butler, Clerk Pro Tem. | John E. Gunter, Commissioner |

May 19, 1887
Docket #152   **KUHN**   John L. McCoy, Atty.
Rolls 1835 to 1852

Baltimore, MD

#	NAMES	AGE	SEX
1	Marian L.	9	f
2	Joseph	7	m
3	Ruthy* E.	7	f
4	Robt. B.	5	m

Ancestor: Ruthy E. Kephart

Tahlequah, May 29, 1889

The applicants in this case are Marian L. Kuhn, aged 9 years, Ruthey* E. Kuhn, aged 7 years, Joseph Kuhn aged 7 years (twins), and Robert B. Kuhn, aged 5 years, are the minor children of Mary Abigrail(sic) Kuhn, nee House, deceased; and are the grand-children of Ruth E. House, nee McCoy; whose name appears on the roll of Cherokees taken in the year 1852.

They are of Cherokee blood and the Commission so decided, and also that they are entitled to citizenship in the Cherokee Nation under the provisions of the act dated Dec. 5, 1888, creating this Commission. Post Office, #66 Pace Street, Baltimore, MD.

	Will P. Ross, Chairman
	J.E. Gunter, Comm.
Attest, E.G. Ross, Clerk	R. Bunch, Comm.

(***NOTE:** Name spelled both ways.)

Cherokee Citizenship Commission Docket Books
Tahlequah, Cherokee Nation (1880-84, 1887-89)
Volume I

Tahlequah, Oct. 22, 1889
Docket #151

Alexander Barnes vs The Cherokee Nation

The above case was called three several times for an hour and no response from applicant. The Commission therefore rejected this case on the 25th day of April, 1889.

And now comes the above applicant and asks for a reconsider of his case, and in doing so makes the following statement upon oath, his age is 30 yrs old and I live at Briar Town, Canadian Dist, Cherokee Nation. I did not know that my application for Cherokee citizenship was on file before the Commission on Citizenship until I heard that I was rejected. This was my first knowledge of the fact.

The Commission now upon the above statement does hereby agree to reconsider the above case and in so doing now proceed to take and hear the testimony of one Elis Brown who swears that his age is 40 years old and that he resides at Briar Town and that his mother's name was Elizabeth Brown, nee Crossland, a sister to Richard Crossland. The applicant's mother was named Mary Barnes, nee Brown. She was a sister of mine(sic), a daughter of Elizabeth Brown. The applicants, Alexander, Hiram and John Brown(sic) are her heirs and they are Cherokees by blood.

Now the Commission after an investigation of the testimony and upon an examination of the census rolls taken and made in the year 1852, on the Old Settler Rolls find the name of Elizabeth Brown, the ancestor of applicants.

Now in view of the above facts, the Commission decided that Alexander Barnes, Hiram Barnes, and John Barnes, are Cherokees by blood and are hereby re-admitted to all the rights and privileges of Cherokee citizens.

J.E. Gunter, Act. Chair.
R. Bunch, Comm.

May 19, 1887
Docket #153   **HAUSE***   John L. McCoy, Atty.
Rolls 1835 to 1852

Baltimore, MD

#	NAMES	AGE	SEX
1	Che-nah-sah M.	34	f

Ancestor: Ruthy E. Kephart

Tahlequah, May 29, 1889

It having been proven to the satisfaction of the Commission that the applicant in the above case is the daughter of Geo. W. House (dec.) and Ruth E. Kephart, nee House, nee McCoy, who is the daughter of Daniel McCoy, deceased, and who was formerly a Circuit Judge of the Nation and whose name is found on the census rolls of Cherokees by blood taken and made in the years 1835-52. It is adjudged by the Commission that Che-nah-sah M. House* is of Cherokee blood and is entitled to the rights of citizenship in the Cherokee Nation in accordance with the provisions of the "Act" creating this Commission on Citizenship dated Dec. 5, 1888.

Will P. Ross, Chairman

J.E. Gunter, Commissioner

Attest, E.G. Ross, Clerk   R. Bunch, Commissioner

(*NOTE: Name spelled both ways.)

May 19, 1887
Docket #154   **BACON**   John G. Harnage, Atty.
Roll 1835

Overton, TX

#	NAMES	AGE	SEX
1	Sabina*	30	f
2	Irena	8	f
3	Willie	5	f
4	Harnage	2	m

Ancestor: Nancy Harnage

Now on this the 21st day of May, 1887, comes the above case for final hearing. And having made application pursuant to the provisions of an act of the National Council approved Dec. 8, 1886, and all the evidence being duly considered and found to be sufficient and satisfactory to the Commission. It is adjudged and determined by the Commission that Sabrina* Bacon, Irene* Bacon, Willie Bacon, and Harnage Bacon, are Cherokees by blood and they are hereby re-admitted to all the rights, privileges, and immunities of Cherokees by blood.

And a certificate of said decision of the Commission and of re-admission was made and furnished said parties accordingly.

Cherokee Citizenship Commission Docket Books
Tahlequah, Cherokee Nation (1880-84, 1887-89)
Volume I

J.T. Adair, Chairman
John E. Gunter, Commissioner
Henry Eiffert, Clerk
D.W. Lipe, Commissioner

(***NOTE:** Names spelled both ways.)

May 19, 1887
Docket #155   **HARNAGE**   John G. Harnage,Atty.
Roll 1835
Overton, TX

#	NAMES	AGE	SEX
1	Nancy	67	f

Ancestor: Jessie Mayfield

Now on this the 21st day of May, 1887, comes the above case for final hearing. And having made application pursuant to the provisions of an act of the National Council approved Dec. 8, 1886. And all the evidence being considered and found to be sufficient and satisfactory to the Commission; It is adjudged and determined by the Commission that Nancy Harnage is a Cherokee by blood and she is hereby re-admitted to all the rights, privileges, and immunities of Cherokee citizens by blood.

And a certificate of said decision of the Commission and of re-admission was made and furnished said parties accordingly.

J.T. Adair, Chairman
John E. Gunter, Comm.
Henry Eiffert, Clerk
D.W. Lipe, Comm.

May 19, 1887
Docket #156   **BEAN**   John G. Harnage, Atty.
Roll 1851
Kilgore, TX

#	NAMES	AGE	SEX
1	C. Starr	67	m
2	Mary Ann	58	f
3	Wirt	25	m

Ancestor: Ruth Bean

Now on this day the 24th of January A.D, 1889, comes the above case of C. Starr Bean, his wife, Mary Ann Bean, and their son Wirt Bean, for final

243

hearing. And having made application pursuant to the provisions of the act of the National Council approved Dec. 8, 1886. And all the evidence being considered and found to be sufficient to establish the fact that the applicant C. Starr Bean is the son of Ruth Bean, a Cherokee Indian whose name appears on the Old Settler Rolls of 1851, and his wife Mary Ann Bean, is the granddaughter of John Martin, a Cherokee Indian.

It is adjudged and determined that C. Starr Bean, his wife, Mary Ann Bean, and their son, Wirt Bean, are Cherokees by blood and they are hereby re-admitted to all the rights, privileges, and immunities of citizens of the Cherokee Nation by blood under the Constitution and laws of said Nation.

And a certificate of the decision of the Commission and of re-admission was made and furnished said persons accordingly.

Will P. Ross, Chairman

E.G. Ross, Clerk — Rabbit Bunch, Commissioner

May 19, 1887
Docket #157 — **ROLAND*** — J.G. Harnage, Atty.
Roll 1851

Bellview, TX

#	NAMES	AGE	SEX
1	Emily	22	f

Ancestor: Ruth Bean

Now on this the 25th day of May, 1887, comes the above case for final hearing. And having made application pursuant to the provisions of an act of the National Council, approved Dec. 8, 1886. And all the evidence being duly considered and found to be sufficient and satisfactory to the Commission. It is adjudged and determined by the Commission that Emily Rowland* is a Cherokee by blood and that she is hereby re-admitted to all the rights, privileges, and immunities of a Cherokee citizen by blood.

And a certificate of said decision of the Commission and of re-admission was made and furnished said party accordingly.

J.T. Adair, Chairman
John E. Gunter, Comm.

Henry Eiffert, Clerk — D.W. Lipe, Comm.

May 20, 1887
Docket #158 — **BEAN** — J.G. Harnage, Atty.
Roll 1851

Kilgore, TX

Cherokee Citizenship Commission Docket Books
Tahlequah, Cherokee Nation (1880-84, 1887-89)
Volume I

#	NAMES	AGE	SEX
1	Jack	19	m
2	Henrietta	42	f
3	Nathaniel	13	m
4	Collus	6	m
5	Grover C.	3	m

Ancestor: Ruth Bean

Now on this the 21st day of May, 1887, comes the above case for final hearing. And having made application pursuant to the provisions of an act of the National Council, approved Dec. 8, 1886. And all the evidence being duly considered and found to be sufficient and satisfactory to the Commission; It is adjudged and determined by the Commission that Henrietta Bean, Jack Bean, Nathaniel Bean, Collus Bean, and Grover C. Bean, are all Cherokees by blood and they are hereby re-admitted to all the rights, privileges, and immunities of Cherokee citizens by blood.

And a certificate of said decision of the Commission and of re-admission was made and furnished said parties accordingly.

J.T. Adair, Chairman
John E. Gunter, Comm.

Henry Eiffert, Clerk   D.W. Lipe, Comm.

May 20, 1887
Docket #159   **MAYFIELD**   J.G. Harnage, Atty.
Roll 1835

Bellview, TX

#	NAMES	AGE	SEX
1	Sally	80	f

Ancestor: Sally Mayfield

Now on this the 21st day of May, 1887, comes the above case for final hearing. And having made application pursuant to the provisions of an act of the National Council, approved Dec. 8, 1886. And all the evidence being duly considered and found to be sufficient and satisfactory to the Commission; It is adjudged and determined by the Commission that Sally Mayfield is a Cherokee by blood and that she is hereby re-admitted to all the rights, privileges, and immunities of Cherokee citizens by blood.

And a certificate of said decision of the Commission and of re-admission was made and furnished said parties accordingly.

Cherokee Citizenship Commission Docket Books
Tahlequah, Cherokee Nation (1880-84, 1887-89)
Volume I

J.T. Adair, Chairman
John E. Gunter, Comm.
D.W. Lipe, Comm.

Henry Eiffert, Clerk

May 20, 1887
Docket #160   **WYACHE**   John G. Harnage, Atty.
Roll 1835

Bellview, TX

#	NAMES	AGE	SEX
1	John	19	m
2	Bettie	17	f

Ancestor: Jessie Mayfield

Now on this the 21st day of May, 1887, comes the above case for final hearing. And having made application pursuant to the provisions of an act of the National Council approved Dec. 8, 1886. And all the evidence being duly considered and found to be sufficient and satisfactory to the Commission; It is adjudged and determined by the Commission that John Wyache and Bettie Wyache are Cherokees by blood and are hereby re-admitted to all the rights, privileges, and immunities of Cherokee citizens by blood.

And a certificate of said decision of the Commission and of re-admission was made and furnished said parties accordingly.

J.T. Adair, Chairman
John E. Gunter, Comm.
D.W. Lipe, Comm.

Henry Eiffert, Clerk

May 20, 1887
Docket #161   **STILL**   J.G. Harnage, Atty.
Roll 1835

Bellview, TX

#	NAMES	AGE	SEX
1	William	27	m
2	Ann	6 mo	f

Ancestor: Jessie Mayfield

Now on this the 26th day of May, 1887, comes the above case for final hearing. And having made application pursuant to the provisions of an act of the National Council approved Dec. 8, 1886. And all the evidence being duly considered and found to be sufficient and satisfactory to the Commission; It is adjudged and determined by the Commission that William Still and Ann Still are Cherokee citizens by blood.

And a certificate of said decision of the Commission and of re-admission was made and furnished said parties accordingly.

J.T. Adair, Chairman
John E. Gunter, Comm.

Henry Eiffert, Clerk   D.W. Lipe, Comm.

May 20, 1887
Docket #162   **CARR**   John G. Harnage, Atty.
Roll 1851

Bellview, TX

#	NAMES	AGE	SEX
1	Mary	35	f
2	Walter	15	m
3	John	13	m

Ancestor: John G. Harnage

Now on this the 26th day of May, 1887, comes the above case for final hearing. And having made application pursuant to the provisions of an act of the National Council approved Dec. 8, 1886. And all the evidence being duly considered and found to be sufficient and satisfactory to the Commission; It is adjudged and determined by the Commission that Mary Carr, Walter Carr, and John Carr, are Cherokees by blood and they are hereby re-admitted to all the rights, privileges, and immunities of Cherokees by blood.

And a certificate of said decision of the Commission and of re-admission was made and furnished said parties accordingly.

J.T. Adair, Chairman
John E. Gunter, Comm.

Henry Eiffert, Clerk   D.W. Lipe, Comm.

May 20, 1887
Docket #163   **MURPHEY**   J.G. Harnage, Atty.
Rolls 1835

Center, TX

#	NAMES	AGE	SEX
1	Jessie	26	f

Cherokee Citizenship Commission Docket Books
Tahlequah, Cherokee Nation (1880-84, 1887-89)
Volume I

2	Gus	5	m
3	Iris	3	f
4	Bunny	1	f

Ancestor: Sarah Mayfield

Now on this the 21st day of May, 1887, comes the above case for final hearing. And having made application pursuant to the provisions of the act of the National Council approved Dec. 8, 1886. And all the evidence being duly considered and found to be sufficient and satisfactory to the Commission. It is adjudged and determined by the Commission that Jessie Murphey, Gus Murphey, Iris Murphey, and Bunny Murphey, are Cherokees by blood and they are hereby re-admitted to all the rights, privileges, and immunities of Cherokee citizens by blood.

And a certificate of said decision of the Commission and of re-admission was made and furnished said parties accordingly.

J.T. Adair, Chairman
John E. Gunter, Comm.

Henry Eiffert, Clerk   D.W. Lipe, Comm.

May 20, 1887
Docket #164   **LUMPKIN**   I.B. Hitchcock, Atty.
Rolls 1835, 1848, 1851 & 1852

Tahlequah, C.N.

#	NAMES	AGE	SEX
1	Sally	30	f
2	Charles	17	m
3	Patsey	15	f
4	Lizzie	12	f
5	Frank	7	m
6	Kate	5	f
7	Henry	2	m

Ancestor: Martha Lasley

Now on this date, the above case coming up for final hearing. It is adjudged and determined by the Commission on Citizenship, that Sally Lumpkin and her six children, viz: Charles, Patsey, Lizzie, Frank, Kate, and Henry Lumpkin, are not Cherokees by blood and are not entitled to the rights and privileges of such, for the following reasons, to wit: First, Sally Lumpkin does not appear herself upon any of the census or pay rolls mentioned in the 7th Sec. of the act in relation to citizenship, approved Dec. 8, 1886, neither does the

248

name of Martha Lasley, or that of Martha Buckingham appear upon any of these records of Cherokees.

It is useless to give a summary of the testimony in this case as the Commission is entirely confined to the rolls in making up its judgment, and when the parties or their alleged Cherokee ancestors' names do not appear on these rolls, the Commission cannot re-admit them to Cherokee citizenship, and are therefore <u>rejected</u>. This July 20, 1888.

D.W. Lipe, Act. Chairman
John E. Gunter, Commissioner

May 20, 1887
Docket #167(sic)   **<u>BOON</u>**   (No Atty. given.)
Roll 1835

Kilgore, TX

#	NAMES	AGE	SEX
1	Nancy	29	f
2	Volney	7	m
3	Frank	5	m
4	Earle	3	m
5	Emma	1	f

Ancestors: Jessie and Sally Mayfield

Now on this the 25th day of May, 1887, comes the above case for final hearing. and having made application pursuant to the provisions of an act of the National Council approved Dec. 8, 1886. And all the evidence being duly considered and found to be sufficient and satisfactory to the Commission; It is adjudged and determined by the Commission that Nancy Boon, Volney Boon, Frank Boon, Earle Boon, and Emma Boon, are Cherokees by blood and they are hereby re-admitted to all the rights, privileges, and immunities of Cherokee citizenship by blood.

And a certificate of said decision of the Commission and of re-admission was made and furnished said parties accordingly.

J.T. Adair, Chairman
John E. Gunter, Comm.

Henry Eiffert, Clerk   D.W. Lipe, Comm.

April 21, 1887
Docket #168(sic)   **<u>FLIPPIN</u>**   J.M. Bryan, Atty.

249

Cherokee Citizenship Commission Docket Books
Tahlequah, Cherokee Nation (1880-84, 1887-89)
Volume I

Charged with obtaining citizenship through former Commissions by fraud and bribery. Case called and continued until Aug. 18, 1887.

#	NAMES	AGE	SEX
1	Hannah		
2	Louisa		
3	John O.		
4	Giles		
5	Bell Z.		
6	Mary J.		
7	Caroline		
8	Virginia		
9	Tennessee		

(**NOTE:** No age or sex given for the above names.)

(**NOTE:** The left side of original document too light to read. This is shown in the following as "[. . .]".)

Under an act of the National Council passed Dec. 8, 1886, authorizing this Commission to cite certain persons therein named to appear and answer a complaint of the Cherokee Nation charging said parties with having obtained citizenship by fraud and bribery and show cause why the decrees of (the) Courts and Commissions shall not be set aside on account of fraud having been practiced in obtaining the same. Hannah Flippin, et.al. ordered to appear before the Commission as provided for. It appears that the said Hannah Flippin, et.al. at the September term, 1884, did obtain a decree of [. . .] before what is known as the Spears Court on Citizenship. It also appears that the said Hannah Flippin in filing her declaration before the said Commission alleged that she was the descendant of one John Bryant of Gibson Co, TN, whom she claims was a Cherokee by blood. There were only two witnesses [. . .] before said Commission who pretended to testify definitely as to Cherokee blood of the said John Bryant, to wit: Aaron Bellew who is the [. . .] of the said Hannah Flippin, and the affidavit of J.H. Edwards before the Clerk of Montague Co, TX. It will be noticed in the affidavit of [. . .] he does not explain how he became possessed of the knowledge that Bryant was a Cherokee Indian by blood, but simply asserts that he knew Bryant [. . .] Cherokee Indian the same that he did to be part white man. None of the witnesses in behalf of Flippin before the Spears Court had at any time been residents of the Cherokee Nation East or West or that they had the slightest acquaintance with Cherokee Indians so far as their testimony shows [. . .] Commission admitted the affidavits wholly exparte and totally unknown to the Commission and especially that of Edwards' glaringly suspicious [. . .] can only be accounted for in the light of subsequent events. The investigation of the case before the Commission as charged, the defense [. . .] and the non-jurisdiction of this Comm. which was overruled. The deposition of parties taken in Gibson Co, TN, throws much light on [. . .] part in the investigation. The deposition of Zack Bryant, a grandson of the said John Bryant and a man twenty years old, states positively that he had no [. . .] of this man. J.H. Edwards and father of Edwards had ever lived in the vicinity of his grand-father he would have known this. The deposition of Geo. W. Robinson [. . .] Gibson Co, TN, and a man fifty-seven years old and was acquainted with John Bryant in his life term, and states that [. . .] a man named Jack Edwards but does not remember his middle name who now lives in Gibson Co, but who left said Co. [. . .] years ago under disreputable circumstances. Edwards at that time bought a drove of hogs and went south with them leaving his [. . .] never returning to them nor to pay for the hogs he had bought . From the statements of said Robinson , said Edwards [. . .] when in the state of Texas about the time his affidavit was procured heretofore [. . .].

Under this state of circumstances, this Commission cannot attach the least importance [. . .] affidavit of the said J.H. Edwards qualified to before the Clerk of Montague Co, TX. [. . .] great disparity that much have existed between the age of this man Edwards and the [. . .] John Bryant and the unknown origin of said John Bryant, as testified to by his grand-son, Zack Bryant, renders it morally certain to this Commission he [Edwards] [. . .] not have known when he swore to us references to John Bryant's Cherokee blood [. . .] that the presentation of said affidavit of said Edwards as aforesaid in behalf of Hannah [. . .] besides virtually testifying in his own behalf to establish and [. . .] inheritance in the Cherokee Nation is only hear say and subject to the same objectives when taken in connection with the statements Zack* Bryant testifies that the father and mother of his grand-father, John Bryant, was unknown nor was it known even when he was born.

The truth is, it appears to this Commission from the testimony of Zac* Bryant, who certainly has the best opportunity of knowing or at least as good as any one now living that this claim set up by the Defendants that John Bryant was a Cherokee by blood rests upon a vague hint on caused remark. It may have been uttered by him [John Bryant] even fifty years ago. Certainly common and would require something more definite and tangible to establish a right to citizenship in this Nation. The corrupt methods resorted to by John Flippin, a son of Hannah Joe Bowers and Sam Skinner [. . .] of said Hannah and proceeding the decree of Spears Commission as overwhelmingly established by every witness for the Nation. This Commission has no hesitancy in coming to the conclusion that the decree of the former Commissions in favor of Hannah Flippin, et.al, was obtained in the midst of debauchery, bribery, and corruption in which one member of the Commission was criminally implicated and the clerk of the said Commission was particeps(sic) coercion.

Therefore, the Commission agrees and declares the decree of the former Commission admitting Hannah Flippin, et.al. to Cherokee citizenship null and void to all intents and purposes, to wit: Hannah Flippin, Louisa Flippin, Jno. O. Flippin, Giles Flippin, Bell Z. Flippin, Mary Jane Flippin, Caroline Flippin, Virginia Flippin, and Tennessee Flippin. August 29, 1887.

J.T. Adair, Chairman
D.W. Lipe, Commissioner

(*NOTE: Name spelled both ways.)

May 25, 1887
Docket #167   **PARRIS**   L.B. Bell, Atty.
Roll 1835

Chelsea, I.T.

#	NAMES	AGE	SEX
1	Lemuel	37	m
2	Mattie	9	f
3	Susan	6	f
4	Archabal	4	m

Ancestors: John Vann Maney, Lemuel & Catharen Childers

Now on this the 17th day of August, 1887, comes the above case for final hearing and having made application pursuant to the provisions of an act of the National Council, approved Dec. 8, 1886. And all the evidence having been duly made and considered to be sufficient and satisfactory and the ancestors, Lemuel Childers' name appearing on the Emigrant Roll of 1835; It is adjudged and determined by the Commission that Lemuel Parris, Mattie Parris, Susan Parris, and Archabal Parris are Cherokees by blood.

And a certificate of said decision of the Commission and of re-admission was made and furnished to said parties accordingly.

J.T. Adair, Chairman
John E. Gunter, Comm.
Henry Eiffert, Clerk   D.W. Lipe, Comm.

252

May 25, 1887
Docket #168   **UNSELL**   (No Atty. given.)
Rolls 1835, 1848, 1851 & 52

Texas

#	NAMES	AGE	SEX
1	S.C.	27	m

Ancestors: William Lynn and Hannah Hunt

Now comes the above named case for the final hearing. The applicant in his application sets forth that he is the gr-grand-son of William Lynn and Hannah Hunt, whose names would be found on the census rolls of Cherokees made and taken by the United States of Cherokees by blood in the years of 1835, 1848, 1851, and 1852. On the exparte affidavits of witnesses in Texas and Kentucky indefinent(sic) as to whether Hannah Hunt or Hannah Hunter is the proper name of the ancestor and as to the roll on which it would be found, but as to the Indian blood of the claimant; while no such name as that of William Lynn or Hannah Hunt or Hunter are found on the rolls referred to in the 7th Sec. of the Act of Dec. 8, 1886, creating this Commission on Citizenship.

The Commission therefore adjudges that S.C. Unsell is not of Cherokee blood and is not entitled to citizenship in the Cherokee Nation. Post Office address Unitia, Texas. Rejected, this April 26, 1889.

                                        Will P. Ross, Chairman
D. S. Williams, Clerk   John E. Gunter, Comm.

May 26, 1887
Docket #169   **OLIVER**   L.B. Bell, Atty.
Roll 1852

Atlanta, GA

#	NAMES	AGE	SEX
1	Lewis H.	31	m

Ancestor: Emily Blackburn

Now on this the 13th day of October, 1887, comes the above case for a final hearing and the parties having made application pursuant to the provisions of an act of the National Council, approved Dec. 8, 1886. And all the evidence being duly examined and found to be sufficient and satisfactory to the Commission and the name of the ancestor, Emily Blackburn, appearing on roll (of) 1852. It is adjudged and determined by the Commission that Lewis H. Oliver, is a Cherokee by blood and is hereby re-admitted to all the rights, privileges, and immunities of Cherokees by blood.

And a certificate of said decision of the Commission and re-admission was made and furnished to said party accordingly.

> J.T. Adair, Chairman
> John E. Gunter, Comm.

May 26, 1887
Docket #170   **OLIVER**   L.B. Bell, Atty.
Roll 1852

Atlanta, GA

#	NAMES	AGE	SEX
1	John Francis	4	m

Ancestor: Emily Blackburn

Now on this the 13th day of Oct, 1887, comes the above case for a final hearing. And the parties having made application pursuant to the provisions of an act of the National Council, approved Dec. 8, 1886. And all the evidence being duly examined and found to be sufficient and satisfactory to the Commission and the name of the ancestor, Emily Blackburn, appearing on the roll of 1852; It is adjudged and determined by the Commission that John Francis Oliver is a Cherokee by blood and is hereby re-admitted to all the rights, privileges, and immunities of Cherokees by blood.

And a certificate of said decision of the Commission and re-admission was made and furnished to said party accordingly.

> D.W. Lipe, Act. Chairman
> John E. Gunter, Commissioner

May 26, 1887
Docket #171   **CHRISTIAN**   L.B. Bell, Atty.
Roll 1835

Cass Station, GA

#	NAMES	AGE	SEX
1	Kate F.	35	f

Ancestor: George M. Waters

Now on this the 13th day of Oct, 1887, comes the above case for a final hearing and the parties having made application pursuant to the provisions of an act of the National Council, approved Dec. 8, 1886. And all the evidence being duly examined and found to be sufficient and satisfactory to the Commission and the name of the ancestor, George M. Waters, appearing on the rolls of 1835; It is adjudged and determined by the Commission that Kate F. Christian is a Cherokee by blood, and is hereby re-admitted to all the rights and privileges of Cherokees by blood.

And a certificate of said decision of the Commission and re-admission was made and furnished to said parties accordingly.

D.W. Lipe, Act. Chairman
John E. Gunter, Comm.

May 26, 1887
Docket #172   **OLIVER**   L.B. Bell, Atty.
Roll 1852

Atlanta, GA

#	NAMES	AGE	SEX
1	Joshua	40	m

Ancestor: Emily Blackburn

Now on this the 12th day of Oct, 1887, comes the above case for a final hearing. And the parties having made application pursuant to the provisions of an act of the National Council approved Dec. 8, 1886. And the evidence being duly examined and found to be sufficient and satisfactory to the Commission and the name of the ancestor, Emily Blackburn appearing on the rolls of 1852; It is adjudged and determined by the Commission that Joshua Oliver is a Cherokee by blood and (is) re-admitted to all the rights, privileges, and immunities of Cherokees by blood.

And a certificate of said decision of the Commission and re-admission was made and furnished to said parties accordingly.

D.W. Lipe, Act. Chairman
John E. Gunter, Comm.

May 26, 1887
Docket #173   **HAMILTON**   L.B. Bell, Atty.
Roll 1852

Atlanta, GA

#	NAMES	AGE	SEX
1	Georgia O.*	42	f
2	John Oliver	15	m

Cherokee Citizenship Commission Docket Books
Tahlequah, Cherokee Nation (1880-84, 1887-89)
Volume I

Ancestor: Emily Blackburn

Now on this the 14th day of Oct, 1887, comes the above case for a final hearing and the parties having made application pursuant to the provisions of an act of the National Council, approved Dec. 8, 1886. And all the evidence being duly examined and found to be sufficient and satisfactory to the Commission, and the name of the ancestor, Emily Blackburn, appearing on the rolls of 1852; It is adjudged and determined by the Commission that Georgia H.* Hamilton and John Oliver Hamilton are Cherokees by blood and are hereby re-admitted to all the rights, privileges, and immunities of Cherokees by blood.

And a certificate of said decision of the Commission and re-admission was made and furnished to said parties accordingly.

J.T. Adair, Chairman
John E. Gunter, Comm.

May 24, 1887
Docket #174   **SHOEBOOTS**   (No Atty. given.)
Rolls 1835 to 1852

Tahlequah, C.N.

#	NAMES	AGE	SEX
1	William	64	m
2	Lizzie	31	f
3	Nellie	27	f
4	Ruffus*	27	m
5	Prisley*	?	m
6	Floyd+	?	f(sic)
7	James	15	m
8	Sophia	12	f

Ancestor: John Shoeboots

The above case being submitted, it was taken up and carefully examined. William Shoeboots alleging as his Cherokee ancestor one John Shoeboots, the name [John Shoeboots] fails to appear on any of the rolls of Cherokees mentioned in the laws of Dec. 8, 1886, and Feb. 7, 1888. We the Commission on Citizenship are of the opinion however from the testimony in this case that William Shoeboots is of Cherokee blood, for it shows that he is the son of old Star-la-ke-de-ka, a Cherokee Indian who died before the treaty of 1835 and the brother of Lizzie and Polly Boots, whose names appear on the Emigrant rolls of Cherokees in Delaware District, for the year 1852, as Cherokees.

Cherokee Citizenship Commission Docket Books
Tahlequah, Cherokee Nation (1880-84, 1887-89)
Volume I

Under the 7th Section of act of Dec. 8, 1886, We cannot re-admit William Shoeboots to Cherokee citizenship for he has not proven a lineal descent from a Cherokee ancestor, whose name appears on the rolls of Cherokees cited in the before mentioned laws. William Shoeboots and his seven children, viz: Lizzie, William, Rufus*, Priestly, Brand+, James, and Sophia Shoeboots, have failed to establish their citizenship in the Cherokee Nation under the 7th Section of act of Dec. 8, 1886, and are therefore not citizens of the Cherokee Nation. Nov. 3, 1888.

> J.T. Adair, Chairman
> D.W. Lipe, Commissioner
> H.C. Barnes, Commissioner

(***NOTE:** Names spelled both ways.) (**+NOTE:** Both names given.)

May 27, 1887
Docket #175   **STEPHENS**   (No Atty. given.)
Roll 1835

Vinita, Ind. Terr.

#	NAMES	AGE	SEX
1	Belle	27	f
2	Marshall C.	7	m
3	Laura	5	f
4	Carrie Lee	4	f

Ancestors: Joe V.* Crutchfield

Now on this the 2nd day of September, 1887, comes the above case for a final hearing and the parties having made application pursuant to the National Council approved Dec. 8, 1886. And all the evidence being duly examined and found to be sufficient and satisfactory to the Commission and the names of the ancestor, James* Crutchfield appearing on the rolls of 1835; It is adjudged and determined by the Commission that Belle Stephens, Marshall C. Stephens, Laura Stephens, Carrie Lee Stephens, are Cherokees by blood and are hereby re-admitted to all the rights, privileges, and immunities of Cherokees by blood.

And a certificate of said decision of the Commission and re-admission was made and furnished to said parties accordingly.

> J.T. Adair, Chairman Comm.
> John E. Gunter, Comm.

(***NOTE:** Both names given.)

May 28, 1887
Docket #176   **DEWEESE**   E.C. Boudinot, Atty.
Rolls 1835 to 1852

Blandville, (TX)

#	NAMES	AGE	SEX
1	Elizabeth	65	f

Ancestor: Hunt or Hunter

Now comes the above case for final hearing. The applicant who was about 65 years of age at the filing of this application on the 26th day of May, 1887, alleges that she is the grand-daughter of one Hunt or Hunter whose name would be found on the census rolls of Cherokees by blood taken by the United States in (the) years 1835, 48, 51, or 52. The evidence is the same as that in the case of S.C. Unsell and the name of the ancestor is not found on either of the rolls mentioned. It is therefore adjudged that Elizabeth Deweese is not of Cherokee blood and not entitled to citizenship in the Cherokee Nation. Post Office address Blandville, TX. Rejected this April 26, 1889.

                                        Will P. Ross, Chairman
                                        John E. Gunter, Comm.
D.S. Williams, Clerk   R. Bunch, Comm.

May 27, 1887
Docket #177   **HAYES**   L.B. Bell, Atty.
Rolls 1835 to 1852

Mossey Creek, TN

#	NAMES	AGE	SEX
1	Harvey	65	m

Ancestor: John Wright

Tahlequah, June 25, 1889
    There being no evidence submitted in support of the application in the above case, the Commission decides that Harvey Hayes is not of Cherokee blood. Post Office Mossey Creek, TN.

                                        Will P. Ross, Chairman
                                        J.E. Gunter, Comm.
Attest, D.S. Williams, Clerk   R. Bunch, Comm.

May 27, 1887
Docket #178   **WARWICK**   L.B. Bell, Atty.
Roll 1852

Tilton, GA

#	NAMES	AGE	SEX
1	Jacob M.	24	m
2	Geo F.	3	m
3	Elbert S.	2	m

Ancestor: Henrietta Scudder

Now on this the 14th day of Oct, 1887, comes the above case for a final hearing and the parties having made application pursuant to the provisions of an act of the National Council approved Dec. 8, 1886. And all the evidence being duly examined and found to be sufficient and satisfactory to the Commission, and the name of the ancestor, Henrietta Scudder, appearing on the rolls (of) 1852; It is adjudged and determined by the Commission that Jacob M. Warwick, Geo. F. Warwick, and Elbert S. Warwick, are Cherokees by blood. And are hereby re-admitted to all the rights, privileges, and immunities of Cherokees by blood.

And a certificate of said decision of the Commission and re-admission was made and furnished to said parties accordingly.

D.W. Lipe, Acting Chairman
John E. Gunter, Comm.

May 27, 1887
Docket #179   **HELVINGSTON**   L.B. Bell, Atty.
Roll 1852

Tilton, GA

#	NAMES	AGE	SEX
1	S.A.	28	f
2	Mary H.	5	f

Ancestor: Henrietta Scudder

Now on this the 14th day of Oct, 1887, comes the above case for a final hearing. And the parties having made application pursuant to the provisions of an act of the National Council approved Dec. 8, 1886. And all the evidence being duly examined and found to be sufficient and satisfactory to the Commission. And the name of the ancestor, Henrietta Scudder, appearing in the rolls of 1852; It is adjudged and determined by the Commission that S.A.

Helvingston and Mary Helvingston are Cherokees by blood and are hereby re-admitted to all the rights, privileges and immunities of Cherokees by blood.

And a certificate of said decision of the Commission and re-admission were made and furnished to said parties accordingly.

J.T. Adair, Chairman
John E. Gunter, Comm.

May 27, 1887
Docket #180
Roll 1852

WARWICK   L.B. Bell, Atty.

Tilton, GA

#	NAMES	AGE	SEX
1	Francis H.	52	f
2	Elizabeth M.	35	f
3	Leni*	33	f
4	Laura M.	18	f
5	Thomas A.	16	m

Ancestor: Elizabeth Blackburn

Now on this the 13th day of Oct, comes the above case for a final hearing. And the parties having made application pursuant to the provisions of an act of the National Council approved Dec. 8, 1886. And all the evidence being duly examined and found to be sufficient and satisfactory to the Commission and the name of the ancestor, Elizabeth Blackburn, appearing on the rolls of 1852; It is adjudged and determined by the Commission that Francis H. Warwick, Elizabeth m. Warwick, Lenie* Warwick, Laura M. Warwick, and Thomas A. Warwick, are Cherokees by blood and are hereby re-admitted to all the rights, privileges, and immunities of Cherokees by blood.

And a certificate of said decision of the Commission and re-admission was made and furnished to said parties accordingly.

D.W. Lipe, Acting Chairman
John E. Gunter, Commissioner

(***NOTE:** Name spelled both ways.)

May 30, 1887
Docket #181
Rolls 1835 to 1852

GOOING   B.H. Stone, Atty (Dec'd)
                                  C.H. Taylor, Atty.

Tahlequah, C.N.

Cherokee Citizenship Commission Docket Books
Tahlequah, Cherokee Nation (1880-84, 1887-89)
Volume I

#	NAMES	AGE	SEX
1	P.T.	28	?
2	Dresser	3	?
3	(No name given.)	3	?

Ancestor: Thomas Barnett

See decision in this case in that of Maggie Cleveland in this book on page #146 (Docket #92). Adverse to claimant. Sept. 25, 1888.

Cornell Rogers, Clerk

May 30, 1887
Docket #182   **LEACH**   B.H. Stone, Atty.
Rolls 1835 to 1852

Jackbourough, TX

#	NAMES	AGE	SEX
1	John B.	29	?
2	Jessie G.	1	?

Ancestor: Thomas Barnett

See decision in this case in that of Maggie Cleveland in this book, page #146 (Docket #92). Adverse to claimant. Sept. 25, 1888.

Cornell Rogers, Clerk

May 31, 1887
Docket #183   **PACK**   A.E. Ivey, Atty.
Rolls 1835 to 1852

Chelsea, C.N.

#	NAMES	AGE	SEX
1	Mary	66	f
2	Effie	7	f
3	Benson	5	m

Ancestor: Charles Ivans

Now on this the 10th day of November, 1887, comes the above case for a final hearing. The parties having made application pursuant to the provisions of an act of the National Council, approved Dec. 8, 1886. And all the evidence having been duly examined and found not to be sufficient and satisfactory to the Commission, and the name of the ancestor not appearing on the rolls as claimed in the application; It is adjudged and determined by the Commission that Mary Pack, Effie Pack, and Benson Pack, are not Cherokees by blood and are hereby rejected and declared intruders.

J.T. Adair, Chairman

Attest, C.C. Lipe, Clerk   John E. Gunter, Comm.

May 31, 1887
Docket #184   **SNYDER**   A.E. Ivey, Atty.
Rolls 1835 to 1852

Chelsea, Ind. Terr.

#	NAMES	AGE	SEX
1	Martha J.	28	f
2	Samantha	11	f
3	Hailey	9	f
4	James	2	m

Ancestor: Charles Ivans

The application in this (case) filed (the) 31st day of May, 1887, is supported by no evidence and is therefore decided against the applicant, Martha J. Snyder, Samantha Snyder, Hailey Snyder, and James Snyder.

Geo. O. Butler, Asst. Clerk

May 31, 1887
Docket #185   **PINKSTON**   A.E. Ivey, Atty.
Rolls of 1835 to 1852

Chelsea, I.T.

#	NAMES	AGE	SEX
1	James	21	m

Ancestor: Charles Ivans

The above application was filed on the 31st day of May, 1887, and is supported by no evidence and the Commission therefore decides that James Pinkston, and his Post Office at the time of filing was Chelsea, I.T, is not a Cherokee by blood and is not entitled to citizenship in the Cherokee Nation.

Will P. Ross, Chairman
R. Bunch, Comm.

Geo. O. Butler, Asst. Clerk   John E. Gunter, Comm.

May 31, 1887
Docket #186   **SCRUGGS**   A.E. Ivey, Atty.

Rolls 1835 to 1852

Chelsea, I.T.

#	NAMES	AGE	SEX
1	John P.	18	m
2	James C.	16	m
3	Polly M.	13	f
4	George G.	6	m

Ancestor: Charles Ivans

This application filed 31st day of May, 1887, is supported by no evidence. The Commission therefore decides adversely to applicants, John P. Scruggs, Polly M. Scruggs, James C. Scruggs, and George G. Scruggs. The sons and daughter of G.W. and J.A. Scruggs. P.O. Chelsea, I.T.

Will P. Ross, Chairman
R. Bunch, Comm.
George O. Butler, Asst. Clerk   John E. Gunter, Comm.

May 31, 1887
Docket #187   **TEEL**   A.E. Ivey, Atty.
Rolls 1835 to 1852

Mayesville, AR

#	NAMES	AGE	SEX
1	Lafayette	29	m
2	Manerva	7	f
3	Carrie A.	5	f
4	Wm. L.	1	m

Ancestor: Ose Morgan

See decision next page (case, Docket #188). Adverse to claimant. Aug. 7, '88.

Cornell Rogers, Clerk

May 31, 1886
Docket #189   **BROWN**   A.E. Ivey, Atty.
Rolls 1835 to 1852

South West City, MO

#	NAMES	AGE	SEX
1	Martha W	28	f
2	Cassee	9	f

3	Wm. D.	6	m
4	Lula J.	4	f
5	Martha	1	f

Ancestor: Hosie Morgan

Tahlequah, Aug. 7, 1888

Martha W. Brown, et.al.   Lafayette Teel, et.al.

The above two cases, that of Martha W. Brown, et.al, and Lafayette Teel, et.al, applicants for Cherokee citizenship in the Cherokee Nation, were filed in this office on the 30th day of May, 1887. Both claiming a descent from one Hosie Morgan, who they ally was of Cherokee Indian blood.

Martha W. Brown, nee Fleetwood, is the grand-daughter of Hosie Morgan, and Lafayette Teel is the son of Martha W. Brown, sister - name unknown - consequently her nephew and the great grand-child of Hosie Morgan. They both claim rights in the Cherokee Nation through the same source, that of begin descended from Hosie Morgan. The attorney, Miss Ivey and Hitchcock, for Plaintiff, agreed with the Nation's Atty. Hon. A.F. Wyly, that these two cases should be tried and determined upon the same evidence as they are identically the same in respect to Cherokee citizenship - i.e. if one is a Cherokee the other must be.

These cases were submitted to the Commission on Citizenship on the 4th day of August, 1888. All the evidence being in upon which to base an opinion. The evidence of Charles Wickliff on part of the Plaintiff in this cause, goes to show that he is 68 years old and that he had known Lucy Fleetwood for about 58 years, and that he knew her back in the Old Nation and that she went to school at that time at Valley Town Mission in the state of North Carolina, and that this school was established for Cherokees and that he never knew any other than Cherokee children to attend this school, and that Lucy Fleetwood, had two brothers that went to this mission with her and that their names were Sam and Jerry and that he knew Hosie Morgan, who was the father of Lucy, Sam and Jerry and that he, Hosie Morgan, looked like an Indian but that he did not speak the Cherokee language, but understood it, and that he was considered a Mexican or Spaniard.

Mr. Wickliff further says that when a part of the Cherokees left Calhoun in the Old Nation in the year 1834, that he understood Hosie Morgan and family came to this country with them, and that he came to this Nation in the year 1839, but did not know if Hosie Morgan and family were ever reognized(sic) here as Cherokees. He further says that he was 10 or 11 years old when he went to this Mission School before mentioned, in North Carolina, and that it was during this time that Hosie Morgan and family came into that section of country from the state of Georgia, and that he remained there about two years, but did not know if Hosie Morgan and family had any kin-folks among the Cherokees, or not, but did know that the wife of Hosie Morgan had curley, kinky or negro hair.

    The evidence of Mrs. Nancy Starr, a full blood Cherokee woman, in behalf of claimant, taken before Judge J.L. Ward, District Judge of Delaware District, Cherokee Nation, on the 20th day of June, 1887, is wholly denied by said Nancy Starr on a cross examination made by the Nation's Attorney, Hon. R.F. Wyly, on the 11th day of May, 1888. A letter of Judge J.L. Ward, over his affixed signature, on file in this office, goes to show that Nancy Starr cannot speak or understand the English language, and that he had an interpreter, Lafayette Teel, one of the applicants in this cause, to interpret the statement that should have been made by said Nancy Starr, and that he, Ward, does not understand the Cherokee language himself, and only recorded that which Lafayette Teel gave him to understand Nancy Starr should have said.

    The testimony of Sam Johnson, taken before a former Commission on Citizenship, under date of Sept. 19, 1883, in the Lucy Fleetwood case [tried before a former Commissioner and decision adverse to her on the 29th day of Sept, 1888] and that the claimants in the cause were recognized as Cherokees - that the boys had served as guards &c - but upon the cross examination, he said that they never participated in the per capita payment of that year of Cherokees.

    William Wilson states in the matter of the claim of Lucy Fleetwood, the mother of Martha W. Brown, and grand-mother of Lafayette Teel, before a Commission on citizenship, under date of Oct. 1st, 1883, that he knew Lucy Fleetwood, but did not know of what blood she was, that she looked like a half Negro and that he had her sons hired under a permit to do work for him in Delaware District, and that at one time they tried to pass by him before the United States Court, that they were Cherokees, but failed. Mr. B.W. Alberty, who gave testimony before a former Commission in the Fleetwood case for citizenship, says that he is 52 years old and a Cherokee by blood, and that he was acquainted with the Fleetwood family in 1852, and that they removed into his section of country from Kansas, and that he knew them up to the year 1861, and that he had three of Lucy Fleetwood's boys employed under permit to work for him, and that they were regarded and known as Catawba, and that he had them employed the same as if they had been white man, and that he know them during the "Old Settler" payment in this country, and that they never applied for money, claiming they had no right to participate in the distribution of this fund.

The statement of John G. Harnage in the Lucy Fleetwood case, taken Sept. 29, 1884, shows that he took the census of the "Old Settler" Cherokees, preparatory to making the payment to them, in the year 1851, and that while doing so, he met Lucy Fleetwood in Delaware District, and she claimed to be an "Old Settler" Cherokee, and asked to be enrolled as such. Mr. Harnage says that she failed to satisfy us, the census takers, that she was <u>ever</u> a Cherokee, and that her name was not taken. She brought an Atty and witnesses to Tahlequah, the capital of the Cherokee Nation, where the census rolls of "Old Settlers" was being completed, to have her claim adjusted. The evidence was taken before a Commission, says Mr. Harnage, composed of Judge Drew, Cherokee Agent Brown, Lewis Rogers, and myself, in which it was shown that Lucy Fleetwood came to this Nation with a detachment of Cherokees in the year 1834, but failed to prove that she was of Cherokee Indian descent, this was about the year, 1850.

The testimony of Moses Ward, taken before this Commission on the 17th day of May, 1888, shows that he is 72 years old and that he was acquainted with one Winnie Fleetwood who afterwards married a man by the name of Brown, and lived in Delaware Dist, Cherokee Nation, and that she is the daughter of Lucy Fleetwood and that he was acquainted with her and was some-what with Fleetwood, a white man, her husband. The names of Lucy Fleetwood's children are, says Mr. Ward, Edward, Miles, Aquilla, Jerry, Thomas, Sarah, and Winnie, and one other, the mother of Starr Edwards and Lafayette Teel. After the war, he says at one election in Delaware District, in which he was Judge, these Fleetwoods presented themselves to vote, but were not allowed to do so, as they were not recognized as citizens of the Cherokee Nation. That he was once speaking of these folks to Mr. Bill Ingram, now dec'd, when Ingram remarked that it was either his father or his grand-father that once owned Lucy Fleetwood's mother as a slave, and that Bill Ingram was once a Deputy Marshall and stood as high for truth and knew many men in Benton Co, AR.

The evidence of James Wofford in this case is both conclusive and satis-factory, as it now only shows that he was acquainted with the Fleetwood fami-ly in this Nation, but that he knew them in the Old Nation prior to the treaty of 1835. Mr. Wofford is a man of fair education and great intregrity, he is now 82 years old and was a member of the Senate of the Cherokee Council in the Old Nation, which position he held for several years until he removed to this country and that he was often interpreter for courts and ministers of the gospel.

Cherokee Citizenship Commission Docket Books
Tahlequah, Cherokee Nation (1880-84, 1887-89)
Volume I

Mr. Wofford says that he knew Hosie Morgan in the Old Nation, and that he lived in the North Eastern District of the Nation, next to the North Carolina line, and that he then had a family, some of which was grown, and that Hosie Morgan claimed to be a Catawba Indian, and that his wife was a colored woman, and had family, been a slave, and that Hosie Morgan left that country before the treaty of 1835. Mr. Wofford further states, that Hosie Morgan made application to the Council in the Old Nation for citizenship among the Cherokees, but that his request or petition was not granted, on the grounds that he was not a Cherokee, but was allowed on account of him being a Catawba Indian, to open up a field in the Cherokee Nation, upon which to make a living. That he knew Hosie Morgan well, and that he, Hosie Morgan, told him that he was a Catawba Indian, and was so regarded; and that Mr. Ingram who use to own Hosie Morgan's wife, the mother of Lucy Fleetwood, and grand-mother of Martha W. Brown, and great-grand-mother of Lafayette Teel, as a slave, lived near the line of North Carolina, and that this man Ingram, just spoken of, was the father of William Ingram, who is now dead, that use to live in Arkansas near the Cherokee line, who was once a Deputy Marshall and a man well thought of by all who knew him.

We, the Commission on Citizenship after taking into consideration the evidence in this case, are of the opinion that the applicants, Martha W. Brown, et.al, and Lafayette Teel, et.al, are not Cherokees by blood, and the testimony is conclusive in its proof that they are of Catawba and negro blood, with no evidence whatever, other than the allegations contained in the application for citizenship, that they are Cherokees which they have failed to establish. The fact of Hosie Morgan's children going to a Mission School established for Cherokee children, is no proof that they were Cherokees, only the supposition, which in the form of contradictory testimony sets this aside as being unworthy testimony. For the Missionary schools of that day and time, and down to the present, were governed and controlled by the Missionary Courts of the churches, and Indians have nothing to do with support - they being wholly under the supervision of the Missionaries; and while their object was and is naturally, to benefit the Indian, it is a well known fact that children of many races, white, negro, and Cherokee, attended these schools.

This Fleetwood family lived and continuously resided in the Cherokee Nation, going out into the states and returning at intervals. As to who Hosie Morgan was, the ancestor alleged in this case provisions to his coming into the Old Cherokee Nation, is wholly unknown to this Commission or even of what race of people he might have been, other than what he said himself - that he was a Catawba Indian.

Cherokee Citizenship Commission Docket Books
Tahlequah, Cherokee Nation (1880-84, 1887-89)
Volume I

The evidence of Charles Wickliff and James Wofford was shown to indicate that he might have been of Mexican descent. On this point, there is nothing definite.

We fail to find the name of Hosie Morgan upon any of the rolls of Cherokees mentioned in the 7th Section of the act approved Dec. 8, 1886, in relation to citizenship and known as the rolls of 1835-1848-1851 and 1852, or upon the "Old Settler" rolls of the year 1851, neither do we find the name of the applicants on any of these rolls first mentioned, and do hereby declare, that Martha W. Brown, and her four children, viz: Cassee, William D, Lula J, and Martha Brown; and Lafayette Teel and his three children, viz: Manerva J, Carrie A, and William L. Teel, are not Cherokees by blood and are not entitled by virtue of their blood to any of the rights and privileges of Cherokee citizens and are intruders upon the public domain of the Cherokee Nation.

John T. Adair, Chairman

H.C. Barnes, Commissioner

June 2, 1887
Docket #189   **HILL**   A.E. Ivey, Atty.
Rolls 1835 to 1852

Bartlesville, I.T.

#	NAMES	AGE	SEX
1	Manerva	50	f
2	Susan	11	f
3	Nancy	9	f
4	Andrew	?	m

Ancestor: Annie Jones

In the matter of the above applicant and her children, we the Commission fail to find sufficient proof for them to establish their Cherokee blood, and fail to (find) their ancestor, Annie Jones, on any of the rolls as the law requires. The testimony in their case is of an exparte nature, with the exception of Winnie Ratliff, who makes two affidavits in this case, and they conflict in ones taken in 1887, she states she was acquainted with them in Tenn, and in the other taken in 1886, she said she was acquainted with them in Alabama.

We the Commission are satisfied they are not of Cherokee blood, and not entitled to any rights and privileges in the Cherokee Nation, and we do hereby declare Manerva Hill and her three children, viz: Susan, Nancy, and Andrew Hill to be intruders upon the public domain of the Cherokee Nation. Sept. 24, 1888.

Cherokee Citizenship Commission Docket Books
Tahlequah, Cherokee Nation (1880-84, 1887-89)
Volume I

J.T. Adair, Chairman
D.W. Lipe, Comm.
H.C. Barnes, Comm.

June 3, 1887
Docket #190   **JOHNSON**   C.H. Taylor, Atty.
Roll 1835

Harrison, AR

#	NAMES	AGE	SEX
1	Rena	55	(f)

Ancestor: Cynthia Smith

The above named case comes this day taken up for final motion. The applicant bases her claim upon the descent (of) Jean Cynthia Smith, nee Cynthia Kell, the wife of Robert Smith and in addition to evidence accompanying her own application referred to that in the case of Lucinda Addington. The Commission having examined said papers and also the decision of the Commission rendered the 29th day of Sept, 1887, regarding the application of said Lucinda Addington's case. In the opinion of the late Commission in said case and applying the same to the case now before them, adjudge that Rena Johnson is not of Cherokee blood and is not entitled to citizenship in the Cherokee Nation. Post Office address, Harrison, AR.

J.E. Gunter, Comm
Attest, D.S. Williams, Asst. Clerk   R. Bunch, Comm.

June 3, 1887
Docket #191   **ELLIOTT**   C.H. Taylor, Atty.
Rolls 1835 to 1852

Cooygah, I.T.

#	NAMES	AGE	SEX
1	Thomas J.	38	m

Ancestor: David Elliott

See decision in the case in that of John W. Elliott, in this book (Docket #244). Adverse to claimant. Oct. 16, 1888.

Cornell Rogers, Clerk

June 3, 1887
Docket #192   **BATES**   C.H. Taylor, Atty.

Cherokee Citizenship Commission Docket Books
Tahlequah, Cherokee Nation (1880-84, 1887-89)
Volume I

Rolls 1835 to 1852

Cooy-g-ah, I.T.

#	NAMES	AGE	SEX
1	Matilda A.	30	f
2	Roxie	3	f

Ancestor: David Elliott

See decision in this case in that of John W. Elliott, in this book, (Docket #244). Adverse to claimant. Oct. 16, 1888

Cornell Rogers, Clerk

June 3, 1887
Docket #193   **HARRIS**   C.H. Taylor
Rolls 1835 to 1852

Cooygah, I.T.

#	NAMES	AGE	SEX
1	James H.	25	m
2	David H.	20	m
3	Florence A.	18	f
4	Lillie A.	13	f

Ancestor: David Elliott

See decision in this case in that of John W. Elliott, in this book (Docket #244). Adverse to claimant. Oct. 16, 1888.

Cornell Rogers, Clerk

June 3, 1887
Docket #194   **ELLIOTT**   C.H. Taylor, Atty.
Rolls 1835 to 1852

Cooygah, I.T.

#	NAMES	AGE	SEX
1	David	25	m
2	Benj. F.	5	(m)

Ancestor: David Elliott

See decision in this case in that of John W. Elliott, in this book (Docket #244). Adverse to claimant. Oct. 16, 1888.

Cornell Rogers, Clerk

June 7, 1887
Docket #195   **HILL**   (No Atty. given.)
Rolls 1835 to 1852

Vinita, I.T.

#	NAMES	AGE	SEX
1	Rachael	45	f
2	Robert L.	18	m

Ancestor: Martin Davis

Now on this the 7th day of June, 1887, comes the above case for final hearing. And having made application pursuant to the provisions of an act of the National Council approved Dec. 8, 1886. And all the evidence being duly considered and found satisfactory to the Commission; It is adjudged and determined by the Commission that Rachael Hill and Robert Lee Hill, are Cherokees by blood and they are hereby re-admitted to all the rights, privileges, and immunities of Cherokees by blood.

And a certificate of said decision of the Commission and re-admission was made and furnished to said parties accordingly.

                                        J.T. Adair, Chairman
Attest, Henry Eiffert, Clerk   John E. Gunter, Comm.

June 7, 1887
Docket #196   **SAYRES**   A.E. Ivey, Atty.
Rolls 1851 & 52

Adair, I.T.

#	NAMES	AGE	SEX
1	D.H.	24	m

Ancestor: Nancy J. Sayres

July 11, '88

Hon. Joel B. Mayes, Principal Chief, C.N.

We the Commission on Citizenship have the honor today before you the application of D.H. Sayres, for Cherokee citizenship. The case was submitted on this date. After examination of the testimony, we are convinced beyond a doubt that D.H. Sayres is the person he represents himself to be, and that he is of Cherokee descent, though the rolls mentioned in the 7th Sec. of the Act approved Dec. 8, 1886, on citizenship, and the amendment thereto, approved Feb. 7, 1888, do not contain the name of (the) applicant or any of his ancestors. The grand-mother of the applicant and the mother of Judge J. Scales, died on her way to this country in the year 1836. The grand-father of the applicant and father of Judge Scales, was a white man, and was not allowed per capita in the year 1851, in this country or an "Old Settler" in consequence of the fact that he was a white man.

The mother of the applicant Mrs. Jane Sayres, was residing in Williamson Co, in the state of Texas, in the year 1851, but does not appear upon the census rolls of Cherokees taken in that year. William T. Sayres, a brother of the applicant, was unadmitted to Cherokee citizenship by the Commission on Citizenship on the 16th day of Sept, 1884.

The Commission cannot under the 7th Section of the Act of 1886, in relation to citizenship, re-admit Mr. D.H. Sayres, the applicant, to citizenship in this Nation. We are satisfied however, from the evidence that the applicant is of Cherokee blood by descent, and would respectfully recommend that you take such action in the premises as you may deem necessary.

Very respectfully,

D.W. Lipe, Acting Chairman of Comm.

John E. Gunter, Commissioner

June 8, 1887
Docket #197   **POOL**   C.H. Taylor, Atty.
Roll 1835

Booneville, AR

#	NAMES	AGE	SEX
1	Alfred	60	m
2	Boney P.	38	m
3	Bettie	37	f
4	John A.	36	m
5	Daniel B.	29	m
6	W.H.	27	m

Ancestor: Aaron Pool

(**NOTE:** The entire right side of the original document very difficult to read.)

The application of Alfred Pool for citizenship in the Cherokee Nation was filed June 3, 1887, and is based upon the grounds that he is the son of one Aaron Pool, who was enrolled upon the census rolls of Cherokees by blood, citizens of the Cherokee Nation taken and made in the year 1835, and who died at Bolivar, Hardeman Co, TN, as appears from the ex parte affidavit of one John Vantouce, taken July 10, 1885, before E.A. Clark, County Clerk, who states that Aaron Pool had a (unable to read) with the Cherokee Indians in blood being about one-fourth Indian on his Father's side. Besides the insufficiency of such statement to (unable to read) the fact alleged the name of Aaron Pool is not found in the census rolls of 1835 referred to. The Commission therefore decrees that Alfred Pool is not of Cherokee blood and is not entitled to citizenship in the Cherokee Nation. This decree includes the applicants, Alfred Pool, Boney Pool, Bettie Pool, John A. Pool, Daniel B. Pool, W.H. Pool, L.A. Daniels, Alice Blanchard, Charles Pool [her brother], Mary A. Blanchard, Nancy Blanchard, Tabitha Vantouce, Wm Vantouce, Benjamin Vantouce, John Vantouce, George R. Vantouce, Joseph A. Vantouce, F. Vantouce, and Jane V. Vantouce. Post Office address, Booneville, AR. <u>Rejected</u>, this April 18, 1889.

	Will P. Ross, Chairman
Attest, D.S. Williams, Clerk	John E. Gunter, Comm.

June 8, 1887
Docket #198   **TUNSTALL**   (No Atty. given.)
Roll 1835

Delaney, AR

#	NAMES	AGE	SEX
1	Martha G.	48	f
2	Dollie V.	17	f
3	Edward B.	11	m
4	Rebecca E.	8	f
5	Martha G.	6	f

Ancestor: Nancy J. Adair

Now on this the 19th day of June 1887, comes the above case for final hearing and all the evidence having been submitted and the applicants having filed with the law as provided for pursuant to an act of the National Council approved Dec. 8, 1886. We the Commission after a thorough examination of the Rolls of 1835, 1848, 1851 & 52, and the evidence in the case of Martha G. Tunstall, Dollie V. Tunstall, Edward B. Tunstall, Rebecca E. Tunstall, and Martha G. Tunstall, find that the evidence is not sufficient to justify the above named applicants to any rights or privileges of Cherokees by blood and they are declared intruders.

	J.T. Adair, Chairman
Attest, Henry Eiffert, Clerk	John E. Gunter, Comm.

June 8, 1887
Docket #199 <u>**VANTRASE***</u> (No Atty. given.)
Roll 1835

Booneville, AR

#	NAMES	AGE	SEX
1	Tabitha	65	f
2	William	45	m
3	John W.	43	m
4	Benjamin F.	40	m
5	Mary F.	38	f
6	Jane V.	36	f
7	George R.	34	m
8	Joseph A.	28	m

Ancestor: Aaron Pool

See decision in this case in that of Alfred Pool, in this book on page 202 (Docket #197). Adverse to claimant. <u>Rejected</u>, rendered on the 18th day of April, 1889.

D.S. Williams, Clerk
(***NOTE:** Name spelled different as that in Docket #197.)

June 8, 1887
Docket #200 <u>**DANIELS**</u> C.H. Taylor, Atty.
Roll 1835

Booneville, AR

#	NAMES	AGE	SEX
1	L.A.	44	m

Ancestor: Aaron Pool

See decision in this case in that of Alfred Pool, on page 202 (Docket #197). Adverse to claimant. <u>Rejected</u>, rendered on the 18th day of April, 1889.

D.S. Williams, Clerk

June 8, 1887
Docket #201 <u>**BLANCHARD**</u> C.H. Taylor, Atty.
Roll 1835

Booneville, AR

#	NAMES	AGE	SEX

Cherokee Citizenship Commission Docket Books
Tahlequah, Cherokee Nation (1880-84, 1887-89)
Volume I

1	Alice	25	f
2	Mary A.	3	f
3	Nancy	1	f
4	Charles Pool	21	m

Ancestor: Alfred Pool

See decision in this case in that of Alfred Pool on page 202 (Docket #197). Adverse to claimant. <u>Rejected</u>, rendered on the 18th day of April, 1889.

D.S. Williams, Clerk

June 9, 1887
Docket #202   **MOOR***   L.B. Bell, Atty.
Rolls 1852 & 52

McLendon, TX

#	NAMES	AGE	SEX
1	Mary E.	21	f
2	Walter	4	m
3	Alice	1	f

Ancestor: Henrietta Sanders

July 3, 1889

It having been proven to the satisfaction of the Commission on Citizenship that the applicant in this case, Mary E. Moor is the daughter of Francis H. Warwick, whose name appears on the census rolls of Cherokees taken and made in 1852 and the grand-daughter of Polly Blackburn, nee Daniel, whose name appears on the roll of 1835.

It is decided by the Commission that Mary E. Moore* and her son Walter Moore and daughter Alice Moore, are Cherokees by blood and entitled to citizenship in the Cherokee Nation under the Constitution and laws thereof.

J.E. Gunter, Comm.
Attest, D.S. Williams, Asst. Clk.   R. Bunch, Comm.

(***NOTE:** Name spelled both ways.)

June 9, 1887
Docket #203   **MOOR**   L.B. Bell, Atty.
Roll 1835

Sheltonville, GA

#	NAMES	AGE	SEX
1	Sarah L.	42	f

2	Felix	15	m
3	Elizabeth	10	f
4	Emma L.O.	5	f

Ancestor: William Rogers

Now on this the 14th day of Oct, 1887, comes the above case for a final hearing. And the parties having made application pursuant to the provisions of an act of the National Council approved Dec. 8, 1886. And all the evidence being duly examined and found to be sufficient and satisfactory to the Commission and the name of the ancestor, Wm Rogers, appearing on the rolls of 1835; It is adjudged and determined by the Commission that Sarah L. Moor, Felix Moor, Elizabeth Moor, and Emma L.O. Moor, are Cherokees by blood, and are hereby re-admitted to all the rights, privileges, and immunities of Cherokees by blood.

And a certificate of said decision was made and furnished to said parties accordingly.

D.W. Lipe, Acting Commissioner

John E. Gunter, Comm.

June 9, 1887
Docket #204 **BELL** L.B. Bell, Atty.
Roll 1835

Sheltonville, GA

#	NAMES	AGE	SEX
1	Robert H.	27	m
2	Sala M.	6	f
3	Raymond B.	4	m
4	Henry C	1	m

Ancestor: L.B. Bell

Now on this the 13th day of Oct, 1887, comes the above case for a final hearing. And the parties having made application pursuant to the provisions of an act of the National Council, approved Dec. 8, 1886, and all the evidence being duly examined and found to be sufficient and satisfactory to the Commission; and the name of the ancestor, William Rogers, appearing on the rolls of 1835; It is adjudged and determined by the Commission that Robert H. Bell, Sala M. Bell, Raymond B. Bell, (Henry C. Bell's name omitted) are Cherokees by blood and are hereby re-admitted to all the rights, privileges, and immunities of Cherokees by blood.

And a certificate of said decision of the Commission and re-admission was made and furnished to said parties accordingly.

D.W. Lipe, Act. Commissioner
John E. Gunter, Comm.

June 9, 1887
Docket #205   **DUNLAP**   A.E. Ivey, Atty.
Roll 1835

Fort Gibson, I.T.

#	NAMES	AGE	SEX
1	J.W.	52	m
2	Sabria E.	19	f
3	Lynda	8	f

Ancestor: Margarett Blackburn

May 1, 1889

The application in this case was filed the 9th day of June, 1887, but is supported by no evidence. The case having been called three several times at intervals of not less than one hour apart and no answer returned. The Commission decided adversely to applicant and his daughters Sabria E. Dunlap and Lynda Dunlap. Post Office Fort Gibson, Ind. Terr. Rejected this May 1, 1889.

Will P. Ross, Chairman
Attest, D.S. Williams, Clerk   John E. Gunter, Comm.

June 9, 1887
Docket #206   **THOMPSON**   A.E. Ivey, Atty.
Rolls 1835 to 1852

Ft. Graham, TX

#	NAMES	AGE	SEX
1	E.J.	37	f
2	Jonis P.	15	m
3	Wm. Carrol	8	m
4	Geo. Taylor	6	m
5	Ora L.	4	f
6	Stella S.	3	f
7	Rebecca F.	10 mo.	f

Ancestor: Polly Blevins

(**NOTE:** No other information given.)

June 10, 1887
Docket #207   **LONG**   E.C. Boudinot, Atty.
Rolls 1835 to 1852

Coffeyville, KS

#	NAMES	AGE	SEX
1	Lucinda	68	f
2	Robert	21	m
3	Henry	18	m

Ancestor: Lewis Dishon

May 18, 1889

Now comes this case for final hearing. Lucinda Long, the applicant alleges that she is the daughter of one Lewis Dishon, whose name will be found on the census rolls of Cherokees by blood taken and made by the United States in the years 1835-48-51 & 52, and therefore, asks for re-admission to citizenship in the Nation for herself and sons. The evidence offered as certified by the ex parte affidavits taken before a Notary Public in Montgomery County, Kansas, and which are not admissible under the rules of this Commission, fail to show that the father of applicant was a Cherokee Indian nor does his name appear on the rolls of Cherokees by blood named above. The Commission therefore decides that Lucinda Long and her two sons, Robert Lincoln Alexander Long and Henry Long, are not of Cherokee blood and not entitled to citizenship in the Cherokee Nation.

                                        J.E. Gunter, Comm.
Attest, D.S. Williams, Asst. Clerk   R. Bunch, Comm.

June 10, 1887
Docket #208   **MAHEW**   E.C. Boudinot, Atty.
Rolls 1835 to 1852

Chetopa, KS

#	NAMES	AGE	SEX
1	Henry	64	m
2	Elijah	14	m
3	Tillie Jane	10	f
4	Henry, Jr.	10	m

Elizabeth Curtis

Cherokee Citizenship Commission Docket Books
Tahlequah, Cherokee Nation (1880-84, 1887-89)
Volume I

Now comes this case for the final hearing. The claim of the applicant was filed the 10th day of June, 1887. He alleges that he is the son of one Elizabeth Curtis, whose name would be found on the census rolls of Cherokees by blood taken and made in the years 1835-48-51 & 52, the only evidence in support of the application is that of James Long and Lucinda Long, as ex parte affidavits, made in the state of Kansas, the 31st day of May, 1887, that they were born in North Carolina respectively, in the year 1818 and 1829, and knew Betsey Curtis and other persons named and knew them to be Cherokees, but this is no identification of the parentage of Henry Mayhew* as the son of Betsey Curtis nor does her name appear on the rolls mentioned above. It is therefore adjudged and decreed by the Commission on Citizenship that Henry Mayhew and his children, Elijah Mayhew, Henry Mayhew, Tillie Jane Mayhew, are not of Cherokee blood and not entitled to re-admission to the Cherokee Nation as citizens. Rejected, this April 26, 1889.

	Will P. Ross, Chairman
D.S. Williams, Clerk	John E. Gunter, Comm.

(**NOTE:** Spelled differently as that on page 206.)

June 14, 1887
Docket #209   **LENOIR**   C.J. Harris, Atty.
Roll 1852

Duluth, GA

#	NAMES	AGE	SEX
1	Annie C.	65	f
2	Mary O.	42	f

Ancestor: John Rogers

Now on this the 14th day of June, 1887, comes the above applicants for a final hearing and having made application pursuant to the provisions of an act of the National Council approved, Dec. 8, 1886, and all the evidence having been duly considered and found to be sufficient and satisfactory to the Commission; It is adjudged and determined by (the) Commission that Annie C. Lenoir and Mary O. Lenoir, are Cherokees by blood and they are hereby re-admitted to all the rights and privileges of Cherokee citizens by blood.

And a certificate of said decision of the Commission and of re-admission was made and furnished said parties accordingly.

J.T. Adair, Chairman Commission

Attest, Henry Eiffert, Clerk   John E. Gunter, Commissioner

June 14, 1887
Docket #210   **LOWE**   C.J. Harris, Atty.
Roll 1852
                            Duluth, GA

#	NAMES	AGE	SEX
1	Cynthia	66	f
2	Julia P.	41	f
3	Nancy O. Nickols	34	f

Ancestor John Rogers

On this the 14th day of June, 1887. comes the above case for final hearing and having made application pursuant to the provisions of the National Council, approved December 8, 1886, and all the evidence having been duly considered and found to be sufficient and satisfactory to the Commission; It is adjudged and determined by the Commission that Cynthia Lowe and Julia Lowe are Cherokees by blood and they are hereby re-admitted to all the rights, privileges, and immunities of Cherokee citizenship by blood.

And a certificate of said decision of the Commission and of re-admission was made and furnished said parties accordingly.

                              J.T. Adair, Chairman
Henry Eiffert, Clerk   John E. Gunter

(**NOTE:** Nancy O. was not mentioned in the above explanation.)

June 14, 1887
Docket #211   **LOWE**   (No Atty. given.)
Roll 1852
                            Duluth, GA

#	NAMES	AGE	SEX
1	John J.	38	m
2	Mary	10 mo	f

Ancestor: Cynthia Lowe

Now on this the 14th day of June, 1887, comes this case for final hearing and the parties having made application pursuant to an act of the National Council approved Dec. 8, 1886, and all the evidence having been examined and found to be sufficient and satisfactory to the Commission; It is adjudged and determined by the Commission that John J. Lowe and Mary Lowe are Cherokees by blood and they are hereby re-admitted to (all the) rights, privileges, and immunities of Cherokee citizens by blood.

And a certificate of said decision of the Commission and of re-admission was made and furnished said parties accordingly.

J.T. Adair, Chairman Commission

Henry Eiffert, Clerk   John E. Gunter, Commissioner

June 14, 1887
Docket #212   **<u>MOOR</u>**   (No Atty. given.)
Roll 1852

Duluth, GA

#	NAMES	AGE	SEX
1	Sarah A.	36	f
2	Cynthia A.	4	f
3	Clifton	2	m
4	John	1	m

Ancestor: Cynthia Lowe

Now on this the 14th day of June, 1887, comes the above case for final hearing, and the parties having made application pursuant to the provisions of an act of the National Council approved Dec. 8, 1886, and all the evidence having been examined and found to be sufficient and satisfactory to the Commission; It is adjudged and determined by the Commission that Sarah A. Moor, Cynthia A. Moor, Clifton Moor, and John Moor, are Cherokees by blood.

And a certificate of said decision of the Commission and of re-admission was made and furnished said parties accordingly.

J.T. Adair, Chairman Commission

Henry Eiffert, Clerk   John E. Gunter, Commissioner

June 14, 1887
Docket #213   **<u>ROBERTS</u>**   (No Atty. given.)
Roll 1852

Duluth, GA

#	NAMES	AGE	SEX
1	Anna	34	f
2	Annie	6	f

3	Leona	4	f
4	Marion	2	m
5	John H.	1	m

Ancestor: Annie C. Lenoir

Now on this the 14th day of June, 1887, comes the above case for final hearing and the parties having made application pursuant to the provisions of an act of the National Council approved Dec. 8, 1886, and all the evidence having been examined and found to be sufficient and satisfactory to the Commission; It is adjudged and determined by the Commission that Anna Roberts, Annie Roberts, Leona Roberts, Marion Roberts, and John H. Roberts, are Cherokees by blood and they are hereby re-admitted to all the rights, privileges, and immunities of Cherokee citizens by blood.

And a certificate of said decision of the Commission and of re-admission was made and furnished said parties accordingly.

J.T. Adair, Chairman Comm.

Henry Eiffert, Clerk

John E. Gunter, Comm.

June 14, 1887
Docket #214　　　　　　　　　　**ROBERTS**　　　　　(No Atty. given.)
Roll 1852

Duluth, GA

#	NAMES	AGE	SEX
1	Emma E.	30	f
2	Mary E.	4	f
3	Estella C.	2	f
4	Fannie L.	1	f

Ancestor: Annie C. Lenoir

Now on this the 14th day of June, 1887, comes the above case for final hearing and the parties having made application pursuant to the provisions of an act of the National Council approved Dec. 8, 1886, and all the evidence having been examined and found to be sufficient and satisfactory to the Commission; It is adjudged and determined by the Commission that Emma E. Roberts, Mary E. Roberts, Estella C. Roberts, and Fannie L. Roberts, are Cherokees by blood and they are hereby readmitted to all the rights, privileges, and immunities of Cherokee citizens by blood.

And a certificate of said decision of the Commission and of re-admission was made and furnished said parties accordingly.

Cherokee Citizenship Commission Docket Books
Tahlequah, Cherokee Nation (1880-84, 1887-89)
Volume I

J.T. Adair, Chairman Comm.
Henry Eiffert, Clerk   John E. Gunter, Comm.

June 14, 1887
Docket #215   **HARLIN**   A.E. Ivey, Atty.
Rolls 1835 to 52

South West City, MO

#	NAMES	AGE	SEX
1	W.T.	33	m
2	R.H.	31	m

Ancestor: James E. Harlin

Now on this the 14th day of June, 1887, comes the above case for final hearing and the applicant having made application pursuant to the provisions of an act of the National Council approved Dec. 8, 1886. And all the evidence being duly considered and examined and found to be sufficient and satisfactory to the Commission; It is adjudged and determined by the Commission that W.T. Harlin and R.H. Harlin, are Cherokees by blood and they are hereby re-admitted to all the rights, privileges, and immunities of Cherokee citizenship by blood.

And a certificate of said decision of the Commission and of re-admission was made and furnished said parties accordingly.

J.T. Adair, Chairman Comm.
Henry Eiffert, Clerk   John E. Gunter, Comm.

June 15, 1887
Docket #216   **NICKOLS**   (No Atty. given.)
Roll 1852

Duluth, GA

#	NAMES	AGE	SEX
1	Octavia	34	f

Ancestor: Cynthia Lowe

Now on this the 14th day of June, 1887, comes the above case for final hearing, and the applicant having made application pursuant to the provisions of an act of the National Council approved Dec. 8, 1886, and the evidence having been duly considered and examined and found to be sufficient and satisfactory to the Commission; It is adjudged and determined by the Commission that

Cherokee Citizenship Commission Docket Books
Tahlequah, Cherokee Nation (1880-84, 1887-89)
Volume I

Octavia Nickols is a Cherokee by blood and she is hereby re-admitted to all the rights, privileges, and immunities of a Cherokee citizen by blood.

And a certificate of said decision of the Commission was made and furnished said parties accordingly.

J.T. Adair, Chairman

Henry Eiffert, Clerk   John E. Gunter, Comm.

June 15, 1887
Docket #217   **JOHNSON**   C.H. Taylor, Atty.
Roll 1835

Chetopa, KS

#	NAMES	AGE	SEX
1	Edward	28	m

Ancestor: William Johnson

Now on this date, the 17th of Oct, 1888, comes the above case up for final disposition. It having been submitted by Plaintiff's Atty. When the testimony was duly considered, as well as the rolls mentioned in the 7th Section of Act of Dec. 8, 1886, in relation to citizenship. We, the Commission on Citizenship, fail to find the name of William Johnson enrolled on said rolls, in the absence of which important fact, we are of the opinion that Edward Johnson is not a Cherokee by blood, and not entitled to any of the rights of citizens of the Cherokee Nation on account of his blood, and should he be now residing within the confines of said Cherokee Nation, is an intruder upon the public domain of the same, and the Commission do hereby so declare.

J.T. Adair, Chairman

H.D. Barnes, Comm.

June 16, 1887
Docket #218   **JOHNSON**   C.H. Taylor, Atty.
Roll 1835

Chetopa, KS

#	NAMES	AGE	SEX
1	William	68	m
2	Josephine	28	f
3	Mary	21	f

Ancestor: Molly Johnson

284

The above case being submitted to the Commission on Citizenship on the 16th, and all the testimony being duly read, was considered, as well as the rolls of Cherokees mentioned in the 7th Section of Act of Dec. 8, 1886, in relation to citizenship. We find, that the name of Molly Johnson, from whom the parties claim a Cherokee descent, fail to appear on said rolls, consequently in our opinion, the applicants are not Cherokees by blood, but from the testimony of themselves are colored folks, as they admit having ever been in a condition of servitude, and William Johnson, Josephine Johnson, and Mary Johnson, are not entitled to the rights and privileges of citizens of the Cherokee Nation, and should they be within the bounds of said Nation, are intruders therein. Oct. 17, 1888.

J.T. Adair, Chairman
H.C. Barnes, Comm.

June 16, 1887
Docket #219   **SWAGERTY**   C.H. Taylor, Atty.
Roll 1835

Tahlequah, C.N.

#	NAMES	AGE	SEX
1	Mary	48	f

Ancestor: John Shoeboots

Now comes this case for final hearing. The applicant alleges that she is 48 years of age and is the daughter of one John Shoeboots, whose name may be found on the census rolls of Cherokees by blood, made and taken in the year 1835, but there is no proof to establish her identity as the daughter of John Shoeboots from whom she claims to have derived her Cherokee blood.

The Commission, therefore decides that Mary Swagerty, is not of Cherokee blood and not entitled to citizenship in the Cherokee Nation. Rejected, April 27, 1889.

Will P. Ross, Chairman
D.S. Williams, Clerk   John E. Gunter, Comm.

June 16, 1887
Docket #220   **STEPHENS**   C.H. Taylor, Atty.
Roll 1851

Coffeyville, KS

#	NAMES	AGE	SEX
1	William	60	m

Cherokee Citizenship Commission Docket Books
Tahlequah, Cherokee Nation (1880-84, 1887-89)
Volume I

Ancestor: William Shoeboots

The above case was submitted by Plaintiff's Attorney, Mr. C.H. Taylor. Wm Stephens alleging his Cherokee ancestor, one William Shoeboots, who the testimony shows was his uncle and not an ancestor under the law when it says a lineal descendant. [See Sec. 7 of the Act of Dec. 8, 1886.] Consequently, this Commission cannot re-admit such persons to Cherokee citizenship. We are however satisfied from the testimony in this cause, that William Stephens, the applicant, possesses Cherokee blood as his uncle, William Ellington Shoeboots appears on the resident Old Settler Rolls of Cherokees of the year 1851, and that he, William Shoeboots, is the son of Old Sar-sa-ki-ar-ka, a Cherokee Indian who died before the date of 1835; who was the grand-father of the applicant, William Stephens. William Stephens, has failed under the 7th Section of the Act of Dec. 8, 1886, to establish his citizenship in the Cherokee Nation, as is therein required; and is therefore, under the law, declared not to be a citizen of the said Cherokee Nation. Nov. 3, 1888.

J.T. Adair, Chairman Comm.
D.W. Lipe, Comm.
H.C. Barnes, Comm.

June 16, 1887
Docket #221   **McKINLEY**   A.E. Ivey, Atty.
Rolls 1835 to 1852

Denison, TX

#	NAMES	AGE	SEX
1	Nancy J.	39	f
2	Charles H.	18	m
3	Daniel D.W.	15	m
4	Margarett M.	12	f
5	Louis R.	9	m
6	Eugenia G.	6	f
7	Jennie	2	f

Ancestor: Elizabeth Looney or Bledson

Now on this the 1st day of June, 1888, comes the above case up for final hearing. The husband of the applicant having submitted the case in person.

The application of Nancy J. McKinley, et.al, alleges Elizabeth Looney nee Bledson, as being a Cherokee by blood, and her ancestor. Under the 7th Section of the law creating this Commission, approved Dec. 8, 1886, says the

286

applicant must prove a lineal descent from some person whose names appear on the census rolls taken by the United States Govt. taken after the Treaty of 1835, and known as the rolls of 1835, also the rolls of 1848, 1851, and 1852.

The testimony of R.T. and J.R. Peak, in this case, shows that they were not positive as to the Bledson's being of Cherokee blood; they state that they were recognized in the community where they lived as Cherokees and heard them say as themselves.

The evidence of J.L. McCoy, who was partly raised in Marshall Co, AL, shows that he resided there previous to the emigration, and that he never heard of any Bledsons that were of Cherokee blood.

The testimony of Patrick Henry, who now resided in Marshall Co, AL, shows that he was acquainted with the Bledson family, and knows nothing of their Cherokee blood, and in his dealings with Hodges, who married a Bledson, never heard him say that his wife was a Cherokee, and Hodges was aware that he [Henry] was of Cherokee blood.

The rolls of 1835, 1851, and 52, show no such name as Bledson, either in the state of Alabama or Tennessee. The Commission after carefully and impartially investigating the case, find that the applicants, Nancy J, Charles H, Daniel W.D*, Margaret M, Louis R. Eugene G, and Jennie McKinley, fail to prove their Cherokee blood, and are hereby rejected and declared to be intruders upon the public domain of the Cherokee Nation.

> J.T. Adair, Chairman
> John E. Gunter, Comm.
> D.W. Lipe, Comm.

(***NOTE:** Initials reversed.)

June 16, 1887
Docket #222   **RUSSELL**   A.E. Ivey, Atty.
Rolls 1835 to 1852

St. Louis, MO

#	NAMES	AGE	SEX
1	Thomas F.	34	m
2	Kate E.	10	f
3	Mary E.	8	f
4	Thomas F, Jr.	5	m

Ancestor: John Russell

May 1, 1889

The applicant in the above case filed his application the 8th day of June, 1887, as the son of John Russell or Joseph Russell, but which he does not remember. It came before the Commission without evidence and having been called three several times at intervals of not less than an hour apart and no answer returned.

The Commission adjudged adversely to the applicant, Thomas F. Russell and children, Kate E. Russell, Mary E. Russell, and Thomas F. Russell (Jr.). Post Office Saint Louis, MO. Rejected May 1, 1889.

	Will P. Ross, Chairman
D.W. Williams, Clerk	John E. Gunter, Commissioner

June 20, 1887

Docket #223 **KEYS** A.E. Ivey, Atty.

Rolls 1851 & 52

(No Post Office given.)

#	NAMES	AGE	SEX
1	T.S.	27	m
2	Mary A.	34	f
3	L.J.	24	f

Ancestor: Richard Keys

Now on this the 20th day of June, 1887, comes the above case for a final hearing and having made application pursuant to the provisions of an act of the National Council, approved Dec. 8, 1886. And all the evidence being duly considered and found to be sufficient and satisfactory to the Commission; It is adjudged and determined by the Commission that T.S. Keys, Mary A. Keys, and L.J. Keys, are Cherokees by blood and are hereby re-admitted to all the rights, privileges, and immunities of Cherokee citizens by blood.

And a certificate of said decision of the Commission and re-admission was made and furnished to said parties accordingly.

	J.T. Adair, Chairman
Henry Eiffert, Clerk	John E. Gunter, Commissioner

June 20, 1887

Docket #224 **ROBERTS** A.E. Ivey, Atty.

Rolls 1835 to 1852

Bartlesville, I.T.

#	NAMES	AGE	SEX
1	Martha A.	35	f
2	William Jones	15	m

3	Albert Roberts*	3	m

Ancestor: Annie Jones

May 1, 1889

The above named case was filed the 20th day of June, 1887, No evidence accompanied the application and the case having been called three several times at intervals of not less than one hour apart. The Commission decided adversely to the claimant, Martha A. Roberts, and her sons, William Jones and Albert Jones*. Post Office Bartlesille, Ind. Terr. Rejected May 1, 1889.

Will P. Ross, Chairman

D.S. Williams, Clerk   John E. Gunter, Comm.

(*NOTE: Both names given.)

June 20, 1887
Docket #225   **JONES**   A.E. Ivey, Atty.
Rolls 1835 to 52

Bartlesville, I.T.

#	NAMES	AGE	SEX
1	W.H.	39	m

Ancestor: Annie Jones

May 1, 1889

The application in the above case was filed June 20, 1887, but being accompanied by no evidence, the Commission, therefore after having the case called three several times and no answer being returned, decide adversely to claimant. Post Office Bartlesville, I.T. Rejected May 1, 1889.

Will P. Ross, Chairman

D.S. Williams, Clerk   John E. Gunter, Comm.

June 20, 1887
Docket #226   (No Atty. given.)
Roll 1835

Camp Creek, I.T.

#	NAMES	AGE	SEX
1	Margaret	45	f
2	Arragina	24	f
3		21	m
4	Margaret J.	19	f

289

5	Davis M.	19	m
6	John B.	14	m
7		10	f

Ancestor: ? Waters

(**NOTE:** This docket extremely difficult to read, print faded.)

June 20, 1887
Docket #227   <u>COODY</u>   E.C. Boudinot, Atty.
Roll 1835

Tahlequah, C.N.

#	NAMES	AGE	SEX
1	Arthur	45	m
2	Luther	15	m
3	Arthur	?	m

Ancestor: Elizabeth Coody

Now on this the 20th day of June, 1887, comes the above case for final hearing and having made application pursuant to the provisions of an act of the National Council approved Dec. 8, 1886. And all the evidence having been duly considered and found to be sufficient and satisfactory to the Commission; It is adjudged and determined by the Commission that Arthur Coody, Luther Coody, and Arthur Coody, Jr, are Cherokees by blood and they are hereby entitled to all the rights, privileges, and immunities of Cherokee citizens.

And a certificate of said decision of the Commission and re-admission was made and furnished said parties accordingly.

J.T. Adair, Chairman Commission
Henry Eiffert, Asst. Clerk   John E. Gunter, Commissioner

June 23, 1887
Docket #228   <u>BOUDINOT</u>   E.C. Boudinot, Atty.
Roll 1835

New York City

#	NAMES	AGE	SEX
1	Frank B.	24	m

Ancestor: Elias Boudinot

Now on this the 28th day of June, 1887, comes the above case for final hearing, and having made application pursuant to the provisions of an act of the National Council approved Dec. 8, 1886, and all the evidence being duly considered and found to be sufficient and satisfactory to the Commission; It is adjudged and determined by the Commission that Frank B. Boudinot is a Cherokee by blood and is hereby re-admitted to all the rights, privileges, and immunities of a Cherokee by blood.

And a certificate of said decision of the Commission and of re-admission was made and furnished said parties accordingly.

J.T. Adair, Chairman
John E. Gunter, Comm.

C.C. Lipe, Clerk   D.W. Lipe, Comm.

June 25, 1887
Docket #229   **FOURT**   B.H. Stone, Atty.
Rolls 1835 to 1852

Tahlequah, C.N.

#	NAMES	AGE	SEX
1	M.J.	40	f
2	Cordelia	?	f
3	Edward A.	?	m
4	Malissa	?	f
5	Camer	?	m
6	Hardin	?	m

Ancestor: David Whitaker

May 1, 1888

The application in the above case was filed the 24th day of June, 1887. Without evidence and having been called three several times on the 30th of April and again called on this day and no one answering; the Commission decides adversely to the applicant, M.J. Fourt as a Cherokee by blood and her children, Cordelia Fourt, Edward A. Fourt, Malissa Fourt, Camer Fourt, and Hardin Fourt, are not entitled to citizenship in this Cherokee Nation. Rejected this May 20, 1889.

Will P. Ross, Chairman

D.S. Williams, Clerk   John E. Gunter, Comm.

June 26, 1887
Docket #230   **WARD**   E.C. Boudinot, Atty.
Roll 1835

Honey Grove, TX

Cherokee Citizenship Commission Docket Books
Tahlequah, Cherokee Nation (1880-84, 1887-89)
Volume I

#	NAMES	AGE	SEX
1	John	40	m
2	Andy	12	m
3	Nancy	10	f
4	Jerry	2	m

Ancestor: Jerry Ward

(**NOTE:** Page 1 of original docket is illegible, print too light.)

. . . the statement of his daughter, Henrietta shows that she was born in Illinois after her father left Tennessee, that after remaining there until she was about six years old, he moved to Missouri and again in 1837 to Texas. This witness also alleges that the father of Jeremiah Ward was one Jack Ward. It appears to the Commission that if any doubt was present, these statements in support to the testimony of Jeremiah Ward that the fact is clearly shown by the statements made before the present Commission by Darius Ward of Tahlequah District. Bryant Ward and Moses Ward of Illinois, who fully trace the genealogy of the Wards who are of Cherokee blood from Jack Ward, a white man and Kate McDaniel, a part Cherokee woman. These witnesses give the names of the Cherokee Wards descended from Jack Ward and show that no Jerry or Jeremiah Ward descended from him and that they have neither known or heard of any such Ward and that those who hear the name and have and Indian blood line within the limits of the Cherokee Nation. These facts in connection with the additional one which shows that the name of Jerry or Jeremiah Ward appears on some of the rolls and found to have no doubt in their minds of the conclusion that John Ward, the son of Jerry or Jeremiah Ward, is not of Cherokee blood and is not entitled to citizenship in the Cherokee Nation and they hereby so decide.

Will P. Ross, Chairman
J.E. Gunter, Commissioner

June 25, 1887
Docket #231   **STEVENS**   A.E. Ivey, Atty.
Rolls 1835 to 1852

Prairie City, I.T.

#	NAMES	AGE	SEX
1	Susan V.	32	f
2	S.L.	17	m
3	John	6	m

Cherokee Citizenship Commission Docket Books
Tahlequah, Cherokee Nation (1880-84, 1887-89)
Volume I

Ancestor: Jeremiah Ward
Adverse. Embraced in decision (above, docket #230) of John Ward case.
E.G. Ross, Clerk of Commission

June 25, 1887
Docket #232   **YATES**   A.E. Ivey, Atty.
Roll 1835 to 1852
Prairie City, I.T.

#	NAMES	AGE	SEX
1	Henrietta	62	f

Ancestor: Jerry Ward

Adverse. Embraced in decision (above, docket #230) of John Ward.
E.G. Ross, Clerk of Commission

June 25, 1887
Docket #233   **YATES**   A.E. Ivey, Atty.
Rolls 1835 to 1852

Prairie City, I.T.

#	NAMES	AGE	SEX
1	Albert J.	27	m

Ancestor: Jerry Ward

Adverse. Embraced in decision in (this) book, page #216 in John Ward
case (See docket #230).
E.C. Ross, Clerk

June 25, 1887
Docket #234   **BOND**   A.E. Ivey, Atty.
Rolls 1835 to 1852
Blue Jacket, I.T.

#	NAMES	AGE	SEX
1	Sarah A.	62	f

Ancestor: Isham* Sizemore
Sept. 19, 1888

Sarah A. Bond, et.al.   James C. Sizemore, et.al.

293

Cherokee Citizenship Commission Docket Books
Tahlequah, Cherokee Nation (1880-84, 1887-89)
Volume I

Now on this the above written date, comes the Attorney for the applicants, and submits the above cases, together with all the applications claiming a descent from Isom* Sizemore, Joal Sizemore, Richard Sizemore, and Henry Sizemore, of which he may have control.

We, the Commission on Citizenship, after duly considering the testimony in these cases, and the rolls laid down in the 7th Section of the Act of December 8, 1886, fail to find the names of the alleged ancestors thereon, or the names of the applicants themselves, therefore:

Sarah A. Bond, William Stout, James C. Sizemore, America A. Sizemore, Ida Sizemore, Geo. C. Dobin, James H. Sizemore, H.H. Sizemore, J.R. Sizemore, Noah E. Sizemore, Patience L. Sizemore, Manda J. Sizemore, Margaret R. Sizemore, Mary Sizemore, Isom R. Bond, Almeda Bond, Irva H. Bond, Ida Bond, Earl Bond, Ethel Bond, Mabel Bond, Abel J. Bond, J.H. Bond, Christina Bond, Laura Bond, Bertha Bond, Ana P. Bond, John S. Bond, Anna Bond, Percy Ellen Sizemore, Alvis Caswell Sizemore, J. Henry Sizemore, A.R. Sizemore, Wm. A. Sizemore, Louisa J. Sizemore, Mary K. Hall, Minni J. Hall, Daisy M. Hall, Perly L. Hall, Effie M. Hall, Archie C. Hall, Wm. A. Hall, Willis D. Sizemore, Leander Sizemore, Tennessee Sizemore, Sarah E. Sizemore, Wm. Sanford Sizemore, L.D. Sizemore, Isom F. Sizemore, Sarah Keith, James M. Keith, Minnie Keith, Jefferson Keith, Stella Keith, Elmer Keith, Elizabeth David, Maude Davis, Wm F. Sizemore, Andrew J. Sizemore, Sizzie(sic) A. Sizemore, Mary A. Gaylor, Bertha R. Gaylor, America O. Gaylor, Garland H. Gaylor, Richard G. Sizemore, Jas. A. Sizemore, Hattie G. Sizemore, Della V. Sizemore, Charles A. Sizemore, Jesse Sizemore, Allen Grant, Gertrude Sizemore, Adolph A. Sizemore, James H. Sizemore, and Gracie May Sizemore, are not Cherokees by blood and are not entitled to the rights, privileges, and immunities of Cherokee citizens by blood, and those who are now residing, of these applicants, within the confines of the Cherokee Nation are declared to be intruders upon the public domain of the Cherokee Nation.

J.T. Adair, Chairman
D.W. Lipe, Comm.
[76 persons]   H.C. Barnes, Comm.
(*NOTE: Both names given.)

June 25, 1887
Docket #235   **WICKED**   A.E. Ivey, Atty.
Roll 1852

Morehead, I.T.

Cherokee Citizenship Commission Docket Books
Tahlequah, Cherokee Nation (1880-84, 1887-89)
Volume I

#	NAMES	AGE	SEX
1	William	53	m
2	Minnie D.	17	f
3	S.A.	15	f
4	James P.	12	m
5	Samantha	9	f

Ancestor: Jas. Wicked

Now on this the 25th day of June, 1887, comes the above case for final hearing. And having made application pursuant to the provisions of an act of the National Council approved, Dec. 8, 1886, and all the evidence being duly examined and found to be sufficient and satisfactory to the Commission; It is adjudged and determined by the Commission that William Wicked, Minnie D. Wicked, S.A. Wicked, James P. Wicked, and Samantha Wicked are Cherokees by blood and are hereby re-admitted to all the rights, privileges, and immunities of Cherokees by blood.

And a certificate of said decision of the Commission and re-admission was made and furnished to said parties accordingly.

                                    J.T. Adair, Chairman
Henry Eiffert, Asst. Clerk   John E. Gunter, Commissioner

June 25, 1887
Docket #236   **PETERS**   A.E. Ivey, Atty.
Rolls 1851 & 52

Morehead, I.T.

#	NAMES	AGE	SEX
1	Annie A.	23	f
2	Thomas L.	4	m
3	Viola E.	3	f
4	Bessie E.	2	f
5	Lorenzo M.	4 mo	m

Ancestor: William Wicked

Now on this the 25th day of June, 1887, comes the above case for final hearing and the applicant having made application pursuant to the provisions of an act of the National Council approved Dec. 8, 1886. And all the evidence having been duly examined and found to be satisfactory to the Commission; It is adjudged and determined by the Commission that Annie A. Peters, Thomas L. Peters, Viola E. Peters, Bessie E. Peters, and Lorenzo M. Peters are Chero-

295

kees by blood and are hereby re-admitted to all the rights, privileges, and immunities of Cherokees by blood.

And a certificate of said decision of the Commission and re-admission was made and furnished to said parties accordingly.

J.T. Adair, Chairman Commission

Henry Eiffert, Clerk   John E. Gunter, Commissioner

June 25, 1887
Docket #237   **CHURCH**   E.C. Boudinot, Atty.
Roll 1835

Washington, CA

#	NAMES	AGE	SEX
1	Mary B.	30	f

Ancestor: Elias Boudinott

Now on this the 28th day of June, 1887, comes the above case for final hearing and having made application pursuant to the provisions of an act of the National Council, approved Dec. 8, 1886. And all the evidence being duly considered and found to be sufficient and satisfactory to the Commission; It is adjudged and determined by the Commission that Mary B. Church is a Cherokee by blood and she is hereby re-admitted to all the rights, privileges, and immunities of a Cherokee by blood.

And a certificate of said decision of the Commission and of re-admission was made and furnished said parties accordingly.

J.T. Adair, Chairman Comm.
John E. Gunter, Comm.

C.C. Lipe, Clerk   D.W. Lipe, Comm.

June 25, 1887
Docket #238   **McNAIR**   W.A. Thompson, Atty.
Rol 1835

Sheep Ranch, CA

#	NAMES	AGE	SEX
1	Clement V.	73	m
2	Clement A.	31	m
3	Nicholas G.	29	m
4	Ezra A.	25	m
5	Mary E.	21	f

Cherokee Citizenship Commission Docket Books
Tahlequah, Cherokee Nation (1880-84, 1887-89)
Volume I

Ancestor: David McNair

Now on this the 23rd day of August, 1887, comes the above case for final hearing and having made application pursuant to the provisions of an act of the National Council, approved Dec. 8, 1886. And all the evidence being duly considered and found to be sufficient and satisfactory to the Commission; It is adjudged and determined by the Commission that Clement V. McNair, Clement A. McNair, Nicholas G. McNair, Ezra A. McNair, and Mary E. McNair, are Cherokees by blood and are hereby re-admitted to all the rights, privileges, and immunities of a Cherokee by blood.

And a certificate of said decision of the Commission and of re-admission was made and furnished said parties accordingly.

J.T. Adair, Chairman

Henry Eiffert, Clerk   D.W. Lipe, Commissioner

June 27, 1887
Docket #239   **HENRY**   W.A. Thompson, Atty.
Roll 1835

Sheep Ranch, CA

#	NAMES	AGE	SEX
1	Amelia D.	27	f
2	Eva M.	9	f
3	Archie B.	11	m
4	Ada A.	8	f
5	Elsie A.	6	f
6	Mabell	1	f

Ancestor: David McNair
Admitted. (No other information given.)

June 27, 1887
Docket #240   **FISHER**   W.A. Thompson, Atty.
Roll 1835

Sheep Ranch, CA

#	NAMES	AGE	SEX
1	Leoda F.	23	f
2	Grover C.	2	m
3	Viva L.	1	f

Ancestor: David McNair

Admitted. (No other information given.)

June 27, 1887
Docket #241   **LANGLEY**   A.E. Ivey, Atty.
Rolls 1835, 51 & 52

Ellijay, GA

#	NAMES	AGE	SEX
1	Lock, Jr.	43	m
2	Sidney* J.	17	m
3	Susan M.	15	f
4	Thomas J.	15	m
5	Manda C	13	f
6	Wm. F.	12	m
7	Francis M.	10	f
8	Sam B.	8	m
9	Milly M.	6	f
10	Mary M. +	6	f
11	Joseph H.	4	m
12	Alice A.	1	f

Ancestor: Susan Langley

Now on this the 26th day of Sept, 1887, comes the above case for final hearing and the parties having made application pursuant to the provisions of an act of the National Council, approved Dec. 8, 1886. And all the evidence being duly examined and found to be sufficient and satisfactory to the Commission. And the name of the ancestor appearing on the rolls of 1835, 51 & 52; It is adjudged and determined by the Commission that Lock Langley, Jr, Sindy* J. Langley, Susan M. Langley, Thomas J. Langley, Wm. F. Langley, Manda Langley, Francis M. Langley, Sam B. Langley, Milly M. Langley, Joseph H. Langley, Alice A. Langley, are Cherokees by blood and are hereby re-admitted to all the rights, privileges, and immunities of Cherokees by blood.

And a certificate of said decision of the Commission and of re-admission was made and furnished said parties accordingly.

J.T. Adair, Chairman

John E. Gunter, Commissioner

(***NOTE:** Both names given.) (**+NOTE:** Mary M. was omitted from explanation.)

Cherokee Citizenship Commission Docket Books
Tahlequah, Cherokee Nation (1880-84, 1887-89)
Volume I

June 27, 1887
Docket #242   **PRATHER**   W.P. Boudinot and
Roll (None given.)   E.C. Boudinot, Jr, Atty.

(No P.O. given.)

#	NAMES	AGE	SEX
1	R.A.	?	?
2	Caroline	?	?

(No Ancestor given.)

Cherokee Nation vs Prather

Case called June 27, 1887, and by consent of parties was continued until Aug. 11, 1887.

The above case was tried Aug. 18, 1887, and has since that time been awaiting the action of the Commission on Citizenship upon the charge of fraud and bribery; having been made in securing the judgment of the Commission, granting said Prather citizenship in the Cherokee Nation [See 18th Sec. of an Act of Dec. 8, 1886]. The case was duly tried and the Nation's Atty. Hon. R.F. Wyly, used every endeavor to carry out the alleged charge. This case was tried and admitted to citizenship Dec. 19, 1870, by the "Bob Daniels" Court of Commission.

The witnesses in this case are all about dead, and the original testimony upon which the Commission based their opinion has nearly all been lost in consequence of which the Attorney for the Nation had but the margin to work on.

We the Commission on Citizenship fail to find that fraud or bribery had been resorted to be said Prather in obtaining their citizenship in the Cherokee Nation, on Dec. 19, 1870. We find for the defendants in this cause. Nov, 1888.

J.T. Adair, Chairman
D.W. Lipe, Comm.
H.C. Barnes, Comm.

June 27, 1887
Docket #243   **WHITAKER**   C.H. Taylor, Atty.
Rolls 1835 and 51

Valleytown, NC

#	NAMES	AGE	SEX
1	Stephen D.	33	m
2	Austin	11	m
3	Victor	9	m

| 4 | Caroline | 7 | f |
| 5 | Adaline | 4 | f |

Ancestor: Elizabeth Whitaker

Now on this the 9th day of February, 1888, comes the above case for a final hearing. And the parties having made application pursuant to the provisions of an act of the National Council, approved Dec. 8, 1886. And all the evidence being duly considered and found to be sufficient and satisfactory to the Commission; It is adjudged and determined by the Commission that Stephen D. Whitaker, Austin Whitaker, Victor Whitaker, Caroline Whitaker, and Adaline Whitaker, are Cherokees by blood and they are hereby re-admitted to all the rights, privileges, and immunities of Cherokee citizens by blood.

And a certificate of said decision of the Commission and of re-admission was made and furnished said parties accordingly.

J.T. Adair, Chairman Commission

Attest, C.C. Lipe, Clerk   John E. Gunter, Commissioner

June 27, 1887
Docket #244   **ELIOTT***   C.H. Taylor, Atty.
Rolls 1835 & 51

Cooyah, C.N.

#	NAMES	AGE	SEX
1	John W.	42	m
2	Odorothy	12	f
3	John B.	9	m

Ancestor: David Eliott

Oct. 16, 1888

John W. Elliott*, et.al   Mattie J. Miller, et.al

Now on this the 16th day of Oct, 1888, comes the above entitled case up for final hearing. The applicants claiming a Cherokee descent from Joseph and David Elliott. The evidence was duly considered both pro and con. This is one of the most important citizenship cases that has ever been before the Council and Commission of the Cherokee Nation for determination. As the question dates back to the year 1828, some 60 years ago when George Elliott, a brother of David Elliott, petitioned the National Council of the Old Cherokee Nation at Newechota (New Echota), for the rights of citizenship, and was rejected. Joseph Vann states further under date of the 23rd of Oct, 1872, that he was a member of the National Committee in the Old Nation when this case was taken before it for action, and gives as his reason, why the Elliotts were rejected was that several of the members knew George Elliott and knew him not to be a Cherokee, and further, the reason of Joseph Elliott, the father of George, being allowed a reservation as provided for under the provisions of the Treaty of 1817 and 1819, was that he was a great friend of Dick Riley's, who used his influence in obtaining this reservation for said Elliott, and that Dick Riley was at that time the 3rd Chief of the Old Cherokee Nation, and was very influential, and that he, Jos Vann, came to this country in the year 1829, and was again a member of the Senate or National Committee, as it was then called, of the Cherokee Nation, and that George Elliott again petitioned the National Council [here] for citizenship, he having removed to this country too, and that his cause for citizenship was again lost.

Luney Riley states under date of July 26, 1878, that he was a brother of Dick Riley, before spoken of as the 3rd Chief of the Old Cherokee Nation, and that his brother Dick went in company with Joseph Elliott, before mentioned, to an Agent to procure a certificate for a reservation for Elliott, and that Dick said to the Agent, "Elliott wants a reservation", and the Agent asked "who Elliott was and if he was a Cherokee", and that his brother, Dick answered by taking off his hat and saying to the Agent, "look at us and our hair", and the Agent without further inquiry gave Elliott a certificate that would entitle him to a reservation, the same as if he was an acknowledged Cherokee. Which reservation he got and afterwards relinquished to the United States for due compensation, as the papers before this Commission attest.

The testimony of D.L. Nicholson, who gave evidence in the John W. Elliott case for citizenship before the Chambers Commission, goes to show that he knew George Elliott in North Alabama, and that he was the reported owner of a reservation in Jackson Co, of that state, and that said George Elliott told persons he was a Cherokee, but that public opinion was, that he was not, on the contrary, that he was part Negro and white, probably an admixture of equal portions, and that he understood that the reservation obtained by the Elliotts under the terms of the before mentioned treaties was gotten by unfair practice. There is a great deal of other testimony both for and against the claim of these parties for Cherokee citizenship, but we deem it of no use to recount it.

Mr. Siler, who took the census of the Cherokees in the states of North Carolina, Tennessee, Georgia, and Alabama in the year 1851, preparatory to the Government of the United States paying out monies under the Treaty of 1835, says; [for he enrolled this family of Elliotts, and submitted their names together with the evidence taken to the Commissioner of Indian Affairs for his consideration] in a note, "Joseph Elliott from whom the families named above

Cherokee Citizenship Commission Docket Books
Tahlequah, Cherokee Nation (1880-84, 1887-89)
Volume I

[David Elliott, Martha A. Elliott, Catharine Elliott, John Elliott, Richard Elliott, Joseph Elliott, and Thomas Elliott, in one family; and Matilda Elliott, Ovitta Elliott, and Mary Elliott, in one family; Nancy Elliott, David Elliott, Louisa Elliott, and Josiah Elliott, in one family; and Mary Vaughn, Josiah Elliott, Martha Vaughn, Mary Vaughn, and David Vaughn, in one family; and Matthew Killingsworth, William Killingsworth, Martha Killingsworth, and Mary Killingsworth, in one family; and Matilda Dukes, William Dukes, and Mahala Dukes, in one family; and Caroline Johnson, Mary Johnson, and Tabitha Johnson, in one family; and Sarah A. Johnson by herself; and Mahala Hillian, Jesse Hillian, Winford Hillian, James Hillian, Thomas Hillian, and Nancy J. Hillian, in another family; and George Elliott, by himself] descended was recognized as for as to be allowed a reservation near Larkinsville, Alabama. He claimed that he was half Indian and seemed to have enjoyed many if not all the primary benefits accruing to the individuals of the Cherokee Nation under the treaty with the Government of the U.S., from the best account, if the history of the family, that I was able to procure, their claims were always disputed. I can find nothing to show that the authorities of the Cherokee Nation has ever reorganized them, and several persons of good character and intelligence are inclined to believe that the Cherokees decline to receive them in the Nation. I found no other native who believes that the Elliotts were Cherokees, in appearance I did not think they had the features of the Indian though their complexion is sufficiently dark. The rolls also shows that they were rejected.

Mr. Siler was a conscientious Agent and a man, who it has been thoroughly proven, was a friend to the right, and his opinion whenever expressed, was always good and clear, and based upon facts clearly set forth. He has shown himself a true friend to the Cherokee Indian.

The fact that a reservation was granted these Elliotts, as before mentioned, is not conclusive in itself that these parties were Cherokees, only the supposition, which in the face of contradictory testimony clearly set up, must fall to the ground. This seems to be the strongest points, this family have presented and upon which the have solely relied to establish their citizenship in the Cherokee Nation. In this they have failed, but, should persistence have been one of the requisites whereby claimants could have been re-admitted, they would have been recognized long ago.

We, the Commission on Citizenship, do therefore declare, that David Elliott, Benjamin Elliott, Millie J. Miller, Alexander Miller, James J. Miller, Ida L. Miller, John W. Elliott, Odorothy J. Elliott, John B. Elliott, Matilda A. Bates, Roxie Bates, Thomas J. Elliott, James H. Harris, David L. Harris, Florence A. Harris, and Lillie A. Harris, are not Cherokees by blood and are not

Cherokee Citizenship Commission Docket Books
Tahlequah, Cherokee Nation (1880-84, 1887-89)
Volume I

entitled to the rights and privileges of citizens of the Cherokee Nation on account of their blood or their residence within the limits of the Nation for the last 60 or 70 years, and are intruders upon the public domain of the Cherokee Nation.

J.T. Adair, Chairman Commission
H.C. Barnes, Commissioner
(*NOTE: Name spelled both ways.)

June 27, 1887
Docket #245   **HILLIER***   C.H. Taylor, Atty.
Roll 1851

Cooyah, C.N.

#	NAMES	AGE	SEX
1	Pinkney H.	20	f (?)
2	Joseph F.	?	m
3	Bessie G.	?	f

Ancestor: Polly Vaughn

April 27, 1889

Now on this day comes the above named case for the final hearing. The application was filed the 27th (of) June, 1887, and alleges that the applicant, is the son of Polly Vaughn, formerly Polly Elliott, whose name would be found on the census roll of Cherokees by blood taken in the year 1851. The application being supported by no evidence and the name of ancestor not being found on the census roll of 1851, the Commission decrees that Pinkney H. Hiller* is not of Cherokee blood and not entitled to re-admission to citizenship in the Cherokee Nation.

Will P. Ross, Chairman
R. Bunch, Commissioner
Attest, E.G. Ross, Clerk   John E. Gunter, Commissioner

(*NOTE: Name spelled both ways.)

June 27, 1887
Docket #246   **MILLER**   C.H. Taylor, Atty.
Rolls 1835 and 51

Cooyah, C.N.

#	NAMES	AGE	SEX
1	Millie J.	49	f
2	Alexander	20	m

3	James J.	17	m
4	Ida L.	6	f

Ancestor: Joseph Eliott*

See decision in this case in that of John W. Elliott* in this book on page 223 (Docket #244). Adverse to claimant. Oct. 16, 1888

Cornell Rogers
Clerk

(*NOTE: Name spelled both ways.)

June 28, 1887
Docket #247   **McCART**   A.E. Ivey, Atty.
Rolls 1835 and 52

Prairie City, I.T.

#	NAMES	AGE	SEX
1	L.C.	43	f
2	R.J.	18	m
3	J.W.	16	m
4	Lilla M.	14	f
5	Rosa Lee	11	f
6	L.A.	3	m

Ancestor: Jerry Ward

Adverse. Embraced in decision in (this) book, page 216 (Docket #230), in John Ward case.
E.G. Ross, Clerk

June 28, 1887
Docket #248   **HOWELL**   A.E. Ivey, Atty.
Rolls 1835 and 52

Pryors Creek, I.T.

#	NAMES	AGE	SEX
1	L.E.	46	f
2	J.H.	15	m
3	Mary E.	14	f
4	Emma L.	13	f
5	Wm. G.	9	m

Ancestor: Jerry Ward

Cherokee Citizenship Commission Docket Books
Tahlequah, Cherokee Nation (1880-84, 1887-89)
Volume I

Adverse. Embraced in decision in (this) book, page 216 (Docket #230).
E.G. Ross, Clerk

June 28, 1887
Docket #249   **GOINS**   A.E. Ivey, Atty.
Rolls 1835 to 1852

Vian, I.T.

#	NAMES	AGE	SEX
1	Polly	54	f
2	Riley	30	m
3	Elisha	24	m
4	Shannon	20	m
5	Adam	16	m
6	Mary E.	14	f

Ancestor: George Fields

Now on this the 26th day of August, 1887, comes the above case for a final hearing. And submitted by agreement between the Attorney for Plaintiff and the Atty. on part of the Nation on the evidence taken and submitted in this case of Polly Goins; We the Commission on Citizenship after a careful and impartial investigation of the testimony and having also examined the census rolls of 1835 to 52, we failed to find the name of ancestor, George Fields. And the evidence in behalf of applicant not being sufficient. The Commission therefore declares that the above named parties are not Cherokees by blood and not entitled to any of the rights or privileges of Cherokee citizens.

J.T. Adair, Chairman
D.W. Lipe, Commissioner

June 28, 1887
Docket #250   **GOINS**   A.E. Ivey, Atty.
Rolls 1835 and 1852

Vian, I.T.

#	NAMES	AGE	SEX
1	Corzina	48	f
2	Alice	18	f
3	Martha	12	f
4	Nancy	14	f
5	Cherokee	10	f

6	James B.	16	m

Ancestor: George Fields

Now on this the 9th day of Nov, 1887, comes the above case for a final
hearing and submitted by agreement between the Attorney for Plaintiff and the
Atty. on part of the Nation, on the evidence taken and submitted in this case of
Corzina Goins, Alice Goins, Nancy Goins, Cherokee Goins, James B. Goins;
We the Commission on Citizenship after a careful and impartial investigation
of the testimony and having also examined the census rolls of 1835 to 52, and
failed to find the name of the ancestor, George Fields. And the evidence in behalf of applicants not being sufficient; The Commission therefore declares that
the above named parties are not Cherokees by blood and not entitled to any of
the rights or privileges of Cherokee citizens.

J.T. Adair, Chairman
D.W. Lipe, Commissioner

June 28, 1887
Docket #251   **KREBBS**   A.E. Ivey, Atty.
Rolls 1835 and 1852

Vian, I.T.

#	NAMES	AGE	SEX
1	Cassandra	26	f
2	Lillie M.	3	f

Ancestor: George Fields

Now on this the 9th day of Nov, comes the above case for a final hearing
and submitted by agreement between the Attorney for Plaintiff and the Atty. on
part of the Nation, on the evidence taken and submitted in this case of Cassandra Krebbs, Lillie M. Krebbs; We the Commission on Citizenship after a careful and impartial investigation of the testimony and having also examined the
census rolls of 1835 to 52, and failed to find the name of the ancestor, George
Fields. And the evidence in behalf of applicants not being sufficient; The
Commission therefore declares that the above named parties are not Cherokees
by blood and not entitled to any of the rights or privileges of Cherokee citizenship.

J.T. Adair, Chairman
John E. Gunter, Comm.

June 28, 1887

Docket #252   **FIELDS**   A.E. Ivey, Atty.
Rolls 1835 to 1852

Vian, I.T.

#	NAMES	AGE	SEX
1	Martin	43	m
2	Sarah J.	16	f
3	James Riley	13	m
4	Julia A.	12	f

Ancestor: George Fields

Now on this the 26th day of August, 1887, comes the above case for final hearing had having made application pursuant to the provisions of an act of the National Council approved Dec. 8, 1886, and all the evidence having been duly considered and from the evidence given by applicants' witnesses, it is clearly proven that George Fields, the ancestor, and his descendants are not Cherokees by blood. Therefore the Commission unanimously agreed and decided that the applicant Martin Fields, Sarah J. Fields, James Riley Fields, and Julia A. Fields, are not Cherokees by blood and are not entitled to any rights or privileges of Cherokee citizens.

J.T. Adair, Chairman

Henry Eiffert, Clerk   D.W. Lipe, Comm.

June 28, 1887
Docket #253   **MOORE**   A.E. Ivey, Atty.
Rolls 1835 to 1852

Vian, I.T.

#	NAMES	AGE	SEX
1	Tennessee	18	f

Ancestor: George Fields

Now on this the 9th day of Nov, 1887, comes the above case for a final hearing and submitted by agreement between the Attorney for Plaintiff and the Atty. on part of the Nation, on the evidence taken and submitted in this case of Tennessee Moore; We the Commission on Citizenship after a careful and impartial investigation of the testimony and having also examined the census rolls of 1835 to 52, and failed to find the name of the ancestor. And the evidence in behalf of applicant not being sufficient; The Commission therefore declares that the above named party is not a Cherokee by blood and not entitled to any of the rights or privileges of Cherokee citizens.

J.T. Adair, Chairman
John E. Gunter, Comm.

June 28, 1887
Docket #254   **CROW**   A.E. Ivey, Atty.
Rolls 1835 to 1852

Henderson, TX

#	NAMES	AGE	SEX
1	Ollie	59	f

Ancestor: Mrs. Dunson

May 1, 1889

Now on this day for the final hearing of the above entitled case the Commission after investigating the papers in said case find that the applicant produces no evidence whatever to sustain the allegation set forth in her application. Relying entirely on her application, therefore, the Commission renders a decision adverse to claimant, Ollie Crow, age 59 years. Post Office Henderson, TX. Rejected, May 1, 1889.

Will P. Ross, Chairman
D.S. Williams, Clerk   John E. Gunter, Comm.

June 28, 1887
Docket #255   **HUBBARD**   L.B. Bell, Atty.
Roll (None given.)

Afton, I.T.

#	NAMES	AGE	SEX
1	Caleb	66	m

Ancestor: Ann Crews

Adversely. Rejected July 2, 1889.

J.E. Gunter, Comm.
Attest, D.S. Williams, Asst. Clerk

June 28, 1887
Docket #256   **MEREDITH**   L.B. Bell, Atty.
Roll (None given.)

Afton, I.T.

#	NAMES	AGE	SEX
1	John	82	m

Ancestor: Mary Crews

Aug. 22, 1889

The above application was filed on the 28th day of June, 1888, and on this day the case coming up for final hearing, we find no evidence submitted by applicant in support of his claim, also his Attorney, L.B. Bell, admits that his name or that of his ancestor's does not appear upon the census rolls of Cherokees taken in the year of 1835, 48, 51, and 52. Therefore, we decide that applicant, John Meredith, is not a Cherokee by blood and not entitled to citizenship in the Cherokee Nation.

Will P. Ross, Chairman
R. Bunch, Comm.

Attest, E.G. Ross, Clerk   John E. Gunter, Comm.

June 29, 1887
Docket #257   **CROCKEROON**   A.E. Ivey, Atty.
Rolls 1835 to 1852
Moorehead, I.T.

#	NAMES	AGE	SEX
1	Soloman	73	m

Ancestor: Will Crockeroon

Now on the 17th day of April, 1889, comes the case of Soloman Crockeroon versus the Cherokee Nation for final hearing. The application in this case is made in the name of Soloman Crockeroon, who claims his Cherokee blood from one Will Crockeroon, whose name he believes was duly enrolled upon the census rolls of Cherokees by blood, citizens of the Cherokee Nation, taken and made in the year 1835 and 1852. The statement made before the Commission by the applicant shows that he pronounced his name as spell - Soloman Crockeroon, that when he and some of his descendants came into the Nation several years ago, they were known by the name of Crocker, and that it was since the filing of the application the 28th day of June, 1887, that the effort to change the name to Crockeroon was made. It is further shown that John Crockeroon died about the middle of December, or the later part of that month in 1887, and that applicant and his family had been in the Nation two or three years prior to that time, but that no attempt appears to have been made to obtain his statement, although perhaps the most important witness in the case then living. It also appears conclusively that Soloman Crockeroon made an effort to procure manufactured evidence in his behalf as did his son, L.B. Crockeroon. It does not appear that Soloman Crockeroon, alias Crocker, alias Crockrane, at any time resided within the limits of the Cherokee Nation East of the Mississippi, nor West of that river until within recent years, nor that he sought at any time to have his own name enrolled either in the year 1835 or 1852, although according to his own statement, he was living in Alabama at the time of the payment of funds per capita to the Cherokees in 1852. The Commission sees no sufficient cause to believe that the name of the applicant has been wrongly enrolled or that he is the son of Will Cockran, whose name may be found on the census rolls of 1835 and 1852. It is therefore decreed by the Commission that Soloman Crockeroon is not a Cherokee by blood and is not entitled to citizenship in the Cherokee Nation. This decree embraces the applications of L.B. Crockeroon [recently deceased] and his son, James Crockeroon, aged 22 years, at time of filing application, June 29, 1887; F.W. Crockeroon, age 34 years; L.M. Crockeroon, aged 35 years; L.M. Crockeroon [son] aged 6 years; Julia Z. Crockeroon, female aged 4 years; Luvenia E. Crockeroon, female aged 3 years; W.F. Crockeroon, male aged 1 year; W.B. Crockeroon, aged 27 years; and Maude Crockeroon aged 1 year. The Post Office address June 28, 1887, of L.B. Crockeroon was Tahlequah and that of the others named, Moorehead, Ind. Terr.

<table>
<tr><td></td><td>Will P. Ross, Chairman</td></tr>
<tr><td>Attest, D.S. Williams, Clerk</td><td>John E. Gunter, Comm.</td></tr>
</table>

June 29, 1887
Docket #258 **LYNCH** A.E. Ivey, Atty.
Rolls of 1835 & 1852

Moorehead, I.T.

#	NAMES	AGE	SEX
1	Julia	23	f
2	Kate	6	f
3	Bull	2	m

Ancestor: Wm. Crockeroon

The above case was called and submitted by Atty. A.E. Ivey without evidence in support of claim. The Commission therefore decides that Julia Lynch, and the following children, Kate Lynch and Bull Lynch, are not Cherokees by blood. Post Office, Moorehead, I.T. Rejected Sept. 9, 1889.

<table>
<tr><td></td><td>Will P. Ross, Chairman</td></tr>
<tr><td>Attest, D.S. Williams, Clerk</td><td>J.E. Gunter, Comm.</td></tr>
</table>

July 1, 1887
Docket #259   **CROCKROM***   A.E. Ivey, Atty.
Rolls 1835 to 1851

Moorehead, I.T.

#	NAMES	AGE	SEX
1	S.M.	35	m
2	S.M, Jr.	6	m
3	Julia Z.	4	f
4	Luvenia	3	f
5	W.F.	1	m

Ancestor: Will Crockroon*

Adverse to claimant.

See decision in this case in that of Soloman Crockeroon, on page 230 (Docket #257) this book. <u>Rejected</u> April 17, 1889.

D.S. Williams, Clerk
(***NOTE:** Name spelled all three ways.)

July 1, 1887
Docket #260   **CROCKROM***   A.E.
Ivey, Atty.
Rolls 1835 to 1852

Moorehead, I.T.

#	NAMES	AGE	SEX
1	W.B.	27	m
2	Maude	1	f

Ancestor: Will Crockroon*

Adverse to claimant.

See decision in this case in that of Soloman Crockeroon* on page 230 (Docket #257) this book. <u>Rejected</u> April 17, 1889.

D.S. Williams, Clerk
(***NOTE:** Name spelled all three ways.)

July 1, 1887

Docket #261   **CROCKROM***   A.E. Ivey, Atty.
Rolls 1835 to 53

Tahlequah, I.T.

#	NAMES	AGE	SEX
1	S.B.	49	m
2	James	22	m

Ancestor: Will Crockroon*

Adverse to claimant.

See decision in this case in that of Soloman Crockeroon* on page 230, (Docket #257) in this book. Rejected April 17, 1889.

D.W. Williams, Clerk

       (***NOTE:** Name spelled all three ways.)

July 1, 1887

Docket #262   **CROCKROM***   A.E. Ivey, Atty.
Rolls 1835 to 52

Moorehead, I.T.

#	NAMES	AGE	SEX
1	F.W.	34	m

Ancestor: Will Crockroon*

Adverse to claimant.

See decision in this case in that of Soloman Crockeroon* on page 230 (Docket #257) in this book. Rejected April 17, 1889.

D.S. Williams, Clerk

       (***NOTE:** Name spelled all three ways.)

July 1, 1887

Docket #263   **DAUGHERTY**   (No Atty. given.)
Roll 1848

Joplin, MO

#	NAMES	AGE	SEX
1	Winnie	40	f
2	A.A.	43	m
3	James R.	8	m

4	John M.	4	m
5	Sarah E.	2	f

Ancestor: John Love

Now on this the 19th day of March, 1888, comes the above case for a final hearing, and having made application pursuant to the provisions of an act of the National Council, approved Dec. 8, 1886, and all the evidence being duly considered and found to be sufficient and satisfactory to the Commission; It is adjudged and determined by the Commission that Winnie Daugherty, and her three children, James R. Daugherty, John M. Daugherty, and Sarah E. Daugherty, are Cherokees by blood, and they are hereby re-admitted to all the privileges. rights, and immunities of Cherokee citizens by blood.

And a certificate of said decision of the Commission and of re-admission was made out and furnished said parties accordingly.

J.T. Adair, Chairman
John E. Gunter, Commissioner
Attest, C.C. Lipe, Clerk   D.W. Lipe, Commissioner

July 1, 1887
Docket #264   **WARD**   A.E. Ivey, Atty.
Rolls 1835 and 1852

Honey Grove, TX

#	NAMES	AGE	SEX
1	James	42	m
2	William	15	m
3	Lewis	12	m
4	Sallie	10	f
5	Belle	8	f
6	Gill	6	m
7	Henrietta	4	f
8	Baby	?	?

Ancestor: Jerry Ward

Adverse. Embraced in decision on page 216 (Docket #230), in John Ward Case.
Attest, E.G. Ross, Clerk

July 1, 1887

Docket #265   **WARD**   A.E. Ivey, Atty.
Rolls 1835 and 1852

Honey Grove, TX

#	NAMES	AGE	SEX
1	Lewis M.	27	m

Ancestor: Jerry Ward

Adverse. Embraced in decision of John Ward, this book, page 216 (Docket #230).

Attest, E.G. Ross, Clerk

July 1, 1887
Docket #266   **NORTON**   A.E. Ivey, Atty.
Rolls 1835 and 1852

(No Post Office given.)

#	NAMES	AGE	SEX
1	J.B.	35	m
2	J. Alice	15	f
3	Manda B.	11	f
4	Lewis A.	13	m
5	Lillie	6	f
6	John F.	3	m
7	Cora	1	f

Ancestor: Jerry Ward

Adverse. Embraced in decision in this book, page 216 (Docket #230), in John Ward case.

Attest, E.G. Ross, Clerk

June 29, 1887
Docket #267   **JOLLY**   A.E. Ivey, Atty.
Roll 1835 to 1852

Honey Grove, TX

#	NAMES	AGE	SEX
1	A.M.	44	f
2	Wm. L.	27	m

3	Lelia	22	f
4	Sarah	18	f

Ancestor: Jerry Ward

Adverse. Embraced in decision in this book, page 216 (Docket #230), in John Ward case.

Attest, E.G. Ross, Clerk

June 29, 1887
Docket #268   **YATES**   A.E. Ivey, Atty.
Rolls 1835 to 52

South West City, MO

#	NAMES	AGE	SEX
1	Thomas J.	38	m
2	Mattie B.	12	f
3	Gracie A.	10	f
4	Albert J.	8	m
5	Aggie	6	f
6	J. Henry	3	m

Ancestor: Jerry Ward

Adverse. Embraced in decision in this book, page 216 (Docket #230), in John Ward case.

Attest, E.G. Ross, Clerk

June 30, 1887
Docket #269   **ROGERS**   A.E. Ivey, Atty.
Rolls 1835 to 1852

Checotah, I.T.

#	NAMES	AGE	SEX
1	Kate D.	39	f
2	Wm Penn	16	m
3	W.B.	14	m
4	Delilah P.	10	f
5	Jessie C.	8	m

| 6 | Mary R. | 4 | f |
| 7 | Kate D. | 4 mo | f |

Ancestor: Wm & Delilah Drew

Now on this the 2nd day of October, 1888, comes the above case for a final hearing. And the parties having made application pursuant to the provisions of an act of the National Council approved Dec. 8, 1886, and all the evidence having been duly examined and found to be sufficient and satisfactory. It is adjudged and determined by the Commission, that Kate D. Rogers, and her six children, to wit: William Penn Rogers, W.B. Rogers, Delilah P. Rogers, Jessie C. Rogers, Mary R. Rogers, and Kate D. Rogers, are Cherokees by blood, and are hereby re-admitted to all the rights, privileges, and immunities of other Cherokee citizens.

And a certificate of said decision of the Commission and of re-admission was made out and furnished said parties accordingly.

J.T. Adair, Chairman

Attest, C.C. Lipe, Clerk　　　　　　　　H.C. Barnes, Commissioner

June 30, 1887

Docket #270　　　　　　　**ROBINSON***　　　　(No Atty. given.)

Roll 1835

Fort Gibson, I.T.

#	NAMES	AGE	SEX
1	Sallie A.	32	f
2	F.N.	11	m
3	C.L.	7	m
4	Sallie H.	5	f
5	Nellie Love	2	f

Ancestor: Dillard Love Trammell

The above case was called three several times at intervals of not less than one hour apart and no person answering and there being no evidence to sustain the allegations set forth in the application which was filed the 29th day of June, 1887; It is adjudged that Sallie A. Roberson* and her children, F.N. Roberson, C.L. Roberson, Sallie H. Roberson, and Nellie Love Roberson, are not entitled to re-admission to citizenship in the Cherokee Nation as Cherokees by blood. Post Office Fort Gibson, Ind. Terr. Rejected April 29, 1889.

Will P. Ross, Chairman

D.S. Williams, Clerk   John E. Gunter, Commissioner
(*NOTE: Both names given.)

July 2, 1887
Docket #271   **RAWLSTON***   L.B. Bell, Atty.
Roll 1835

Dalton, GA

#	NAMES	AGE	SEX
1	Nancy	50	f

Ancestor: Lewis Rawlston

Now on this the 13th day of Oct, 1887, comes the above case for a final hearing. And the parties having made application pursuant to the provisions of an act of the National Council approved Dec. 8, 1886. And all the evidence being duly examined and found to be sufficient and satisfactory to the Commission and the name of the ancestor Lewis Rawlston appearing on the rolls of 1835; It is adjudged and determined by the Commission that Nancy Raulston* is a Cherokee by blood and is hereby re-admitted to all the rights, privileges, and immunities of Cherokees by blood.

And a certificate of said decision of the Commission and re-admission was made and furnished to said parties accordingly.

D.W. Lipe, Acting Chairman
John E. Gunter, Commissioner
(*NOTE: Name spelled both ways.)

July 2, 1887
Docket #272   **RAWLSTON***   L.B. Bell, Atty.
Roll 1835

Dalton, GA

#	NAMES	AGE	SEX
1	Agnes P.	39	f
2	Charles C.F.	3	m

Ancestor: Lewis Rawlston

Now on this the 13th day of Oct, 1887, comes the above case for a final hearing. And the parties having made application pursuant to the provisions of an act of the National Council approved Dec. 8, 1886. And all the evidence being duly examined and found to be sufficient and satisfactory to the Commission and the name of the ancestor Lewis Rawlston appearing on the rolls of

1835; It is adjudged and determined by the Commission that Agnes P. Raulston* and Charles C.F. Raulston, Cherokees by blood and are hereby re-admitted to all the rights, privileges, and immunities of Cherokees by blood.

And a certificate of said decision of the Commission and re-admission was made and furnished to said parties accordingly.

D.W. Lipe, Acting Chairman
John E. Gunter, Commissioner

(*NOTE: Name spelled both ways.)

July 2, 1887
Docket #273   **RAWLSTON***   L.B. Bell, Atty.
Roll 1835

Dalton, GA

#	NAMES	AGE	SEX
1	Francis T.	56	f

Ancestor: Lewis Rawlston

Now on this the 13th day of Oct, 1887, comes the above case for a final hearing. And the parties having made application pursuant to the provisions of an act of the National Council approved Dec. 8, 1886. And all the evidence being duly examined and found to be sufficient and satisfactory to the Commission and the name of the ancestor Lewis Rawlston appearing on the rolls of 1835; It is adjudged and determined by the Commission that Francis T. Raulston* is a Cherokee by blood and is hereby re-admitted to all the rights, privileges, and immunities of Cherokees by blood.

And a certificate of said decision of the Commission and re-admission was made and furnished to said parties accordingly.

D.W. Lipe, Acting Chairman
John E. Gunter, Commissioner

(*NOTE: Name spelled both ways.)

July 2, 1887
Docket #274   **RAWLSTON***   L.B. Bell, Atty.
Roll 1835

Dalton, GA

#	NAMES	AGE	SEX

| 1 | Emily E. | 52 | f |

Ancestor: Lewis Rawlston

Now on this the 13th day of Oct, 1887, comes the above case for a final hearing. And the parties having made application pursuant to the provisions of an act of the National Council approved Dec. 8, 1886. And all the evidence being duly examined and found to be sufficient and satisfactory to the Commission and the name of the ancestor Lewis Rawlston appearing on the rolls of 1835; It is adjudged and determined by the Commission that Emily C. Raulston* is a Cherokee by blood and is hereby re-admitted to all the rights, privileges, and immunities of Cherokees by blood.

And a certificate of said decision of the Commission and re-admission was made and furnished to said parties accordingly.

D.W. Lipe, Acting Chairman
John E. Gunter, Commissioner

(**NOTE:** Name spelled both ways.)

July 2, 1887
Docket #275 **RAWLSTON** L.B. Bell, Atty.
Roll 1835

Dalton, GA

#	NAMES	AGE	SEX
1	Robert D.	32	m
2	E.C.	8	f
3	Lillie D.	6	f
4	Mary C.	3	f
5	Robert L.	3 mo	m

Ancestor: Lewis Rawlston

Now on this the 13th day of Oct, 1887, comes the above case for a final hearing. And the parties having made application pursuant to the provisions of an act of the National Council approved Dec. 8, 1886. And all the evidence being duly examined and found to be sufficient and satisfactory to the Commission and the name of the ancestor Lewis Rawlston appearing on the rolls of 1835; It is adjudged and determined by the Commission that Robert D. Rawlston, E.C. Rawlston, Lillia D. Rawlston, Mary C. Rawlston, and Robert L. Rawlston, are Cherokees by blood and are hereby re-admitted to all the rights, privileges, and immunities of Cherokees by blood.

And a certificate of said decision of the Commission and re-admission was made and furnished to said parties accordingly.

D.W. Lipe, Acting Chairman
John E. Gunter, Commissioner

July 2, 1887
Docket #276 **JONES** L.B. Bell, Atty.
Roll 1835

Dalton, GA

#	NAMES	AGE	SEX
1	Agnes E.	9	f
2	Carrie Georgia	8	f
3	Charlie	6	m

Ancestor: Lewis Rawlston

The above case was called three times and no response from applicant or by Atty. and there being no evidence on file in support of claim, the Commission decided that Agnes E. Jones, Cassie Georgia Jones, and Charley Jones, nephew [E.E. Rawlston is guardian for the above minor children], are not Cherokees by blood. P.O. Dalton, GA. Rejected Sept. 16, 1889.

Will P. Ross, Chairman
Attest, D.S. Williams, Clerk J.E. Gunter, Commissioner

July 2, 1887
Docket #277 **HAMPTON** J.M. Bryan and
Rolls 1851 & 52 L.B. Bell, Attys.

Prairie City, I.T.

#	NAMES	AGE	SEX
1	Elizabeth	67	f

Ancestor: James Jones

The decision in this case will be found in this book on (this) page , (Docket #278, below), in the Polly White case. Re-admitted.

Cornell Rogers, Clerk

Cherokee Citizenship Commission Docket Books
Tahlequah, Cherokee Nation (1880-84, 1887-89)
Volume I

July 2, 1887
Docket #278   **WHITE**   J.M. Bryan, Atty.
Rolls 1851 & 52

Prairie City, I.T.

#	NAMES	AGE	SEX
1	Polly	65	f

Ancestor: James Jones

Now on this the 30th day of June, 1888, comes the above entitled case up for final hearing. The case having been submitted by Bell & Bryan, Attorneys for applicants, on the 28th. After a careful investigation of all the evidence, both oral and documentary, submitted by Plaintiff, also the Old Settler Payroll of Cherokees made in the year 1851, find for the Plaintiff for these reasons; to wit:

First: That the name of James Jones, from whom the above applicants have proven a lineal descent, appear upon the Old Settler Pay roll of Cherokees, made in the year 1851, and numbered thereon 57, and further, that the names of Polly White and Elizabeth Hampton, daughter and William Jones, also Martin Jones, now dead, sons of the said James Jones, together with Andrew Hampton, Thomas B. Jones, and Mary White, children of Polly White, Elizabeth Hampton and William Jones and grand-children of James Jones, all appear upon the Old Settler Payroll of 1851.

Secondly: That James Jones took a reservation under the terms of the Treaty of 1817 on the Tennessee River in the state of Tennessee, as the roll of Reservees of that year shows, together with a certified transcript of the bounds of this reservation from the Interior Department of the United States.

Thirdly: The attention of the Commission is called to an act of the National Council, approved Nov. 16, 1849, which reads:

"Be it enacted by the National Council. That James Jones be and he is hereby privileged to return to the Cherokee Nation with his family and reside, and is admitted to the enjoyment of the rights and privileges of citizenship of this Nation.

Tahlequah, November 16th, 1849
Approved - Jno. Ross."

Therefore, we the Commission on Citizenship, a body duly created under the provisions of an act of the National Council, approved Dec. 8, 1886, and rejecting or re-admitting applicants for citizenship, who shall have filed their applications in due season, under the 7th Section of the above act, and the amendment to said act in relation to Old Settler applicants, approved Feb. 7, 1888, do declare that Polly White, Elizabeth Hampton, Thomas Jones and his nine children, viz: William H, Artela, Leroy A. John S, Hatta H.C, Betsy E, J.H, Joel, and Arvilla Jones, and James E, Wm H, and J.S. White, and Mary Jane White, Eli Herod, Polly Brown, Mont Smith, John Smith, and Eliza Smith, and Joseph S. Herod and his two sisters, and brother, Elzena, William W, and Louisa Bell Herod and James Joel Jones, son of Margaret Jones, dead, and Andrew W. Hampton, William C. Mattie J. and Clara May Hampton, and Alabama Hampton, and Emily Jones, and Catharine Hurley, and her child Jancy Hurley, and Theodore Jones, Elizabeth Jones, Caldonia Jones, and Margaret A. Jones, and Sarah A. Blaylock, and her four children, Mary Elizabeth, Milly Jane, Artela, and Lotta Ann Blaylock, and Ruth Ann Atchison, and Josiah White, are entitled to all the rights and privileges of Cherokees by virtue of such blood, and are hereby re-admitted as such.

J.T. Adair, Chairman
D.W. Lipe, Commissioner

July 4, 1887
Docket #279   **SNOW**   A.E. Ivey, Atty.
Rolls 1835 to 1852

Uniontown, AR

#	NAMES	AGE	SEX
1	Joseph	25	m
2	Effie	2	f
3	Mamie	Infant	f

Ancestor: Mary Franklin, nee Deese

Now on this the 31st day of March, 1888, comes the above case up for final disposition. They having made application pursuant to the provisions of an act of the National Council, approved, Dec. 8, 1886, and all the evidence being duly considered and found to be insufficient and unsatisfactory; It is adjudged and determined by the Commission, that Joseph Snow, Effie Snow and Mamie Snow, are not Cherokees by blood, and are not entitled to the rights, privileges, and immunities of such.

(No Chairman or Commissioner given.)

Cherokee Citizenship Commission Docket Books
Tahlequah, Cherokee Nation (1880-84, 1887-89)
Volume I

July 5, 1887   Ridge,

Paschal

Docket #280   **HALL**   E.C. Boudinot, Jr, and

Rolls 1835 51&52   John L. Adair, Atty.

St. Louis, MO

#	NAMES	AGE	SEX
1	Josephann	41	f
2	Jessee	17	f
3	Blanche	14	f
4	James Eugene	20	m

Ancestor: Joseph Rogers

Now on this the 19th day of Oct, 1887, comes the above case for a final hearing. And the parties having made application pursuant to the provisions of an act of the National Council approved Dec. 8, 1886. And all the evidence being duly examined and found to be sufficient and satisfactory to the Commission and the name of the ancestor Joseph Rogers appearing on the rolls of 1835, 51 & 52; It is adjudged and determined by the Commission that Josephann Hall (This is the only name mentioned in the explanation.) is a Cherokee by blood and is hereby re-admitted to all the rights, privileges, and immunities of Cherokees by blood.

And a certificate of said decision of the Commission and re-admission was made and furnished to said parties accordingly.

J.T. Adair, Chairman

John E. Gunter, Commissioner

July 5, 1887   Ridge, Paschal,

Docket #281   **HALL**   E.C. Boudinot, Jr, &

Roll 1835   John L. Adair, Attys.

St. Louis, MO

#	NAMES	AGE	SEX
1	Wm. Oscar	21	m

Ancestor: Joseph Rogers

Now on this the 19th day of Oct, 1887, comes the above case for a final hearing. And the parties having made application pursuant to the provisions of an act of the National Council approved Dec. 8, 1886. And all the evidence being duly examined and found to be sufficient and satisfactory to the Commission and the name of the ancestor Joseph Rogers appearing on the rolls of 1835; It is adjudged and determined by the Commission that Wm. Oscar Hall, is a Cherokee by blood and is hereby re-admitted to all the rights, privileges, and immunities of Cherokees by blood.

And a certificate of said decision of the Commission and re-admission was made and furnished to said parties accordingly.

J.T. Adair, Chairman
John E. Gunter, Commissioner

July 8, 1887
Docket #282   **ROGERS**   C.J. Harris, Atty.
Rolls 1851 & 52

Duluth, GA

#	NAMES	AGE	SEX
1	William A.	26	m
2	Cora Lee	23	f
3	David M.	53	m
4	Love	20	m
5	Lena M.	24	f
6	Mary E.	17	f

Ancestor: William Rogers

Sept. 6, 1888

The above case being submitted by Defendants' Attorney, C.J. Harris, on the date above mentioned. We the Commission on Citizenship after a careful examination of all the evidence and the census rolls of Cherokees mentioned in the 7th Section of the law of Dec. 8, 1886, find that (the) names of David M. Rogers and his five children, viz: William A, Cora Lee, Love, Mary E, and Lena M. Rogers, are Cherokees by blood. And it is adjudged and determined by the Commission that the above named persons are hereby re-admitted to all the rights, privileges, and immunities of Cherokee citizens by blood.

And a certificate of said decision of Commission and re-admission was made and furnished said parties accordingly.

D.W. Lipe, Acting Chairman
H.C. Barnes, Commissioner

(**NOTE:** David M. was marked out on original.)

July 9, 2887
Docket #283   **MELTON**   A.E. Ivey, Atty.
Rolls 1835 to 52

Jacksboro, TX

Cherokee Citizenship Commission Docket Books
Tahlequah, Cherokee Nation (1880-84, 1887-89)
Volume I

#	NAMES	AGE	SEX
1	O.M.	53	m
2	Jerry C.	21	m
3	Alexander B.	19	m
4	Mary Francis	16	f
5	Nellie	12	f
6	Albert Lemans	8	m
7	Charles Fielden	5	m

Ancestor: Elizabeth Badson

On the 1st day of July, 1887, the application of O.M. Melton, Jacksboro, TX, for admission to citizenship in the Cherokee Nation, was filed before the Commission on Citizenship. In it, the applicant alleges that he is the grand-son of Elizabeth Badson, who was of Cheorkee blood and whose name would be found on the rolls of Cherokees by blood; citizens of the Cherokee Nation taken and made in the year 1835 and 1852. There is no evidence to show that Elizabeth Badson was of Cherokee blood nor is her name found on the census rolls of Cherokees taken in 1835-1851 or 52.

It is therefore adjudged that O.M. Melton is not of Cherokee blood and not entitled to citizenship in the Cherokee Nation. This decree includes the children of O.M. Melton, viz: Jerry C. Melton, Alexander B. Melton, Mary Francis Melton, Nellie Melton, Albert Lemans Melton, and Charles Fielden Melton.

Will P. Ross, Chairman
John E. Gunter, Comm.

July 11, 1887
Docket #284   **JOHNSON**   A.E. Ivey, Atty.
Rolls 1835 to 52

Tahlequah, C.N.

#	NAMES	AGE	SEX
1	Mary A.	67	f

Ancestor: James & Elizabeth Cooper

April 29, 1889

Now comes the above case for the final hearing. The application was filed the 2nd day of July, 1887, and submitted by the attorneys for applicant and for the Nation, without evidence to sustain it, the Commission decided that Mary A. Johnson, is not a Cherokee by blood and not entitled to re-admission to citizenship in the Cherokee Nation. Rejected, April 29, 1889.

D.S. Williams, Clerk

Will P. Ross, Chairman
John E. Gunter, Commissioner

July 12, 1887
Docket #285
Roll 1835

BRIGHTWELL

A.E. Ivey, Atty.

Mayesville, AR

#	NAMES	AGE	SEX
1	Elizabeth		

Ancestor: Abraham Scott

April 29, 1889

Now on the day above named comes the above application for the final hearing. The case having been submitted by the Attorneys for both parties. The application which was filed the 8th day of July, 1887, being unsustained by any evidence, the Commission decided that the applicant, Elizabeth Brightwell, is not entitled to re-admission to citizenship in the Cherokee Nation by virtue of having Cherokee blood. Rejected, April 29, 1889.

D.S. Williams, Clerk

Will P. Ross, Chairman
John E. Gunter, Comm.

July 13, 1887
Docket #286
Roll 1835

MYERS

A.E. Ivey, Atty.

Housley, TX

#	NAMES	AGE	SEX
1	Orlenes T.	29	f
2	Cordelia	11	f
3	John S.	9	m
4	Marvin E.	7	m
5	Walter P.	5	m
6	Hiram	3	m

Ancestor: Ibby Hargrove

Docketed twin. Admitted O.T. Myers. Children not admitted, not on the original application.

Cornell Rogers, Clerk

326

343

Index

Lightning Source UK Ltd.
Milton Keynes UK
UKHW010653070922
408471UK00002B/490

9 781649 680587